BION IN FILM THEORY AND ANALYSIS

In *Bion in Film Theory and Analysis: The Retreat in Film*, Carla Ambrósio Garcia introduces the rich potential of the thinking of British psychoanalyst Wilfred Bion for film theory. By so doing, she rethinks the space of the cinema as a space of retreat, and brings new insights into the representation of retreat in film.

Presented in two parts, the book seeks to deepen our understanding of the film experience and psychical growth. Part I places Bion's view on the importance of the epistemophilic instinct at the heart of a critique of the pleasure-centred theories of the cinematic apparatus of Jean-Louis Baudry, Christian Metz and Gaylyn Studlar, proposing an idea of cinema as 'thoughts in search of a thinker'. Garcia then moves from Bion's epistemological period to his later work, which draws on mysticism, in order to posit an emotional experience in the cinema through which the subject can be or become real (or at one with 'O'). Part II examines representations of retreat in four European films, directed by Ingmar Bergman, Pier Paolo Pasolini, Georges Perec and Bernard Queysanne, and Manoel de Oliveira, showing them to articulate a gesture of retreat as an emotionally turbulent transitional stage in the development of the psyche – what Bion conceptualizes as *caesura*.

Through its investigation of the retreat in cinema, the book challenges common understandings of retreat as a regressive movement by presenting it as a gesture and space that can also be future-oriented. *Bion in Film Theory and Analysis* will be of significant interest to academics and students of psychoanalysis, psychotherapy, and film and media studies, as well as psychoanalysts and psychotherapists.

Carla Ambrósio Garcia is a filmmaker and academic who completed her doctorate in Film Studies at King's College London (funded by Fundação Ciência e Tecnologia in Portugal). Her articles on film and psychoanalysis have been published in academic journals and edited collections, and she currently teaches at King's College and Royal Holloway, University of London.

'*Bion in Film Theory and Analysis* is that rare thing: a book that offers a renewed encounter between psychoanalysis and cinema. At once disciplined and productively wayward, this book opens up new ground for thinking about what we do when we use the environment created by a work of art: film, in this instance, but Garcia's intervention has a reach well beyond her immediate concerns. In particular, through her explorations of Bion's writings, the "retreat" becomes a generative figure via which to reflect not only on what psychoanalysis can do to our understanding of the experience of film but, more broadly, the conditions of life and labour in the 21st century. At stake, in effect, is a question about the futures of human mind and being – and what cinema can contribute to our understanding of the forms of resistance made possible by retreat.'

– Prof. Vicky Lebeau, Professor of English, University of Sussex

'This is a sophisticated piece of original research at the intersection of psychoanalysis and film studies. Carla Ambrósio Garcia brilliantly demonstrates why film theory's canonical accounts of spectatorial experience need to be revisited in the light of Wilfred Bion (and object-relations generally), and facilitates a productive thinking space for the ongoing discussion about how we might conceive of a revolutionary psychical metamorphosis in and through the experience of film.'

– Dr Andrew Asibong, Reader in Film and Cultural Studies, Birkbeck, University of London

'Carla Ambrósio Garcia's fascinating book offers a new way of thinking about cinema, and its introduction of Bion to film studies ought to be both noticed and long lasting.'

– Dr Agnieszka Piotrowska, Filmmaker and Reader in Film Practice and Theory, University of Bedfordshire

BION IN FILM THEORY AND ANALYSIS

The Retreat in Film

Carla Ambrósio Garcia

Routledge
Taylor & Francis Group
LONDON AND NEW YORK

First published 2017
by Routledge
2 Park Square, Milton Park, Abingdon, Oxon OX14 4RN

and by Routledge
605 Third Avenue, New York, NY 10017

Routledge is an imprint of the Taylor & Francis Group, an informa business

British Library Cataloguing in Publication Data
A catalogue record for this book is available from the British Library

Library of Congress Cataloging in Publication Data
Names: Ambrósio Garcia, Carla, author.
Title: Bion in film theory and analysis: the retreat in film /
Carla Ambrósio Garcia.
Description: Abingdon, Oxon; New York, NY: Routledge, 2017. |
Includes bibliographical references and index.
Identifiers: LCCN 2016030453| ISBN 9781138193031 (hardback : alk. paper) |
ISBN 9781138193048 (pbk. : alk. paper) | ISBN 9781315639604 (ebook)
Subjects: | MESH: Bion, Wilfred R. (Wilfred Ruprecht), 1897–1979. |
Psychoanalysis | Motion Pictures as Topic
Classification: LCC RC506 | NLM WM 460 | DDC 616.89/17–dc23
LC record available at https://lccn.loc.gov/2016030453

ISBN: 978-1-138-19303-1 (hbk)
ISBN: 978-1-138-19304-8 (pbk)
ISBN: 978-1-315-63960-4 (ebk)

Typeset in Bembo and Stone Sans
by Florence Production Ltd, Stoodleigh, Devon, UK

CONTENTS

FIGURES

PREFACE

The image on the cover of this book was captured in a sea cave near Sesimbra, in Portugal. It was captured by my sister Ana with her digital camera, probably as I loaded my film camera underneath a dark cloth, feeling the film's progress through its interior with the tips of my fingers. Or perhaps as I carefully measured the distance between the film plane and the cave wall with a laser, so that I could turn the focus ring to the appropriate setting. In the process of working with 16 mm film, there are times in which we cannot rely on our eyes. There are stages in which we become aware of not seeing, and of having to wait in order to see. This awareness and waiting are an intrinsic part of the process of working with analogue formats. My interest in analogue formats goes back to my early university years, when I first entered a darkroom to process and print my own photographs. I learned the time that it takes to produce a photochemical image, the time it takes the latent to become visible. The passage of this time, the 'blind' stages that the analogue process involves, make me appreciate the moment of seeing, make me focus on the moment of looking and on the image itself. The importance of the moment of looking and the importance of the object itself at that moment as aspects of my art practice have made their way into the subject of this book, the retreat in film.

As I shall discuss in what follows, the retreat in film effects a diminution of extraneous light, a filtering or focusing of the light. To my mind, this is what Ana's image captures so well. It is a digitally captured image; I am not referring to something inherent to medium or technical support. I am referring to *how we use* different technical or technological supports in the encounter and exchange between ourselves and our world, which is of course only to a certain extent determined by those supports. Distracted or interrupted viewings of a film can be richly associative. Film has a fleeting, transient quality, which can be embraced in various modes of viewing film. But this book is not about them. This book is about a certain space and time for the experience of film that has a certain physical and psychical quality about it. Perhaps paradoxically, this physical and psychical quality can take many forms. This book is about what I will call cinema, or the retreat in cinema. In my definition, cinema can happen in various places and situations other than 'the cinema', as long as those places and situations allow a focused experience of film.

The initial idea for this project came as I was looking at images of the speleothems – or cave formations – in a cave not far from where I ended up filming *Sea Cave Cinema*, a film that I made alongside the writing of this book. The captions of these images classified some of the speleothems metonymically, for example as 'needles', 'curtains' or 'cave flowers'. The strangeness and evocativeness of these cave formations precipitated the thought of an *inversion* of Plato's allegory of the cave. Following this inverted allegory, we would strive to escape the dazzling light of the Sun, cast on a world of images and shadows, and search for Plato's forms *inside* the cave. The true forms of needles, curtains and flowers would exist in the interior of the Earth and would be perceived by the senses.

The British psychoanalyst Wilfred Bion (1897–1979) eventually helped me to develop and refine this idea with his concept of O. But he first came into the project as an intriguing figure in psychoanalysis who read Plato, and the mystics, and who had formulated a concept for a stage of turbulent psychical growth that he named caesura (after Freud's comment in *Inhibitions, Symptoms and Anxiety* on the 'impressive caesura of the act of birth'). So the first of Bion's works that I read were the caesura papers, which he wrote in the last 4 years of his life, and which over the years I have come back to again and again, as they seem to me an inexhaustible source of ideas of great depth and import. I became interested in a conceptualization of the retreat as caesura, and began exploring representations of retreat in film. Part II of this book is the outcome of that investigation.

After the caesura papers, I began reading the work of Bion in a more disciplined chronological order. I also began reading some key texts of apparatus film theory – Jean-Louis Baudry, Christian Metz and then Gaylyn Studlar – and was rather puzzled to find that their argument always seemed to revolve around pleasure: cinema was theorized as something that had pleasure at its core, pleasure as its aim and pleasure as its effect. This was fundamentally and radically at odds with my experience of the cinema, irrespective of film or genre. A film had been enjoyable, or beautiful, or amusing, but . . . Another film had left me feeling sad, or anxious, or irritated, or bored, but . . . This 'but' that occurs so often in a discussion of a film we may have with ourselves and with our fellow filmgoers is only one indication of the ambivalence that I believe shapes our relation to film. At the same time, through the reading of Bion's work that was happening in parallel, I was finding precisely the model of the mind that not only gave substance to these suspicions and experiences, but enabled me to ground and to build a theory of the cinema on Bion's terms. This work constitutes Part I of this book.

With Bion, the retreat can be conceived as a space and time where the pleasure and the reality principles coexist, where neither is precedent nor necessarily dominant. For Bion the pleasure principle and the reality principle do not follow each other in any particular order but they are seen to coexist from the beginning of life. His view that the reality principle operates since the earliest formative stages allows me to place the process of assimilation of emotions in the development of thinking and in psychical growth – a process that also entails unpleasure and pain – at the core of my formulation of a theory of the cinema and the retreat.

Sea Cave Cinema developed into a form of thinking about the space of the cinema, the medium of film and the practice of filmmaking. This film was made in a cave where light is filtered through a hole in its ceiling, refracted and reflected by the moving surface of water. Then, the light was focused by the lens of my camera, and imprinted on a moving strip of film. In both instances, the form of the light was only possible through the form of the surrounding darkness, and it is in surrounding darkness, and silence, that I would like this film to be shown.

ACKNOWLEDGEMENTS

This book developed from research conducted in the Department of Film Studies at King's College London. I am grateful to Fundação para a Ciência e a Tecnologia in Portugal, for having allowed me to pursue my PhD in full-time mode during its last two and a half years, with the award of a doctoral programme grant. I would especially like to thank Sarah Cooper and Patrick ffrench, for their inspiring commitment and support, and all that I have learned with their guidance. I would like to thank Vicky Lebeau, Andrew Asibong and Michele Pierson for their encouraging and thought-provoking comments. Thank you also to my anonymous reviewers for their suggested improvements, and to Susannah Frearson at Routledge for her invaluable help with this publication.

At King's, many friends and colleagues have helped me throughout the writing of this book: Calum Watt, Louis Bayman, Lawrence Webb, Mariana Liz, Kosuke Fujiki, André Hammelmann, Shu-Yi Lin, Barbara Plotz, Alice Guilluy, Alice Haylett Bryan, Christopher Holliday, Kierran Horner, Aaron McMullan, Alexander Sergeant, Martha Shearer, Alissa Timoshkina and Ben Tyrer. I would also like to thank Neil Vickers and the participants of the Bion reading group. I am grateful to Mark Betz, Richard Dyer, Victor Fan, Tom Brown and Belén Vidal for the energy of their teaching and mentoring. Thank you also to Agnieszka Piotrowska for her generous collegiality. From earlier times, but with continued presence, I thank Jayne Parker, John Hilliard, Mick Williamson and Lourdes Sendas, who have been supportive and inspiring.

I would like to thank my sister Ana Ambrósio Garcia for her steadfast contribution in the making of *Sea Cave Cinema*, her patience, courage and sense of humour; and for her beautiful contribution to the book cover. I would like to thank Francisco Luís Rasteiro, João Cláudio dos Santos, Carlos José Cruz, Rui Rodrigues and Francisco Gomes for sharing their passion for the wonders of Serra da Arrábida; and to extend my thanks to Manuel Procópio, Glória Silva and António Silva for also helping with access to the cave.

I am grateful to Susana Gavancha for her invaluable insights in the early stages of this project; and to Joana Ferreira, Bruno Ferreira, Sónia Neves, Arlindo Silva, Steffi Sachsenmaier, Patrick Beveridge, Sotirios Varsamis and Stamatis Zografos for stimulating discussions and contagious optimism.

This book is dedicated to my mother and father, with love and gratitude.

I would like to thank Meg Harris Williams for permission to reproduce excerpts from Donald Meltzer's *The Kleinian Development* (1978); Josef Bull for permission to reprint material in Chapter 3 of this book from the article 'The Sound of the Foghorn as Caesura in Ingmar Bergman's *Through a Glass Darkly*' that was published in *Nautofon*, 1 (2010); Duarte Maria da Silva Bruschy at NOS Lusomundo Audiovisuais for permission to reproduce excerpts from the English subtitles of the films *The Convent* and *Party*, and the interview *Entrevista com Manoel de Oliveira* (2001); Ana Cunha from Babel Editora, Guimarães Editores, and the family of Agustina Bessa-Luís, for permission to use the translation of the excerpt from Agustina Bessa-Luís's book *As Terras do Risco* (1994). Finally I would like to express my gratitude to Bernard Queysanne for his generous permission to reproduce excerpts from the transcript of the English version of the film *A Man Asleep*, and the stills from this film.

I would also like to make the following acknowledgements, thanking the publishers and their representatives, for their kind permissions:

Szeman, Imre. and Blacker, Sarah. (2014). Introduction: 'Between the exception and the rule'. *PUBLIC*, 25 (50), pp. 8–9, 13. Reproduced by permission of *PUBLIC*.

Barthes, Roland. (1979). Lecture in Inauguration of the Chair of Literary Semiology, Collège de France, 7 January 1977. Translated by R. Howard. *October* 8, p. 16. © 1979 October Magazine, Ltd. and the Massachusetts Institute of Technology.

Longhin, Luigi. and Mancia, Mauro. (2000). Kant's philosophy and its relationship with the thought of Bion and Money-Kyrle. *International Journal of Psychoanalysis*, 81 (6), p. 1201, p. 1202, pp. 1202–3. Copyright © Institute of Psychoanalysis, London, 2000. Reprinted with permission of John Wiley & Sons Ltd.

John Wiley & Sons Ltd. for permission to reprint material in Chapter 4 of this book from Ambrósio Garcia, Carla. (2013). Caesura and binocular vision in Pasolini's *Pigsty*. *International Journal of Psychoanalysis*, 94 (3), pp. 575–88. Copyright © 2012 Institute of Psychoanalysis.

Proust, Marcel. (1913). *In Search of Lost Time: The Way by Swann's*. Translated by Lydia Davis. London: Penguin Books, 2002. p. 9. Translation and editorial matter copyright © Lydia Davis, 2002. General Editor's Preface copyright © Christopher Prendergast, 2002. Reproduced by permission of Penguin Books Ltd.

Andrews, Chris. (1996). Puzzles and lists: Georges Perec's *Un homme qui dort*. *MLN*, 111 (4), pp. 783–4. © 1996 The Johns Hopkins University Press. Reprinted with permission of Johns Hopkins University Press.

Perec, Georges. (1974). Species of spaces. In: *Species of Spaces and Other Pieces*. Translated by John Sturrock. London: Penguin Classics, 1997, 1999. pp. 5, 91–2. Translation and Notes copyright © John Sturrock, 1997, 1999. *Espèces d'espaces* copyright © Editions Galilée, 1974. Reproduced by permission of Penguin Books Ltd.

Leak, Andrew. (2009). Phago-citations: Barthes, Perec, and the transformation of literature. *Review of Contemporary Fiction*, 29 (1), p. 136. Reproduced by permission of Dalkey Archive Press.

Sartre, Jean-Paul. (1938). *Nausea*. Translated by R. Baldick. London: Penguin Classics, 2000. pp. 182, 185, 187. Copyright © Librairie Gallimard 1938. This translation copyright © Penguin Books Ltd. 1965. Reproduced by permission of Penguin Books Ltd. Reprinted by permission of New Directions Publishing Corp.

von Goethe, J.W., Arndt, W. and Hamlin, C. (1976). *Faust: A Tragedy*. Translated by W. Arndt. Edited by C. Hamlin. 2nd ed. New York: W.W. Norton, 2001. p. 90. Reproduced by permission of W.W. Norton & Company, Inc.

All efforts have been made to contact copyright holders. Any omissions brought to the attention of the publisher shall be corrected in subsequent editions.

INTRODUCTION

> Instead of trying to bring a brilliant, intelligent, knowledgeable light to bear on obscure problems, I suggest we bring to bear a diminution of the 'light' – a penetrating beam of darkness: a reciprocal of the searchlight. The peculiarity of this penetrating ray is that it could be directed towards the object of our curiosity, and this object would absorb whatever light already existed, leaving the area of examination exhausted of any light that it possessed. The darkness would be so absolute that it would achieve a luminous, absolute vacuum. So that, if any object existed, however faint, it would show up very clearly. Thus, a very faint light would become visible in maximum conditions of darkness.[1]
>
> Wilfred R. Bion, *Brazilian Lectures*

The metaphor of a penetrating beam of darkness directed at an obscure object of investigation is used by Wilfred Bion in various contexts, but perhaps in all of them is implied a change of point of view, or a change of vertex, as he would rather call it. To change vertex is to reconsider what is already known, or believed, in order to learn, or to experience, something new. The metaphor suggests that what is already known can become an obstacle, it can produce too much light, which can blind or make disappear those objects or those characteristics of the object that can only become visible under certain conditions of darkness. Bion's image for psychoanalytic investigation, which occurs within the circumscribed space and time of the analytic situation, is resonant, in my view, with an image of retreat, and with an image of the cinema. The space of retreat and the space of the cinema effect a diminution of the light that comes from the 'outside world'.

The notion of retreat is often surrounded by a mist of negative connotations, such as fear, evasion, indifference; the gesture of retreat is generally interpreted as a regressive, retrograde movement. In psychoanalysis, and within the object relations paradigm that frames this book, John Steiner develops the notion of 'psychic retreat' as a type of withdrawal that 'provides the patient with an area of relative peace and protection from strain when meaningful contact with the analyst is experienced as threatening' (1993, p. 1). Here the retreat is a defensive structure aimed at averting anxiety and pain, an area 'where no realistic development can take place' (p. 41). Examples of recurrent images of the 'psychic retreat' in clinical material are 'a house, a cave, a fortress, a desert island' or, rather than physical locations, organizations of objects represented 'as a business organization, as a boarding school, as a religious sect, as a totalitarian government or a Mafia-like gang' (p. 2). The latter appear in cases of pathological narcissistic organizations of the personality in which destructive parts of the self are idealized (p. 45), and in which the experience of the retreat might be terrifying but nevertheless addictive (p. 52). A perverse quality can also be found in spatial configurations of retreat, in which a desert island, for example, is experienced as both an idealized haven and an arid environment that can barely sustain life (p. 102). In Steiner's conceptualization, only emergence from the retreat is a positive sign of development.

Moving from the specialized field of psychoanalysis to that of art criticism, I encountered an example of the notion of retreat as a regressive movement in a text by Julian Heynen, written for the catalogue of an exhibition of work by the artist Miroslaw Balka. Heynen comments on visual materials that Balka selected as a constellation of ideas pertinent to his creative process at the time, among these a photograph of a soldier next to a foxhole, and a 1941 painting by Henry Moore titled *Tube Shelter*, depicting an underground space in which an assemblage of human figures lie down. Heynen writes:

> This retreat from the light, which scarcely filters into such dwellings, the tendency to shut out the times of day and the seasons, the act of shutting one's own person into that unimaginably vast and different mass that we call Earth, allegedly ensue when life is being lived at a less developed level, when the individuals in question lack the imagination, courage or skill to fit in with and hold their own in the outside world. Thus existing under ground can be seen as the opposite of living in the world, a primitive state or a regressive act that pre-empts what normally only comes after life, the grave, whose final darkness most people want to postpone.
>
> (2009, p. 33)

Heynen then considers a series of Balka's sculptural works that delimit extremely confined spaces evoking the idea of precarious survival, and further on he asks whether it is a tension between non-life and 'the last glimmerings of a highly concentrated life' that the previous images and Balka's work produce (pp. 34–5). Would Heynen extend his ideas on the gesture of retreat to underground places or to austere, claustrophobic spaces such as those created by Balka, to any circumscribed space? In other words, is it the act of separation from the 'outside world', in a wider sense, that is being rejected?

More recently, the Canadian journal *PUBLIC* published an issue titled 'The Retreat', which gathered contributions by academics and artists who met in the mountainside resort town of Banff in the summer of 2012 in order to develop ideas and work around that topic. The topic of retreat was proposed by dOCUMENTA(13) director Carolyn Christov-Bakargiev, in a collaboration between that art event and the Banff Research in Culture group. In the introduction to the issue, Imre Szeman and Sarah Blacker note a general feeling of unease among the participants, as they questioned the validity of their 'retreat about retreat' at a time when the rest of the world seemed to be involved in a 'forward march' (2014, p. 8).[2] They observe that amid the political and economic upheavals that have marked recent years, such as the Arab Spring, the Occupy movement, and the student protests against the rise in tuition fees, their retreat could easily be taken as 'an act of both elitism and escapism' (p. 13). Yet the necessity of retreat as a form of political resistance in late capitalism soon emerges as a central preoccupation:

> Especially in such a system of life and labour, which has become more intensive and extensive in the Wi-Fi era, the need for even a compromised space of retreat – a step back and away from the main circuits of capital – from which to generate the forms of reflection necessary to produce insight into the structures one inhabits cannot but be important. [. . .] It's also hard to know what one is doing when one's body and mind are broken down by the repetition of work, and the work of culture that comes after work, which means that retreat is also a restitution to the body of its forces and a syncopation of time that comes all too infrequently in the hurry-up time of late capital.
>
> (p. 9)

These authors' observations raise the question of whether the cinema is a 'work of culture that comes after work', or whether it could be a space of retreat that does provide the space and time for the restitution of force to the body and mind, for reflection and insight.

The gesture and space of retreat are investigated by Roland Barthes in one of his lectures at the Collège de France. The figure of *Retreat* is presented as one of a series of figures or 'traits' chosen to reflect on the *Neutral*. Barthes states: 'I define the Neutral as that which outplays [*déjoue*] the paradigm, or rather I call Neutral everything that baffles the paradigm' (1978, p. 6). Engaging with various literary, biographical and philosophical texts, he speaks of mystical revelations, intellectual pursuits, work, idleness, the right measure of otherness, places allocated to a split of the personality, organization of space and routine, obsessive rituals . . . and in the last section of his lecture, Barthes links the retreat to the fantasy of a *Vita Nuova*, a radical change of life, 'a decision-desire without concession' for a new life (p. 147). Here, Barthes begins with a quotation by Jean-Jacques Rousseau, in which he writes of renouncing the world on reaching the age of forty. Barthes sees this refusal as the supreme trap of the imaginary, from which the only means of escape is the 'soft benevolence' (p. 148) and 'icy indifference' (p. 243, n. 52) of the Tao way, translated into gestures of retreat that are temporary, and non-systematic. Not being systematic outplays the paradigm, producing a scandalous, baffling image of the subject to the 'outside world'.

But this lecture on the figure of *Retreat* is not the only instance where Barthes uses the expression *vita nuova*, or *vita nova*. Referring to his own life, he recognizes a need to be periodically reborn, in moments where an incisive event determines a transformation. In his inaugural lecture on entering the Collège, this process is seen to entail a certain forgetfulness:

> There is an age at which we teach what we know. Then comes another age at which we teach what we do not know; this is called *research*. Now perhaps comes the age of another experience: that of *unlearning*, of yielding to the unforeseeable change which forgetting imposes on the sedimentation of the knowledges, cultures, and beliefs we have traversed.[3]
>
> (1979, p. 16)

This process of unlearning brings to mind the diminution of light in Bion's metaphor. In a subsequent lecture, after the course on the *Neutral*, Barthes returns to the idea of a new life, this time determined by the need to emerge from his state of mourning. As a writer, this initiates 'the search, the discovery, the practice of a new form' (1982, p. 286). For Barthes, the new form is the Novel (an uncertain form), examples of which provoke, on reading a particular episode, a disruption that is experienced as a 'moment of truth' (p. 287). The recognition of *pathos* as a force of reading (which literary theory does only insufficiently, in his view) and of an amorous, generous energy that animates writing, can be realized in this uncertain form, which Barthes accomplishes in *Camera Lucida* (1980).[4] A few months later, he begins to work on the plan for a novel, of which only exist a small number of pages kept in a folder titled *Vita Nova*, each presenting a somewhat different outline of the project (Barthes, 1995, III, pp. 1299–307). In her study of these pages, Diana Knight (1997, pp. 96–7) identifies an opposition that she believes fascinated Barthes: that between the will to write and the work of writing, and an actively chosen *oisiveté*. Interestingly, in Barthes's earlier text on cinema – 'Leaving the Movie Theater' – there can be found a similar tension, between the idleness or inoccupation of the spectator's body, and an invisible work of affects: 'the movie spectator could easily appropriate the silkworm's motto: *Inclusum labor illustrat*; it is because I am enclosed that I work and glow with all my desire' (1975, p. 346). Work, idleness, enclosure, and transformation are ideas that suggest themselves in Barthes's text on the cinema, which can be linked to his lecture on the figure of *Retreat*.[5]

An in-depth exploration of the notion of retreat remains uncharted territory in the field of film studies; and yet I believe it can be a very productive notion, and especially pertinent to the question of spectatorship, which is one of the main concerns of this book. This book stands as a contribution towards the widening of the understanding of *retreat* within film studies, more precisely, as it might be present in the experience of film, and as it might be represented in films.

In this book I will use the expression 'to experience a film' because it seems more adequate to describe a sensory experience that involves all the senses in a particular relation.[6] To conceive of the particularity of this relation means that the situation in which it happens is also thought to be particular in some way. The cinema situation is my model, because I am interested in what its spatial and temporal conditions aim to create: the cinema aims to obliterate or minimize the influence of the exterior and of extraneous elements to the film, so a focused and intimate engagement with the film is possible (a particular relation). My purpose is to investigate the experience of film as retreat.

Thomas Elsaesser and Malte Hagener comment on what is defined as 'apparatus theory', a strand of film theory that emerged in the 1970s concerned with the ideological effects of film technology: they state that it 'is based first of all on an analysis of the fixed and unchangeable arrangement of (disembodied, captive, and impressionable) spectators, (fixed) screen and (hidden) projector, all of which entertain a specific spatial relationship to one another' (2010, p. 88). The emphasis here seems to be on a certain arrangement of relationships.

Further in their survey of the directions in which film theory has developed since, notably in relation to the positioning of power and embodied perception, Elsaesser and Hagener defend that 'the cinematic apparatus, regardless of how we define it, is less in need of a theory capable of deconstructing it than it is threatened by obsolescence' (p. 106). Theory develops in response to theory, but also in response to history and to the technologies that have been changing the way films are available to be experienced.

It is also interesting to note these authors' contextualizing of apparatus theory within the historical moment in which it appeared. They write:

> In the 1970s and 1980s it even appeared likely that the cinema in which this apparatus had first been used would not only hand over to television and its 'channels', but that cinema as a public place was inevitably condemned to extinction. [. . .] In other words: apparatus theory reacted to the crisis of cinema – which had been caused historically by the development of different audio-visual technologies and by changes in audience behavior – with a certain kind of mourning work vis à vis the cinema in which the loving, nostalgic look of the cinephiles gave way to a special kind of love-hate relationship in the face of cinema's looming demise.
>
> (p. 101)

Following Elsaesser and Hagener, it would appear that to revisit apparatus theory today could be symptomatic of a crisis of cinema, certainly feared but not necessarily real; and that to do so does no longer make much sense anyway since apparatus theory has become obsolete. Nevertheless, at home screens are becoming larger, the sound systems more immersive, and digital projectors – which need surrounding darkness – more popular; in galleries, single screen projections of film are often found in darkened rooms with seating, and sometimes the screenings are scheduled. This leads me to think that even though technologies have changed, there is something about the experience and the arrangements of cinema that seems to last, and to be carried over to other spaces and situations. Thus, despite the dominance conferred by apparatus theory to disembodied vision that no longer holds true, I believe it can still be rewarding to explore the relationships in a certain arrangement of (relatively immobile) spectators, (fixed) screen and (relatively unobtrusive) moving image technology, because the existence of this arrangement is still relevant today.

I mentioned the above examples of the home and the gallery, aware that they present important differences between private and public space, and between the different temporalities that each space permits, to name just two aspects of complexity. And indeed my notion of cinema can extend to other, more improvised or alternative spaces for experiencing film. To have what some might consider to be a rather flexible notion of cinema does not mean that differences between spaces, situations, and media, do not matter.[7] But my discussion of the cinema as apparatus, though it engages with theorists that use the term in their own specific sense, is open to differences in space, situation, and media, provided that the conditions for a focused and dedicated experience of the film are in existence. This experience privileges the original or intended format(s) and presentation(s) of the film. And since I am interested in this arrangement of relationships, I will retain the term 'cinematic apparatus', and move seamlessly between it and 'cinema' and 'space of the cinema', even when I am reappropriating these terms to fit within other modes of experiencing film. What is important in my conceptualization of 'cinema' is the possibility of a relation in which a separation from or diminution of external interference happens. I want to retain the image of a penetrating beam of darkness that focuses on the object of investigation: an image of cinema as retreat.

The re-evaluation of the cinematic apparatus that I undertake in Part I of this book entails an examination of the work of two influential French film theorists, Jean-Louis Baudry and Christian Metz – the major proponents of apparatus theory – and the more recent contribution of United States film scholar Gaylyn Studlar. In line with the broader interests of my thinking, they recognize in certain instances, and in a more or less accentuated form, the position of the subject in the cinema as preserving traces of a relation to a maternal figure. Accordingly, throughout my argument I will move between discussions of spectator and film, infant and caregiver, and analysand and analyst, not only following the parallel drawn between the first two pairings by the film theorists mentioned above, but also the parallel drawn between the latter two by psychoanalysts in their study of the transference. The term 'subject' will refer both to the analytical subject and to the spectator.[8]

I will consider Baudry's and Metz's metapsychological studies of the cinematic apparatus, and certain points in Metz's seminal work 'The Imaginary Signifier'. These articles were first published in the French journal *Communications*, in a 1975 edition devoted to psychoanalysis and cinema.[9] 'The Imaginary Signifier' was translated and published in Britain in the same year by the journal *Screen*. This publication occupied a central position in film theory during the 1970s, a decade that, again, focused attention on the technological apparatus of the cinema and its ideological implications. This tendency in theoretical approaches to film, which is seen by some to have been detrimental to historical research, often drew on semiotics, the philosophy of Louis Althusser, and psychoanalysis (Kuhn and Stacey, 1998, p. 2). In this last discipline, the work of Jacques Lacan has made an immense contribution to studies of film, including those conducted by Baudry and Metz. Greatly indebted to the Lacanian concepts of the mirror stage, and of the scopic and invocatory drives, which determine the subject's endless attachment to the narcissism of the Imaginary realm, Baudry's and Metz's psychoanalytic investigations on subject-positioning in the cinema are centred on the pleasures of specularity. Their psychoanalytic approach, in its preoccupation with the specular, is distinctly apart from the one I take here, founded on Kleinian object relations theory and its legacy.[10]

As it will be seen, Baudry and Metz only refer to Melanie Klein's work in passing. Lacan, who increasingly dominated the French psychoanalytic scene in the 1960s and 1970s, did refer in one of his early articles to the effectiveness of Klein's 'direct, brutal speech' in child analysis, in order to defend the significance of language in 'the constitution of the subject' (Birksted-Breen and Flanders, pp. 5–6). However, Klein did not directly influence the development of French psychoanalysis, only re-entering this discourse via Donald Winnicott, whose work became an important reference to many psychoanalysts who had been Lacan's students in the 1960s (pp. 7–8). The influence of British psychoanalysis in France – in particular of the work of Winnicott and of Bion – has been part of a reaction against Lacan, his avowed 'return to Freud' that really meant a 'return to early Freud', his emphasis on language, and his neglect of pre-verbal experience, meaning and affect.[11]

Departing from Freudian and Lacanian psychoanalytic theory and engaging with semiotics and the philosophy of Gilles Deleuze, Gaylyn Studlar responds to specular conceptualizations of the apparatus, understood in their sadistic aspects, by introducing masochism to the production of filmic pleasures (1988, p. 2, p. 6). Studlar's contribution is pertinent to my argument because it brings into discussion the issue of pain in the cinema; nevertheless, I propose a shift in the emphasis on pleasure that is discernible in Studlar's, Baudry's and Metz's conceptualizations, to a more complex interaction between pleasure, and unpleasure and pain, which cannot be subsumed exclusively under the category of masochism.

The overarching argument of my investigation considers the retreat in connection with the internal world – the internal world as it is conceptualized in Kleinian and post-Kleinian theory. To its proponents, the internal world acquires a new concreteness: it is born from the infant's relation to the mother and her interior; it owes much of its geography and its figures to this relation; and its reality competes in significance with that of the external world. Donald Meltzer, a Kleinian psychoanalyst who was also profoundly influenced by the work of Bion, sees this very concrete conception of the internal world as one of the major contributions of Melanie Klein to psychoanalysis. He writes:

> It requires an immense shift in one's view of the world to think that the outside world is essentially meaningless and unknowable, that one perceives the forms but must attribute the meaning. Philosophically, this is the great problem in coming to grips with Kleinian thought and its implications.
>
> (1978, II, p. 86)

Meaning, and truth, are seen to be dependent on a constant exchange between external and internal. As well as being the first object that the infant loves and hates, the mother is also the first to whom an instinctual thirst for knowledge is directed, especially to the inside of her body. The concept of the epistemophilic instinct, early formulated by Freud, undergoes crucial developments with Klein and Bion; I believe that these developments can bring new insights into film theory, as well as contribute to a different understanding of retreat.

A valuable source in this investigation is *The Kleinian Development* by Meltzer, a work that looks at the progression of psychoanalytic thought from Freud, through Klein to Bion. Meltzer makes important remarks on the development of Freud's ideas over the course of his life, and on how they contain the seeds of what later become fundamental tenets of the Kleinian school. Myriad readings of Freud's work exist, but my investigation – especially the work that I will be doing in the first chapter of Part I – is concerned with those advanced by Meltzer. Bion is deeply influenced by Klein's thinking; however, he develops some of her concepts to such an extent and with such originality that his work is rejected by some Kleinian followers. These and other theoretical disjunctions are pointed to in the course of the text.

The origins of psychoanalysis in bourgeois Vienna at the turn of the century have helped some critics to set limits and limitations on the value of the discipline. However, Meltzer points out that 'the mental apparatus as postulated by Bion [. . .] is universal in that it functions phylogenetically and ontogenetically in terms valid for all individuals' (Longhin and Mancia, 2000, p. 1202).[12] While many would view this as a welcome development in psychoanalysis, some film theorists have criticized apparatus theories that draw on psychoanalysis precisely because they consider them to be universalist, to disregard historical and cultural specificities and subjectivities. Psychoanalytic studies of the apparatus are generally seen to not take into account individual responses to films as a consequence of their positing the spectator as 'an abstract, theoretical entity' (Margolis, 1988, p. xi). Yet I believe that the questions that I raise, of pleasure and unpleasure, thinking and emotions, change and resistance to it, are not necessarily limited to the experience of any particular kinds of films, nor do they concern a particular subject, whether defined by race, class, gender, sexuality or any other aspect that plays a part in the constitution of subjectivity. The questions that I raise may be as equally pertinent to genre broadly considered – for example the experience of comedy or drama – as to the smallest detail in a film, such as an actor's make-up, or a word in the script. It is impossible to predict how certain films or certain aspects of films may affect individual subjects, but it is important to recognize that they do, and do so in unpredictable ways. Therefore, throughout my theorization of the apparatus in Part I, I do not mention any films or genres or make any other reference to content as this would restrict the reader's own thinking and positioning in relation to what is being discussed. In the work done in Part I it is precisely the 'abstract' subject and the absence of film references that allow different subjectivities to relate to it.

In Part II of this book I consider specific films in my exploration of representations of retreat in film. In this part, retreat is conceived of as a stage of turbulent psychical growth. My choice of films can be said to fall under the category of European art cinema, but I must insist that this should in no way be considered to suggest that the domain of my conceptualization of the cinema in Part I is limited to films of that category. The selection of films in the second part of the book has been made with theoretical, conceptual and thematic criteria in mind – of course informed by my access to source materials and by my own interests – but my theory of the apparatus certainly extends beyond art cinema, as I believe will become clear. In Part I my argument has a theoretical basis and follows a theoretical method, but during its writing I had many different kinds of film in mind.

In their engagement with psychoanalysis, Baudry and Metz do not apply the thinking of the authors they draw on in its full breadth to their theories of the apparatus. Baudry draws on Freud but neglects the death instinct; Metz does too, and in his brief references to Klein he overlooks the importance of cinema as a bad object. Thus, in Chapter 1 I will begin by addressing these issues, while at the same time paving the way to Bion by looking at object relations theory and how it has stemmed from Freud. This work is also necessary because Bion uses and develops Kleinian concepts that need prior clarification, and it is the reason for his relatively late appearance in this chapter.

Bion's recognition of an instinctual thirst for knowledge in the subject that plays a fundamental role in the capacity to tolerate unpleasure and pain, and in the development of thinking, is not only vital in making sense of unpleasure and pain in the cinema, it also demonstrates that the retreat may not always be an evasive gesture, or a shelter that provides protection from unpleasurable or painful experiences. In this first chapter the cinema is rethought as a thinking space, through a theory that sees the mind not as being primarily governed by energetic principles, but rather as functioning on the principles of the manipulation of meaning, and of the ability to think about and assimilate emotional experiences.

In the following chapter I consider Bion's concept of O in order to further the investigation of cinema as retreat, while developing a critique of Baudry's analogy between the cinema and Plato's cave. With the formulation of the concept of O, which emerges at a later stage in his work, Bion addresses the problem of resistance in more depth by focusing on how the subject effects the passage from knowing, to being or becoming. O denotes the ultimately real, and Bion posits that while O cannot be known, it can be 'become'. The image of an intense beam of darkness is evoked when Bion explains that contact with O is only possible through giving up memories, desires and understanding, that is, through being completely receptive to the emotional experience of the present. The question of knowledge and emotions in relation to mental growth in the cinema is examined through this theory, and through it the cinema can become detached from the recurrent association with Plato's cave, and from Plato's thinking in a wider sense.

Part II begins with an introduction to my readings of the four films in the subsequent four chapters. As already mentioned, these films are examined in their articulation of retreat as a moment of turbulent psychical change. This research is grounded in Bion's contributions on mental functioning at critical junctures, especially in his concept of caesura, which refers to a transitional stage in the psyche that occurs at different points in life, but is inspired by the incisive moment of birth.[13]

The selection of these four films was initially made as each seemed to address a range of relevant issues to the theme of retreat. Later, I found in a passage of Bion's *Attention and Interpretation* (1970, pp. 84–5), a reference to 'the messianic hope, the Oedipus myth, the Babel myth, and the Eden myth' as models representing a problem of growth; and each of these four models does indeed provide a further contextual layer for the film examined in each of the four chapters.

In Chapter 3 I consider Ingmar Bergman's *Through a Glass Darkly* (1961), the first film in Bergman's 'trilogy of faith'. As its biblical title might suggest, the film is an investigation of the problem of containing the messianic hope. Here I introduce Bion's concept of caesura, a moment of dramatic change in which the past, present and future of the subject are striving to be articulated in some form. The film's spaces of retreat, as well as gestures performed by the characters and other formal elements of the film are seen as articulations of the caesura, in their relation to the characters' emotionally turbulent experiences and to different temporalities in their lives. The survey of this and other aspects of the caesura, such as its link to the maternal, will also provide a basis for the use of this concept in the other three films of Part II.

Chapter 4 provides a reading of Pier Paolo Pasolini's *Pigsty* (1969) through the examination of an early article by Bion titled 'The Imaginary Twin'. In this article he attempts to establish a relation between the capacity to personify splittings of the personality and the process of symbol-formation, the latter seen in its Kleinian formulation, as being dependent on oral-sadistic attacks towards the mother's body and its contents. Bion furthers his inquiry by bringing together clinical material in which a concern with vision and ocular methods of investigation are connected with the emergence of the Oedipus situation. This theoretical framework offers an approach to the content and the form of Pasolini's film, in which the main character retreats to live his Oedipus conflict through an imaginary twin. The twin's cannibalistic acts are performed in a volcanic landscape that is vividly maternal. The main character is able to see himself and the split-off part of his self through an alternating, binocular vision that is here interpreted as a form of the caesura.

Bernard Queysanne's and Georges Perec's *A Man Asleep* (1974), a film based on the homonymous novel by Perec, is discussed in the following chapter. In my argument, the spaces in the film, and the movement of the camera and the protagonist within these spaces, trace geometrical forms and relations among themselves that can be explored through Bion's conceptualization of the point, the line and the circle. These images also occur in the text that is read in voice over, in the sounds that form repetitive, continuous and cyclical patterns, and even in the objects that surround the protagonist. Such elements are used to explore thinking processes, which can be seen to relate to pre-verbal stages, and are in my reading interpreted as articulations of the protagonist's retreat as caesura. The problem of differences in languages that can be discerned in the film, within the individual and within the group, evoke an image of the Babel myth.

The aesthetic dimension of Bion's later thought has been a source of interest in recent psychoanalytic literature,[14] and it seems fitting to 'open' the end of this book by engaging with Meltzer's development of this aspect of Bion's legacy, in work he developed in conjunction with Martha Harris and Meg Harris Williams. The concepts of the aesthetic conflict (Meltzer et al., 1986, p. 182), and the claustrum (Meltzer, 1992, pp. 69–95), will be used in an examination of Manoel de Oliveira's *The Convent* (1995). In this film, the circumscribed spaces of a secluded convent are visited (or intruded into) by a researcher and his wife, and their experiences there are regarded as the crossing of a caesura, in that parts of their personalities (possibly the characters they encounter) will emerge from the claustrum. The claustrum is a compartment of the internal mother that has been intruded into violently or stealthily, opposed to an imaginative, aesthetic relation to the mother's interior that accepts its mystery and respects her privacy. Meltzer's formulation of the conceptions of the inside of the internal mother illuminates the qualities of the film's spaces of retreat. The characters' aims on entering the convent and its library recall the myth of the Tree of Knowledge of Good and Evil.

This book concludes with a recapitulation of the notions of retreat arrived at as well as those that have been challenged throughout its consideration and theorization of the cinematic apparatus and the analysis of the four films. These concluding remarks lead to an overarching notion of retreat as a gesture and space connected with the development of the mind, a gesture and space that can be future-oriented. This future orientation of the retreat not only concerns the development of the individual subject, it also concerns the development of the space and time of the cinema, it concerns the future of cinema.

Notes

1 Bion, W.R. (1973). *Brazilian Lectures*. London: Karnac, 1990. pp. 20–1. The metaphor is inspired by a letter Freud wrote to Lou Andreas-Salomé (see Chapter 2).

2 Szeman, I. and Blacker, S. (2014). Introduction: 'Between the exception and the rule'. *PUBLIC*, 25 (50), pp. 7–18. This and following excerpts reproduced by permission of *PUBLIC*.

3 Barthes, R. (1979). Lecture in Inauguration of the Chair of Literary Semiology, Collège de France, January 7, 1977. Translated by R. Howard. *October*, 8 (Spring, 1979), p. 16. © 1979 by October Magazine, Ltd. and the Massachusetts Institute of Technology.

4 Writing in connection with a utopian, maternal space that functions according to a principle of 'idiorrythmie', a Barthesian concept that refers to a form of living that affords 'the right distance from others', is considered by Patrick ffrench (2009).

5 In addition to the links already made, it is curious that in 'Leaving the Movie Theater' Barthes refers to the king of Spain having Farinelli sing for him the same aria every evening

over fourteen years, in connection with hypnosis and healing, and later, in his lecture, he mentions the same episode, this time in relation to monotony and repetition.

6 Vivian Sobchack (2004) elaborates on existential phenomenology in order to foreground the significance of the lived body experience in the cinema. She writes: 'even at the movies our vision and hearing are informed and given meaning by our other modes of sensory access to the world: our capacity not only to see and to hear but also to touch, to smell, to taste, and always to proprioceptively feel our weight, dimension, gravity, and movement in the world' (p. 60). See also Laura Marks (2000) and Jennifer Barker (2009). The work of these authors is particularly interesting to me in its development of the concept of identification in the cinema, though its focus on the sensorial aspects of experience is generally considered in opposition to psychoanalytic approaches to film.

7 I address the issue of medium specificity in 'Process and Medium in the Practice of Filmmaking: The Work of Jayne Parker' (2015).

8 When referring only to the analytical subject or subject in analysis, the term 'analysand' will be used in my writing; the term 'patient' will only appear in quotations. Even though the distinction between the subject in the cinema and the subject in analysis should be recognized, I will sometimes conflate the two in the same way that analytical discourse theorizes a model of the mind that is not concerned only with the subject in analysis.

9 This issue also features the original publication of the article on cinema by Barthes already mentioned.

10 For studies of film that draw on the theory of Melanie Klein see Sarah Cooper (2001), Suzy Gordon (2004; 2007) and Davina Quinlivan (2015). Andrea Sabbadini (2003; 2007) has edited two collections of film studies that draw on object relations theory (including the work of Bion), though most (but not all) of the contributors have psychoanalytic rather than film studies affiliations. For studies of film that engage with the work of Donald Winnicott see Vicky Lebeau (2009) and Annette Kuhn (2013). See also Bainbridge (2014) for an article that draws on Klein, Bion and Winnicott.

11 Birksted-Breen and Flanders note: 'To this day, French psychoanalysts make much use of Winnicott and also of Bion in their writings, and considerably less of Klein, although they quite regularly use the notion of a "depressive position". It is also true to say that the very style of the writing of both Bion and Winnicott – more poetic than Klein's, and also willing to hold ambiguity when describing phenomena beyond the rational and respecting a sense of an unknowable – appeals to French sensitivity' (p. 17).

12 The quotation is a paraphrase of Meltzer's statement by the authors. Longhin, L. and Mancia, M. (2000). Kant's philosophy and its relationship with the thought of Bion and Money-Kyrle. *International Journal of Psychoanalysis*, 81 (6), p. 1202. Copyright (c) Institute of Psychoanalysis, London, 2000. Reprinted with permission of John Wiley & Sons Ltd.

13 Sergei Eisenstein (1939, pp. 164–5) considers the structure of his film *Battleship Potemkin* (1925), employing the term *caesura* to describe a transitional point between parts of the film, which he notes 'is not merely a transition to a merely *different* mood, to a merely *different* rhythm, to a merely *different* event, but each time the transition is to a sharply opposite quality', e.g. 'a few shots of clenched fists, through which the theme of mourning the dead leaps into the theme of fury'. Bion's concept of caesura and my use of it in my film analyses should not be confused with Eisenstein's.

14 See for example the work of Lia Pistiner de Cortiñas (2009), Meg Harris Williams (2010) and Giuseppe Civitarese (2013).

References

Ambrósio Garcia, C. (2015). Process and medium in the practice of filmmaking: The work of Jayne Parker. In: Piotrowska, A. (ed.) *Embodied Encounters: New Approaches to Psychoanalysis and Cinema*. Hove, East Sussex: Routledge.

Bainbridge, C. (2014). 'Cinematic screaming' or 'all about my mother': Lars von Trier's cinematic extremism as therapeutic encounter. In: Bainbridge, C. and Yates, C. (eds.) *Media and the Inner World: Psycho-Cultural Approaches to Emotion, Media and Popular Culture*. Basingstoke: Palgrave Macmillan.

Barker, J. (2009). *The Tactile Eye: Touch and the Cinematic Experience*. Berkeley: University of California Press.

Barthes, R. (1975). Leaving the movie theater. In: *The Rustle of Language*. Translated by R. Howard. Berkeley: University of California Press, 1989.

Barthes, R. (1978). *The Neutral: Lecture Course at the Collège de France (1977–1978)*. Translated by R.E. Krauss and D. Hollier. New York: Columbia University Press, 2005.

Barthes, R. (1979). Lecture in Inauguration of the Chair of Literary Semiology, Collège de France, January 7, 1977. Translated by R. Howard. *October*, 8, pp. 3–16.

Barthes, R. (1980). *Camera Lucida: Reflections on Photography*. Translated by R. Howard. New York: Hill and Wang, 1981.

Barthes, R. (1982). *Longtemps, je me suis couché de bonne heure . . .* In: *The Rustle of Language*. Translated by R. Howard. Berkeley: University of California Press, 1989.

Barthes, R. (1995). *Vita Nova*. In: Marty, É. (ed.) *Œuvres complètes*, III. Paris: Seuil.

Baudry, J-L. (1975). Le dispositif: Approches métapsychologiques de l'impression de réalité. *Communications*, 23, pp. 56–72.

Bion, W.R. (1970). *Attention and Interpretation*. London: Karnac, 2007.

Bion, W.R. (1973). *Brazilian Lectures*. London: Karnac, 1990.

Birksted-Breen, D. and Flanders, S. (2010). General introduction. In: Birksted-Breen, D., Flanders, S. and Gibeault, A. (eds.) *Reading French Psychoanalysis*. Hove, East Sussex: Routledge.

Civitarese, G. (2013). *The Violence of Emotions: Bion and Post-Bionian Psychoanalysis*. Translated by I. Harvey. Hove, East Sussex: Routledge.

Cooper, S. (2001). Je sais bien, mais quand même . . .: Fetishism, envy, and the queer pleasures of *Beau Travail*. *Studies in French Cinema*, 3 (1), pp. 174–82.

de Cortiñas, L.P. (2009). *The Aesthetic Dimension of the Mind: Variations on a Theme of Bion*. Translated by P. Slotkin et al. London: Karnac.

Eisenstein, S. (1939). The structure of the film. In: *Film Form: Essays in Film Theory*. Edited and translated by J. Leyda. New York: Harcourt Brace Jovanovich, 1949.

Elsaesser, T. and Hagener, M. (2010). *Film Theory: An Introduction through the Senses*. New York: Routledge.

ffrench, P. (2009). How to live with Roland Barthes. *SubStance*, 38 (3), pp. 113–24.

Gordon, S. (2004). *Breaking the Waves* and the negativity of Melanie Klein: Rethinking 'the female spectator'. *Screen*, 45 (3), pp. 206–25.

Gordon, S. (2007). Film, feminism and Melanie Klein: 'Weird lullabies'. In: Bainbridge, C., Radstone, S., Rustin, M. and Yates, C. (eds.) *Culture and the Unconscious*. Basingstoke: Palgrave Macmillan.

Harris Williams, M. (2010). *The Aesthetic Development: The Poetic Spirit of Psychoanalysis – Essays on Bion, Meltzer, Keats*. London: Karnac.

Heynen, J. (2009). That's how it is. In: *Miroslaw Balka: How It Is*. Edited by H. Sainsbury. Translated by F. Elliott. London: Tate Publishing.

Knight, D. (1997). Idle thoughts: Barthes's *Vita Nova*. *Nottingham French Studies*, 36 (1), pp. 88–98.

Kuhn, A. (ed.) (2013). *Little Madnesses: Winnicott, Transitional Phenomena and Cultural Experience*. London: I.B. Tauris.

Kuhn, A. and Stacey, J. (1998). Screen histories: An introduction. In: Kuhn, A. and Stacey, J. (eds.) *Screen Histories: A* Screen *Reader*. Oxford: Clarendon Press.

Lebeau, V. (2009). The arts of looking: D.W. Winnicott and Michael Haneke. *Screen*, 50 (1), pp. 35–44.
Longhin, L. and Mancia, M. (2000). Kant's philosophy and its relationship with the thought of Bion and Money-Kyrle. *International Journal of Psychoanalysis*, 81 (6), pp. 1197–211.
Margolis, H.E. (1988). *The Cinema Ideal: An Introduction to Psychoanalytic Studies of the Film Spectator*. Oxon: Routledge, 2014.
Marks, L. (2000). *The Skin of the Film: Intercultural Cinema, Embodiment, and the Senses*. Durham: Duke University Press.
Meltzer, D. (1978). *The Kleinian Development*. Strath Tay: Clunie Press, 1985.
Meltzer, D. (1992). *The Claustrum: An Investigation of Claustrophobic Phenomena*. London: Karnac, 2008.
Meltzer, D. et al. (1986). *Studies in Extended Metapsychology: Clinical Applications of Bion's Ideas*. Perthshire: Clunie Press.
Metz, C. (1975). Le signifiant imaginaire. *Communications*, 23, pp. 3–55.
Metz, C. (1975). Le film de fiction et son spectateur. *Communications*, 23, pp. 108–35.
Quinlivan, D. (2015). *Filming the Body in Crisis: Trauma, Healing and Hopefulness*. Basingstoke: Palgrave Macmillan.
Sabbadini, A. (ed.) (2003). *The Couch and the Silver Screen: Psychoanalytic Reflections on European Cinema*. Hove, East Sussex: Brunner-Routledge.
Sabbadini, A. (ed.) (2007). *Projected Shadows: Psychoanalytic Reflections on the Representation of Loss in European Cinema*. Hove, East Sussex: Routledge.
Sobchack, V. (2004). *Carnal Thoughts: Embodiment and Moving Image Culture*. Berkeley: University of California Press.
Steiner, J. (1993). *Psychic Retreats: Pathological Organizations in Psychotic, Neurotic and Borderline Patients*. London: Routledge.
Studlar, G. (1988). *In the Realm of Pleasure: von Sternberg, Dietrich, and the Masochistic Aesthetic*. Urbana: University of Illinois Press.
Szeman, I. and Blacker, S. (2014). Introduction: 'Between the exception and the rule'. *PUBLIC*, 25 (50), pp. 7–18.

Filmography

Battleship Potemkin (1925). Directed by Sergei Eisenstein. [DVD] Soviet Union: Goskino.
The Convent (1995). Directed by Manoel de Oliveira. [DVD] Portugal/France: Madragoa Filmes/Gemini Films/La Sept Cinéma.
A Man Asleep (1974). Directed by Georges Perec and Bernard Queysanne. [DVD] France/Tunisia: Dovidis/Satpec.
Pigsty (1969). Directed by Pier Paolo Pasolini. [DVD] Italy/France: IDI Cinematografica/OrsoFilms/INDIEF/CAPAC.
Through a Glass Darkly (1961). Directed by Ingmar Bergman. [DVD] Sweden: Svensk Filmindustri.

PART I

The retreat in cinema

1

RETHINKING THE CINEMATIC APPARATUS WITH BION'S THEORY OF THINKING

Introduction

There are three main points in Jean-Louis Baudry's article titled 'The Apparatus: Metapsychological Approaches to the Impression of Reality in the Cinema' (1975) that I will address. The first is Baudry's contention that the cinematic apparatus engenders a state of artificial regression to a pleasurable moment in the subject's relationship with the breast; the second is his understanding of the cinema as a place where the unconscious, in the Freudian sense, is represented; and the third is the parallel he draws between Plato's cave and the apparatus. My first question is, if traces of regression to a primordial stage are manifest in the subject – and in how the apparatus is constructed – what does this regressive state involve? Then, I ask, if the unconscious is represented in the cinema, how can this be considered beyond Freud's metapsychology? And finally, how can psychoanalysis further expose the implications and inadequacy of the analogy between Plato's scheme and the cinema? I will address the first and second questions in this first chapter, and the third question in Chapter 2.

The *dream-screen*: wish-fulfilment?

In the initial pages of his article, Baudry tries to find a correspondence between Plato's allegorical *topos* and Freud's topographical model of the mind. Baudry speculates whether he can superimpose the outside world with the analyst's conscious, and the philosopher's cave with the unconscious. He is aware of the difficulties of such an endeavour, as he observes that what is real for Plato and what is real for Freud do not share the same location (p. 302). Nevertheless, Baudry pursues his tentative association of the cave, the unconscious and the cinematic apparatus by noting where several aspects of the functioning of these loci seem to overlap.

The most immediate of these aspects is the resemblance of the mode of operation of Plato's cave to that of the cinematic apparatus: the darkness of the space, the projection of light and shadow on the wall, the voices of the hidden passers-by taken for the voices of the projected objects, the immobility of the prisoner-subject. Baudry is also interested in the *impression* of reality experienced by the prisoners in the cave, which he sees as no different from hallucination in a waking state, and dream in sleeping (ibid.). And so he turns to Freud's work on dreams and discovers a few observations that he finds useful for his argument:

> After having shown how the [analytic] treatment gets itself represented [in dreams], Freud comes to the unconscious. 'If the unconscious, insofar as it belongs to waking thought, needs to be represented in dreams, it is represented in them in underground places.' Freud adds the following which, because of the above, is very interesting: 'Outside of analytic treatment, these representations would have symbolized the woman's body or the womb.'
> (pp. 307–8)

This passage in Baudry's text occurs after he refers to the fact that caves have often been considered as representations of the maternal womb (p. 306). Freud's statement introduces an additional signified to the cave, or underground chamber: in dreams, it represents the unconscious. Further on, Baudry quotes Freud again, who states that from a somatic point of view, sleep is a return to the time spent in the body of the mother. The sleeping state induces two types of regression: a temporal regression to a period of hallucinatory satisfaction of desire and to a primal narcissism; and topical regression, which by permitting easier communication among conscious, pre-conscious and unconscious, allows cathetic representations to be perceived (pp. 308–9).

Baudry then moves dream a step closer to the cinematic apparatus by introducing Bertram Lewin's concept of the *dream screen*, inspired by the cinema screen in its unobtrusiveness, and defined as the surface on which a dream appears to be projected (p. 310). The dream screen is a hallucinatory representation of the breast on which the infant used to fall asleep after feeding, and so it reproduces an early state of satisfaction. He describes Lewin's hypothesis of the dream screen as corresponding to the desire to be asleep, and the projected dream images to the desire to be awake; Baudry sees these two forces resulting in a hallucinated *more-than-real*, characteristic of the dream state in its desire for both wished representations and contact with the real. Lewin's concept of the dream screen pertains to the oral phase, specifically to the time before the mirror stage, when the infant still fails to differentiate between representation and perception, and to locate the limits of the body (p. 311).

In a previous article titled 'Ideological Effects of the Basic Cinematographic Apparatus' (1970), it is the scene of the mirror stage that Baudry relates to the cinematic situation. He sees this scene re-enacted not only in the subject's identification with what is represented on the screen, but also in an identification with a transcendental self that operates as the camera, in that it assembles fragments of experience into unifying meaning, like the mirror assembles a fragmented body into an imaginary whole (pp. 293–5). The fact that the screen never (or almost never) reflects the subject's own body, also recognized by Christian Metz (1975a, p. 45),[1] changes Baudry's focus from the mirror stage to an earlier period in the oral phase. But specular processes of identification are not completely disregarded in the subsequent article 'The Apparatus'. The pleasure derived from the operation of these processes is only one of those Baudry finds to explain the subject's relation to the cinematic projection. The darkened theatre, the immobility of the subject and the projection of images are conducive to a regression of the libido to a primal narcissism that is typically experienced by the dreamer, and to a moment of satisfaction in the infant-breast relationship, part of a phase of development where the interior is confused with the exterior (1975, p. 313). Baudry expands on this state of fusion of the body with the environment, experienced by the dreamer and the subject in the cinema, as an effect caused by the succession of images and by the subject's motor inhibition, which subdues reality testing and thus leads the subject to perceive representations as reality. This brings Baudry to his concluding remarks on the issue of the impression of reality in the cinema:

> If the confusion between representation and perception is characteristic of the primary process which is governed by the pleasure principle, and which is the basic condition for the satisfaction produced by hallucination, the cinematographic apparatus appears to succeed in suspending the secondary process and anything having to do with the principle of reality without eliminating it completely.
>
> (p. 314)

For Baudry, the impression of reality in the cinema is precisely engendered by the partial suppression of the secondary process and the reality principle. Still, as Freud postulated, the repetitive phenomenon of traumatic dream is not governed by the pleasure principle, and yet it is a representation passing for perception. In Baudry's article, the only reference to Freud's theory of what is beyond the pleasure principle is made when he considers that Plato's prisoners would rather perpetuate their immobility inside the cave than go outside: 'Initial constraint which seems in this way to turn itself into a kind of spite or at least to inscribe the compulsion to repeat, the return to a former condition' (p. 303). Yet Baudry only takes up this idea of the prisoners' immobility, in his view similar to that of the infant, the sleeper and the subject in the cinema, insofar as it precludes reality testing.

Turning for a moment to Donald Meltzer's commentary on Freud's 'Beyond the Pleasure Principle', it becomes apparent that Baudry does not take into account some of the mechanisms underlying dreams. Meltzer states that Freud realized his dream theory was inadequate to understand the dreams repeatedly had by analysands suffering from traumatic war neuroses. These dreams were mere repetitions of the traumatic experience, or expected traumatic experience, and thus they did not follow a dream structure that could be subsumed under wish-fulfilment dream theory, or failure of wish-fulfilment as in anxiety dream theory. Meltzer explains how Freud resolved this problem:

> At the most primitive levels of instinct, the instincts manifest an economic principle which is in essence a mindless compulsion to repeat: to repeat in a sense that is 'beyond' the pleasure principle, that is, having nothing to do with questions of pleasure or pain, but being simply the tendency to repeat endlessly the experience by which an instinct has manifested itself in the primitive organization of the child's mind and relationships.[2]
>
> (1978, I, pp. 116–17)

Meltzer includes a critique of Freud's theory, which gives some indication of the Kleinian developments that it was to undergo at a later point. Meltzer defends that the 'Project for a Scientific Psychology', written as early as 1895, can be used as a template for recognizing Freud's preconceptions when thinking about clinical data (p. 6). In the first three parts of 'Beyond the Pleasure Principle', Freud proposes the new economic principle of repetition compulsion in an attempt to understand the traumatic neuroses, the repetitiveness of children's play and the reliving of unpleasurable childhood events in the transference. Meltzer considers this to be the clinical part of the paper, but the remainder he sees as an 'extremely elaborate speculation' concerned with the aims of the 'Project', when Freud proposes that the compulsion to repeat is in fact a compulsion to return to an inorganic state (p. 117). Meltzer also underlines that the emotions of love and hate, which are attached to the life and death instincts, have no mention in Freud's paper, and thus his theory is one where affects and meaning have no place. He writes:

> Freud enunciates the significance of a life instinct which is constructive, building greater units; and a death instinct which destructively tears them down, reducing life to an inorganic state; but of course this says nothing about the meaning which these processes have as they manifest themselves in mental life. Therefore it can be (and is) linked with biology and the behaviour of the protozoa; with the 'Project' 's scheme for the distribution of excitations and the reduction of tensions to a minimum; with the constancy principle and the Nirvana principle.
>
> (Meltzer, p. 118)

So what are, in Meltzer's view, Freud's advancements with 'Beyond the Pleasure Principle'? Freud can now conceive of destructiveness as an instinctual force, as opposed to its being simply the outcome of a frustrated sexual instinct. This primary destructiveness is the death instinct, under which category can fall, and which partly elucidates, cruelty, violence and sado-masochism (ibid.). Masochism, the traumatic neuroses and the phenomenon of transference can now be located under the economic principle of repetition compulsion. Still, Meltzer expresses his belief that Freud did not view this new theory of the instincts as introducing any major changes in his conception of mental functioning, but only that it provided a more flexible framework for the manipulation of cathexes. It is worth noting that masochism, about which more will be said later, is the only phenomenon in Meltzer's text to appear both under the death instinct and the repetition compulsion categories.

To continue the review of Baudry's article, it is only necessary at this stage to reiterate that Baudry's use of psychoanalytic theory in his conceptualization of the cinematic apparatus rests in a conception of dream as wish-fulfilment; in pleasurable identification processes rooted in the mirror stage; and in the concept of the dream screen, formed during a pleasurable moment in the oral phase to which the subject in the cinema regresses. The principle of repetition compulsion and the working of the death instinct are omitted from his theory. Nevertheless, in the last footnote of the article, Baudry opens up the issue of the cinematic apparatus to further development, and if his suggestion is followed, the neglected concept of the death instinct is going to feature prominently. He begins by stating that the idea of regression to a moment in the oral phase may seem strange in connection with the cinema, but then he explains that in the cinema situation the visual orifice has taken the place of the mouth. The last sentence reads: 'In the same order of ideas, it may be useful to reintroduce Melanie Klein's hypothesis on the oral phase, her extremely complex dialectics between the inside and the outside which refer to reciprocal forms of development' (p. 318). Baudry did not take this task on, and so to see what these complex dialectics may be, is what I propose to do next.

Kleinian developments

In her 1958 paper on the development of mental functioning, Klein considers Freud's discovery of the life and death instincts as a major breakthrough in the understanding of the mind (p. 236). But Klein places greater emphasis on destructive impulses and aggression than Freud, who gives more importance to the libido. Klein writes:

> Although long before he discovered the life and death instincts he had seen the importance of the destructive component of sexuality in the form of sadism, he did not give sufficient weight to aggression in its impact on emotional life. Perhaps, therefore, he never fully worked out his discovery of the two instincts and seemed reluctant to extend it to the whole of mental functioning.
>
> (p. 245)

The operation of the life and death instincts gives rise to a complex interaction of anxieties, defences and object relations during the first year of the life of the infant, which Klein divides into the paranoid-schizoid position and the depressive position (1952, p. 61). The term 'position' is meant to describe, better than 'phase' or 'stage', particular configurations of object relations that recur throughout life (p. 93).

The paranoid-schizoid position, mostly active during the first three to four months, derives its name from the preponderance of paranoid anxiety and splitting (p. 70). The infant's fear of annihilation and the anxiety produced from the experience of birth and from the loss of the intra-uterine state cause aggressive impulses to be split off from the ego and projected into the breast, or bottle. In this way the primal process of projection is used to deflect the death instinct outwards, turning the breast into a bad, persecuting object, which is hated; the projection of the life instinct in the form of libidinal impulses turns the breast into a loved, good breast (pp. 61–3). The split in the object and the strong opposition of the emotions attached to it are consequences of the lack of integration or cohesion of the early ego. The ego splits the object into good and bad, splits the relation to the object, and so a split occurs within the ego itself. Good and bad objects, of which the external and internalized good breast and bad breast are the prototypes, are established in reality and phantasy, from gratifying and frustrating experiences. These experiences affect and are affected by phantasy: 'Thus the picture of the object, external and internalized, is distorted in the infant's mind by his phantasies, which are bound up with the projection of his impulses on to the object' (p. 63). Therefore, a frustrating moment can lead the infant to attack the breast in phantasy and then perceive it as a vengeful internal and external persecutor.

The intensity of frustration and privation determines the intensity of greed and envy. Greed is an emotion primarily associated with introjection as its aim is to completely scoop out and devour the breast; envy has a projective aspect, as it not only aims to rob the breast of its goodness, but it also seeks to put badness into it. For Klein this destructive process means, in its deepest sense, to destroy the mother's creativeness. She points to the origin of the word 'envy', which lies in the Latin *invideo*, meaning 'to cast an evil eye upon' (1957, p. 181). According to Meltzer (II, p. 23), Klein considers envy to be one of the main manifestations of the death instinct. Meltzer regards the distinction she makes between envy and jealousy as the beginning of 'an important development in psycho-analysis, of finding words with which to dissect emotions' (p. 24). Klein writes:

> Envy is the angry feeling that another person possesses and enjoys something desirable – the envious impulse being to take it away or to spoil it. Moreover, envy implies the subject's relation to one person only and goes back to the earliest exclusive relation with the mother. Jealousy is based on envy, but involves a relation to at least two people; it is mainly concerned with love that the subject feels is his due and has been taken away, or is in danger of being taken away, from him by his rival.
>
> (1957, p. 181)

Envy disturbs the development and stability of good object relations, causing a lack of differentiation between good and bad (p. 230). It can arise in situations of privation, in which the breast is felt to keep all the goodness to itself, but equally in situations of gratification, in which the gifts of the breast are felt to be unattainable (p. 183).

The process of putting bad parts of the self into the breast leads to a particular form of identification discovered by Klein, which she terms 'projective identification'.

In projective identification, parts of the personality are split off and projected into an external object which becomes identified with the projected parts (Klein, 1955, p. 143). This mechanism enables the subject to experience feelings and to live out impulses towards an object that sometimes stands for another. Projective or introjective identification with objects that have characteristics in common with the subject can occur, but also with objects that manifest opposite characteristics, as a defence against an overwhelming identification (pp. 168–9). Excessive projective processes result in an impoverishment of the ego, while a balance between projection and introjection contributes towards integration and the assimilation of internal objects (Klein, 1946, p. 11). The mechanism of projective identification is vital in the early stages of development, since it is the earliest form of empathy and symbol formation (Segal, 1964, p. 36). It is also a fundamental aspect of the experience of film, but one that arguably has not been sufficiently understood in apparatus theory. I will come back to this at later points and elucidate how Bion and Meltzer develop this concept.

When gratifying experiences prevail over frustrating ones, splitting and projection are attenuated, and the distinction between self and object gradually becomes clearer, allowing the transition to the depressive position (p. 37). Manifestation of the depressive position generally begins in the second quarter of the first year (Klein, 1952, p. 71). In this position, in contrast with the previous one that is characterized by relations to part-objects, the infant begins to perceive whole objects and to bring closer together internal and external figures; there is a growing realization that it is the same person, the mother, who comes and goes, who is on occasions good, on others bad, who is sometimes loved, sometimes hated. The infant's main anxieties derive from the discovery of ambivalence, and from a fear of having injured or destroyed the loved object. The intense feelings of loss, guilt and helplessness experienced in the depressive position lead to a wish to restore the external loved objects which are felt to be no longer available, and repair the internal loved objects which are felt to be in bits (p. 77). Reparative and creative impulses are distributed on these objects, among them parts of the self, which become substitutes for the primary object, the mother. These projective processes give rise to symbols and sublimations (p. 83). True reparation is distinguished from manic reparation in that the first is carried out with a genuine concern for the loved object, whereas the latter aims to avert persecutory anxiety caused by a damaged object that becomes equated with a malevolent object (Meltzer, II, p. 99). The assimilation of good objects under favourable circumstances, as well as an increased awareness of psychic reality and external reality, contribute to the working through of depressive anxiety and the gradual strengthening of the ego. Internally, this process is dependent on the dominance of the life instinct over the death instinct (Klein, 1958, pp. 242–3). Nevertheless, Klein's metapsychological approach to the constitution of the ego emphasizes the ceaseless dynamics between the two instincts:

> Even when the life instinct and the capacity for love predominate, destructive impulses are still deflected outwards and contribute to the creation of persecutory and dangerous objects which are reintrojected. Furthermore, the primal processes of introjection and projection lead to constant changes in the ego's relation to its objects, with fluctuations between internal and external, good and bad ones, according to the infant's phantasies and emotions as well as under the impact of his actual experiences. The complexity of these fluctuations engendered by the perpetual activity of the two instincts underlies the development of the ego in its relation to the external world as well as the building up of the internal world.
>
> (p. 239)

The complex dialectics between the internal and external worlds that Baudry mentions in the last footnote to his article are thus theorized to be underlain by the continual operation of the life and death instincts. Following Klein, the subject's regression to a primordial stage in the cinema would most likely involve traces of a whole gamut of emotions such as aggression, anxiety, fear, hatred, greed, envy, jealousy, love, empathy, guilt, helplessness, depression, genuine concern.

Meltzer argues that Klein explicitly works with Freud's model of the mind, as she is not preoccupied with changing it, but that her clinical descriptions actually reveal a very different conception of the mind. Unlike Freud's model, hers does not attempt to explain the causal relations between a mass of psychic energy manipulated by the vicissitudes of instinct, and the demands of the id, the superego and the external world (Meltzer, III, pp. 112–13). Klein describes a developmental process in which an internal geography that is concretely built up in the mind, through projection and introjection, provides the meaning and emotional significance to the forms of the external world. The interaction between the inner and outer worlds, and the view of the inner world as a primary locus for the generation of meaningful emotional relations, is considered by Meltzer to further invaluably the understanding of the mind:

> We see the external world *as*, that is as a reflection of internal relations from the point of view of meaning and significance. There is no such apparatus in Freud's model, the distinction between Pleasure and Reality Principles being so bound to body sensations and gratification of instinctual needs, the alternative to which is hallucinatory wish fulfillment.
>
> (p. 42)

Here Meltzer restates his belief that not only is Freud's discovery of the death instinct not fully integrated in his model of the mind, but also that he never fully conceptualized a concrete inner world where objects live and relate to the ego continuously. But for the moment, my aim is to have shown that an understanding of the cinematic apparatus through Klein's metapsychology entails thinking of processes that go beyond pleasurable identifications and wish-fulfilment.

Klein's theory of object relations has a sparse though explicit presence in Christian Metz's two seminal articles that were originally published in the journal *Communications*, and with which I am concerned here. In 'The Imaginary Signifier', Metz establishes his notion of film as a bad object: 'For the spectator, the film can on occasion be a "bad object": then we have *filmic unpleasure*, [. . .] which defines the relation of certain spectators to certain films, or of certain groups of spectators to certain groups of films' (1975a, pp. 6–7). Metz's definition of film as a bad object is tied with unpleasure, and it denotes the relation of the subject to a film as a whole. In the other article titled 'The Fiction Film and its Spectator: A Metapsychological Study', Metz describes how filmic unpleasure can occur, which, again, he sees as coextensive with films becoming bad objects, or objects that the subject does not like (1975b, pp. 110–12). I will first consider Metz's ideas on the impression of reality in the cinema, since it is the examination of this attribute that leads him to a discussion of filmic pleasure and filmic unpleasure.

Cinema as an integrated object

In 'The Fiction Film and its Spectator: A Metapsychological Study', Metz's main focus is to establish a kinship between fiction film and dream, and between fiction film and phantasy. Out of the forty pages that constitute this article, fewer than three are assigned to a consideration of filmic unpleasure, as the kinship between film and dream that Metz emphasizes is founded on the belief that both film and dream promote a narcissistic withdrawal and the gratifying experience of phantasy, as well as a lack of concern for the exterior world and its real objects (p. 107). Like Baudry, Metz draws largely on Freudian dream theory in its description of the psychical mechanisms operating during sleep, and also in intermediary states between sleeping and waking. For Metz, the fact that the subject is immobile and silent during the projection of the film causes the emergence of a state of sleepiness, and this in turn engenders a dreamlike confusion between film and reality (p. 103). The strength of this confusion, which Metz names 'perceptual transference', fluctuates in an inverted proportion to the state of wakefulness. The subject in the cinema suffers a *paradoxical hallucination*, because the weakening function of reality testing and the confusion between different levels of reality approximate to a real hallucination; still this hallucination is paradoxical in that it is not a purely internal psychical production (p. 104). Metz's explanation for the impression of reality in the cinema is not far from Baudry's, as it is based on a sub-motor, semi-regressive, intermediary state between waking and sleep, which makes the subject particularly receptive to sense impressions from within, while the film itself offers an intense sensory experience from without. Metz argues that it is this perceptual *double reinforcement* that causes the impression of reality in the cinema (p. 118).

The kinship of fiction film with dream is then extended to phantasy. Metz sees this kinship confirmed in the way a film can arouse spirited responses, be they positive or negative, and in the existence of filmic unpleasure itself (p. 110). It is clear how filmic unpleasure can arise from instances that do not accord with the subject's phantasy, as he points out, but why could filmic unpleasure not equally confirm the kinship of fiction film with reality? Further in his argument, Metz compares again film with dream, and states that the latter is more bound to the pleasure principle, whereas film, even though it has pleasure as its final aim, is closer to the reality principle. The reasoning behind this assertion is that film, in its material existence, is not constructed internally by the subject (p. 113). And here again, dream is taken as wish-fulfilment:

> The dream responds to the wish with more exactitude and regularity: devoid of exterior material, it is assured of never colliding with reality (and reality includes other people's phantasy). It is like a film which has been 'shot' from beginning to end by the very subject of the wish – also the subject of fear – a singular film by virtue of its censorship and omissions as much as its expressed content, cut to the measure of its only spectator (this is another sort of *découpage*), a spectator who is also the *auteur* and has every reason to be content with it, since one is never so well served as by oneself.
>
> (Metz, pp. 112–13)

In his exposition of dream theory, Metz mentions the occurrence of dreams that cause excessive fear, but they are only considered insofar as they prevent the subject from continuing to dream or from sleeping (p. 105); such situations are already outside the realm of perceptual transference, and since Metz places this phenomenon at the core of the relation he establishes between film and dream, the dreams that cause fear, as repetitions of unpleasurable experiences, escape formulation in his theory of the apparatus.

It is important now to examine how Metz believes filmic unpleasure is produced. In order to explain the experience of unpleasure in the cinema, he turns to Freud's structural model of the psyche. First Metz describes the instance of unpleasure that occurs when the id is not given enough instinctual satisfaction, that is, when the film is considered boring or dull. Then he describes another instance of unpleasure that arises when the id is so intensely satisfied that the superego and the defences of the ego intervene against the film, which is then experienced as a bad, dangerous object. Metz's examples of films where this may occur include films that are sentimental, pornographic, grotesque, or films that lack verisimilitude. He observes that unpleasure arises from these two psychical paths or from their convergence; these are the sources of dislike for a film (p. 111). Therefore, for Metz, filmic unpleasure exists, but not in its essence: it is rather experienced as not enough pleasure, or as a defence against overwhelming pleasure, or both. This formulation of the emergence of unpleasure in the cinema is undoubtedly influenced by Freud's theory of the libido, which accounts for the deployment of quantitative levels of energy. Donald Meltzer (I, p. 141) argues that Freud's theory, in spite of being undermined by his later work on masochism and the transformations of instincts, still permeates his thinking and that of many psychoanalysts after him. Around 1914, when Freud writes 'On Narcissism', he conceives of the narcissistic stage as in between auto-erotism (in which libidinal impulses are directed towards the infant's own body) and object relations (when object-seeking begins and libidinal impulses are aimed at other people's bodies) (p. 106). Yet Freud's general conception of love at this point, Meltzer defends, is nothing more than a desire for self-gratification: the ego is depleted by investing the object with libido, but always with the purpose of regaining it (p. 84). It follows that mental pain is caused by an impoverished or suppressed libido:

> Freud's attachment to the Libido Theory, which must seek to explain things simply on the basis of the distribution of libido, binds him to the idea that mental pain is radically connected to maldistribution of the libido; that the absence of pleasure derives from either a dammed-up libido or – as he is thinking at this stage – from a drained-out and impoverished libido.
>
> (Meltzer, pp. 84–5)

A year later, with the paper on 'Mourning and Melancholia', Freud begins to think of mental pain as something other than the mere absence of pleasure, or frustration of the libido, which implies thinking of destructiveness and evil as inherent to human nature, not as something derived from the absence of happiness (pp. 86–7). It calls to mind Klein's view of envy as an emotion that can arise in situations of gratification. Freud realizes that pain is something that can shift between the ego and its object, something that may be got rid of into external objects; and that being in pain can involve the 'mysterious process of identification with an object in pain' (p. 86),[3] a problem which cannot be approached with the theory of the economics of the libido.

But before examining these identification processes more closely, what conclusions can be drawn regarding Metz's use of object relations theory? His propositions can be found in 'The Imaginary Signifier', in a subsection titled 'The Imaginary and the "Good Object" in the Cinema and in the Theory of the Cinema'. The polarity of the paranoid-schizoid position and the depressive position is noticeable in Metz's consideration of the nature of film criticism, which for him oscillates between persecutory polemic and depressive reparation of the film-object (p. 10). As discussed above, the ambivalence of object relations is present in his notion of the subject's relation to film. But it is important to note that Metz conceives of a very clear split between films as good objects and films as bad objects; he construes the relation to film as ambivalent, but not the relation to *a* film as ambivalent. Thus he does not consider a film to be an *integrated* object, that can be good or bad at different times or in different aspects; and also that the subject's relation to the same film may be susceptible to change or develop in the course of the subject's life. And still, within this radically split ambivalence, Metz believes that in the theory, as in the consumption of film, it is cinema as a 'good object' that prevails, since the subject becomes a component that produces and consumes film and its discourse in a machinery whose only purpose is pleasure.

He writes:

> Filmic pleasure and filmic unpleasure, although they correspond to the two imaginary objects shaped by the persecutory splitting described by Melanie Klein, are not in my view arranged in positions of antithetic symmetry, since the institution as a whole has filmic pleasure alone as its aim.
>
> (Metz, p. 7)

In his argument, he confines his conceptualization of the cinematic apparatus to film as a cultural production of a capitalist industrial society (p. 3), and to what he describes as narrative film, or fictional, diegetic, novelistic, representational, traditional, or classical, terms which he uses as 'provisional synonyms but which from other points of view must be distinguished' (1975b, p. 139). To a certain extent, his theory can be understood as regarding the 'Once upon a time . . .' of fiction film to be inextricable from dream, phantasy and the profits of the entertainment industry. But a closer inspection reveals that, for Metz, there are no films that fall outside this category. After reflecting on the absence of objects in film, as they are only given as images, he concludes that 'every film is a fiction film' (1975a, p. 44). In another instance, considering erotic and political films, he affirms that 'these genres contradict themselves in their pseudo-rupture of the fiction' and irremediably fail to mobilize the subject, as the screening situation ('*séance*' in French, which can also mean 'sitting') would have to be changed for these films to 'truly begin to exist as *films*' (1975b, p. 117). Thus, even though he writes that narrative fiction film is only one of the possible films (p. 125), Metz gives the impression that these other possible films, for him, do not actually exist.

Is Baudry's theorization of the cinema equally all-encompassing? In 'The Apparatus', Baudry does not specify the kind, or kinds of films he has in mind when he refers to the cinema; he only states that he disagrees with those who think of cinema as an ideologically neutral apparatus whose influence is solely dependent on the content of the film (p. 312). In the earlier 'Ideological Effects of the Basic Cinematographic Apparatus' it is evident, at times, that he is concerned with narrative film, for example when he considers the importance of obtaining narrative continuity from an assemblage of discontinuous elements (frames, shots) for meaning to be constituted (p. 293). In the last section of this article, when he introduces the mirror stage to explain the two levels of identification that occur in the cinema, it is the subject's identification with the camera that is crucial for cinema to exert ideological influence, as long as the camera allows the subject to constitute itself 'in a particular mode of specular reflection' (p. 295). He continues: 'Ultimately, the forms of narrative adopted, the "contents" of the image, are of little importance so long as an identification remains possible' (ibid.). Baudry believes this identification is only possible if cinema's instrumentation is effaced; its revelation disturbs the pleasure of specular reflection. Thus, with the exception of films that reveal the mechanisms by which they are produced, it can be inferred from an examination of these two articles that Baudry considers all other kinds of film shown at the cinema to reproduce ideology in a way that is pleasurable.

It is certain that cinema imparts ideology, but so does any other cultural production; not so obvious is whether cinema does this in a way that is always pleasurable. Furthermore, even in those films excluded by Baudry, in which the pleasures of specularity are disrupted, it can be argued that other kinds of identifications are still possible. Vivian Sobchack (2004, p. 65) approaches the issue of identification, from a phenomenological perspective, by recognizing a sensorial engagement with the film's materiality. Sobchack also mentions Laura Marks's concept of 'ambient identification', which proposes a displacement of the subject from any rigid positionings within and in relation to the filmic image (p. 66). As stated in the introduction to this book, my conceptualization of the apparatus is not circumscribed by any particular kinds of films.

From what has already been examined in Baudry's and Metz's theories of the cinema, it can be observed that for these authors the cinema is a retreat from reality, into wish-fulfilling dreams and phantasies, ideological manipulation, and pleasurable inaction. But is it always the promise of pleasure and its fulfilment that prevail in the cinema?

The centrality of the subject in the scopic arrangement of the cinema is also studied by Metz, and developed in connection with other psychical mechanisms. In the following section, I consider Metz's ideas on these processes while weaving through the work of Gaylyn Studlar, whose response to Metz will further the exploration of questions of pleasure and unpleasure in the cinema.

Absence covered over?

Although each of the three last sections of 'The Imaginary Signifier' deals with a different issue in a psychoanalytic reading of the apparatus, the idea of absence is recurrent in all of them, and so it binds them together. In the first of these sections, dedicated to a study of cinematic identifications, Metz begins by comparing the cinema with the theatre. According to Metz, the action in the theatre unfolds in a space with actors and objects that are really there when they are perceived, while the experience of a film in the cinema and its understanding are dependent on the perception of the object as image, that is, on the perception of the object as absent (p. 57). As mentioned earlier, Metz states that a film does not normally give back an image of the subject; he further comments that this absence of the subject from the screen does not impede the intelligibility of the film, as the experience of the primordial mirror allows the constitution of a world of objects in which the recognition of the subject's own body is still to be fully attained (p. 46).

In addition to the constitution of an imaginary world of objects, Metz believes that the pleasures of mastery connected with the mirror stage are reactivated during the experience of fiction film. In a similar way to the images in the mirror, the images on the screen converge on the vanishing point of the scene represented, and also on the position occupied by the perceiving subject, which merges with the privileged position of the camera-projector (p. 49). This is what Metz calls *primary cinematic identification*, an identification of the subject with the camera-projector as the focus of vision (p. 56).[4] The position of the subject here is inherited from that which shaped the representation of space in the West since the time of *quattrocento* painting, constructed according to laws of perspective that centre on a single point that stands for the eyes of the viewing subject. Metz is aware, as Baudry is too, of the ideological implications of such topographical arrangement. He writes:

> I take no part in the perceived, on the contrary, I am *all-perceiving*. All-perceiving as one says all-powerful (this is the famous gift of 'ubiquity' the film makes its spectator); all-perceiving, too, because I am entirely on the side of the perceiving instance: absent from the screen, but certainly present in the auditorium, a great eye and ear without which the perceived would have no one to perceive it, the instance, in other words, which *constitutes* the cinema signifier (it is I who make the film).
>
> (Metz, p. 48)

Metz states that this all-powerful position 'is that of God himself, or more broadly of some ultimate signified' (p. 49). This is a major point of disagreement between Metz and Gaylyn Studlar. For her, the subject in the cinema is all-perceiving, but not all-powerful (1988, p. 188). Studlar's conceptualization of the apparatus draws on Gilles Deleuze's theory of masochism, which focuses on pre-Oedipal stages of development, when the infant's dependence on the mother is most felt. The process of separation from the mother, initiated at birth and continued by her presence and absence, engenders a feeling of uncertainty of the permanence of the infant's being and of the being of the mother. It is this dependence on the mother that sets Studlar's theorization radically apart from Metz's, as the controlling, sadistic look of the subject that he identifies as operating in the cinema, is inverted in Studlar's formulation: the infant, the masochist and the subject in the cinema submit to the maternal body and gaze (pp. 29–30).

In the following section of 'The Imaginary Signifier', Metz develops the idea of absence in relation to voyeuristic desire. The objects on the screen are absent, inaccessible, distant, and so they do not acknowledge directly the presence of the perceiving subject, who becomes a voyeur. This 'unauthorized scopophilia' is seen to have a special affinity with the primal scene, which unfolds in a space that is separate from the subject, and in which the subject cannot participate (pp. 63–4). The contact with the object is only visual and auditory. Metz uses Lacan's conception of the scopic and invocatory drives, the aim of which is to fill a lack, but also to perpetuate that pursuit so the pleasure of desiring is not extinguished (pp. 58–9). For Metz, the distance maintained between subject and object defines the relation that the scopic and invocatory drives have with their object, an object that is absent because it is distant. This retention of the separation of spaces is seen as a source of sadistic pleasure:

> If it is true of all desire that it depends on the infinite pursuit of its absent object, voyeuristic desire, along with certain forms of sadism, is the

only desire whose principle of distance symbolically and spatially evokes this fundamental rent.

(Metz, p. 60)

Referring to this same statement, Studlar refutes the idea that sadism requires distance between subject and object. Her reading of the Sadian text shows that sadistic pleasure resides in the injury and penetration of the object, that is, in the violation of the object and of boundaries. Instead, Studlar (p. 27) believes that the pleasure derived from the suspension of consummation, which maintains a distance between subject and object and delays their union, is precisely masochistic. Thus scopophilia is seen to originate in the masochistic phantasy, more specifically in its earliest form, which is pre-Oedipal. In Studlar's view, scopophilia reinscribes the conflict between separation and symbiosis with the mother during the infant's oral stage (p. 187). The lack of cohesion of the infant's body and ego engenders the experience of a hallucinated state of fusion with the mother, which is not only seen as the prototype of the masochistic phantasy, but also as the gratifying hallucinated breast that constitutes the dream screen. Citing the work of Baudry and others that use the concept of the dream screen, Studlar brings a masochistic, as well as fetishistic aspect to the pleasure of looking in the cinema:

> Both the hallucinated breast and the cinematic dream screen offer only a temporary and partial gratification of the symbiotic wish. Just as the hallucinated breast cannot offer real nourishment or interaction with the mother, the cinematic apparatus cannot provide intimacy or fusion with real objects. The intimacy of perversion prevails even in the pleasure of cinema: the spectator must disavow an absence.
>
> (Studlar, p. 184)

The intimacy between subject and object in the cinema is described by Studlar as perverse and false, because the object is absent, or, as she puts it, 'merely light and shadow' (p. 180). The dream screen is the disavowal of that absence, it is the fetish, the reconstruction of the mother as inseparable oneness, the transitional object that marks (and masks) the separation from her (p. 43). This conception of fetishism is again very different from the one that Metz uses in the last section of 'The Imaginary Signifier'. Metz turns to Freud and Lacan who believe fetishism is determined in the Oedipal phase, by castration fear: 'the fetish signifies the penis as absent, it is its negative signifier; supplementing it, it puts a "fullness" in place of a lack, but in doing so it also affirms that lack' (p. 71). Here, the fetish is a prop whose function is to assuage the fear of castration. Metz identifies the operation of the fetish in the apparatus of the cinema in that it presents objects that are absent, but also in the fiction film's attempt at verisimilitude, and in the frame of the film for what it reveals and hides from view (pp. 72–8).

Studlar does not question the relevance of Oedipal stages of development to understand the psychodynamics of the apparatus, but her drawing on earlier stages that are not yet sexually differentiated allows her to develop a theory in which gender roles and identifications become fluid (p. 185). Her contribution constitutes an important response to Metz and other Freudian/Lacanian theories of the apparatus, and also to the critiques they received, for they imply and denounce, respectively, a pleasure dynamic in which the male is the active, masterful subject of the look, and the female its passive object.[5]

Now that Metz's articulation of absence in the cinema has been examined, to be returned to when I introduce Bion's theory of thinking, it will be useful to delve deeper into the question of masochism, a question which, as has been shown, is not approached by Metz.

Studlar's review of Freud's work on masochism emphasizes his neglect of the role of pre-genital stages in the formation of the perversion, and consequently, of the mother as a central and independent figure in its structure (pp. 12–15). In her outline of Freud's 'A Child Is Being Beaten', Studlar explains that the male child's desire for the mother turns into desire for the father because of feelings of guilt. The punishment for desiring the mother is to be beaten (a substitute for being castrated) by the father. Conscious phantasies in which the mother is the punishing figure disguise the father and homosexual desire for him; passivity and identification with the mother in copulation and in giving birth are aimed at gaining the father's love.

Reconsidering masochism's etiology with Deleuze's model and recent object relations theory, which locate it within the oral stage, Studlar regards the mother as the crucial object of the child's ambivalence: she is both the loving and the punishing figure, not a disguise or substitute for the father (p. 15). The phantasy of symbiosis with the mother is then elaborated into a phantasy of death:

> Because symbiotic remerger is a physical impossibility, death becomes the fantasy fulfillment to desire. It does not signal the defeat of desire or the end of the masochist's anticipated final triumph; rather, it is the promise of a fantasmical parthenogenetic rebirth from the mother, which is the final mystical solution to the expiation of the father and the symbiotic reunion with an idealized maternal rule.
>
> (Studlar, p. 26)

A tautological statement, as death and rebirth are here understood as the route to reunion with the mother, not as regeneration or transformation of the self. Later in her book Studlar attempts to establish a link between masochistic pleasure and repetition compulsion as a manifestation of the death instinct (p. 182). But this idea is only articulated as a possibility that might be suggested by Deleuze's construct, and although she does not state it as such, she must be aware, as has been shown earlier with Meltzer's comment on 'Beyond the Pleasure Principle', that repetition compulsion was theorized by Freud as a phenomenon separate from questions of pleasure or pain. In a footnote, Studlar mentions Kaja Silverman's investigation of masochism within a framework of instinct theory, but she adds that it is more logical to approach the perversion as an ego function (p. 238). Still, Studlar writes that masochism shows that there is pleasure in repeating situations other than those of mastery, and immediately after this she introduces, quoting Hans Loewald, the force of the life instinct into the working of the death instinct in order to account for the pleasure to be found in pain:

> The repetition of traumatic events, either real ones or imaginary projections formed out of infantile frustration, makes available the pleasure of loss, suffering, and submission. Loewald describes the primordial lure of the traumatic, even self-destructive experience as the pleasure of those 'ecstatic states . . . where love and self-destruction, Eros and Thanatos are merged into one.' For Loewald, the essence of this lure is the resistance to giving up an intense and unique experience, 'whether painful or blissful,' which becomes 'forever longed for'.
>
> (Studlar, pp. 182–3)

This passage suggests that Studlar considers the possibility that such an intensity of experience might be sought with the aim of attaining a fulfilment where it is lacking; or because such an experience is felt to move towards the state in which experience becomes extinct, or turns to nothingness. Studlar makes other attempts to address the difficult problem of 'pleasure in pain'. She considers, alongside other explanations, that masochism's pleasure-pain dynamic could, in effect, be secondary in importance to that of subject positioning: it is rather the symbolic nature of punishment that is key to the understanding of the perversion (pp. 15–16). Drawing on Deleuze's idea of the child's disavowal of phallic inheritance, Studlar states that 'the suspension of orgasmic gratification symbolically expels the father's genital likeness' (p. 16). In a perhaps more persuasive account, Studlar goes on to describe the masochistic structure of pleasure as it is theorized by Deleuze, in terms of Freud's structural model:

> In masochism, the ego is split. Finding its ideal ego in the mother, the narcissistic ego seeks to mystify the superego's repressive demands for pain, which becomes an empty signifier, the masquerade for guilt. [. . .] Rituals of suffering show the masochist's contempt for the superego's expectation that punishment could prevent forbidden pleasure.
>
> (Studlar, pp. 17–18)

In this scheme, masochism affords the pleasure of an ego 'liberated' from the superego. For all its merit in bringing the complex issue of pain to a study of the cinema, as well as defending the importance of the replay of early psychical stages in the subject's maturation (pp. 190–1), Studlar's work is still 'in the realm of pleasure'. Here, masochism is not the mindless repetition of really painful pain, supposedly because pain which is not perverted into pleasure does not enter the definition of masochism. But what about pain that is not mindlessly repeated, or pain that is not perverted into pleasure? In an attempt to begin to answer this question, I will now turn to Donald Meltzer's analysis of Freud's paper 'A Child Is Being Beaten', in the context of the evolution of Freud's thinking.

Unpleasure, anxiety, pain, and the epistemophilic instinct

In Freud's 1915 paper titled 'Instincts and their Vicissitudes', and in a subsequent work 'On Transformations of Instincts', written two years later, Meltzer sees an important development in Freud's way of thinking, the key to which can be found in the use of the terms 'vicissitudes' in the first article, and 'transformations' in the second (Meltzer, I, p. 103). While during this time Freud was also writing about the Wolf Man case, which helps him recognize the complexity of perversions, he was still conceiving of mental life fundamentally in its economic aspects, still thinking in terms of 'psychic energy' (which he saw as something like electricity, hydrostatic energy or heat), and of affects as variable quantities of excitation in the mind, though apprehended with differences in quality (p. 105). 'Instincts and their Vicissitudes' reflects this mode of thought, as Freud is concerned here with the dynamics of the libido. He distinguishes four ways in which this psychic energy can be manipulated: reversing into its opposite, turning upon the self, repression and sublimation; in this paper, he focuses on the first two (p. 106). The main polarities under discussion are activity-passivity and love-hate. And so an instinct can turn from active to passive, such as a sadistic impulse can be inverted into a masochistic one, and the content of an instinct can be converted from love into hate. Meltzer notes that Freud does not explain how these vicissitudes actually happen, but only that they can happen (p. 107).

The paper 'On Transformations of Instincts' reveals an entirely different approach to thinking about instincts from the previous one. Here Freud considers the anal instincts or impulses, and how the relationship of the anus to faeces can be not only significant, but meaningful, in that it can generate a range of phantasies, and in that the different meanings that faeces can take on might not be clearly differentiated. Thus, the meaning of faeces can enter a confusional relation with faeces, penis, baby or gift (pp. 107–8). Meltzer believes that this paper signals the end of the Libido Theory and explains how this shift in Freud's thought inaugurates a new paradigm:

> He has moved from thinking of instincts as simply body tensions requiring satisfaction [. . .] to considering the mind as functioning primarily in relation to the manipulation of meaning. This movement away from an energetics principle, on to the study of the mind as an instrument for the manipulation of meaning, seems to me [. . .] the beginning of ego and object relations psychology.
>
> (Meltzer, p. 108)

And, as has been discussed earlier, it is this new mode of thought that Freud employs in 'A Child Is Being Beaten', insofar as he is trying to find the meaning of that phantasy. While in 'Instincts and their Vicissitudes' he was dealing with the problem of masochism as a sadistic impulse turned against the self, he is now trying to investigate how the masochistic phantasy arrives at one in which a child is being beaten, that is, to what *transformations* the phantasy is subjected (p. 110).

Meltzer reads this paper in the light of the Wolf Man case and in the context of some of the work that Freud had already developed, emphasizing the complexity of identification processes and of the structure of sexual perversions that they reveal. With the Wolf Man, Freud realized that a man having sexual intercourse can be identified with his own penis as a child getting inside the mother's womb, and being copulated with by the father's penis (Meltzer, p. 111). Meltzer's detailing of other material that Freud had available, shows in more or less explicit ways the significance of the mother and her body in identification processes that Meltzer believes can contribute to a formulation of the central masochistic phantasy. This is something that Freud, in Meltzer's opinion, is only on the verge of recognizing:

> And indeed he has constantly been on the verge of this ever since he began talking about Leonardo's homosexuality based on his identification with his mother and loving a young boy the way his mother loved him; since he began talking about Schreber's identification with his wife and how lovely it must be to be a woman being copulated with, and his relation to God as a woman; he has been on the verge of it all through the Wolf Man, in talking about the Wolf Man's identification with his mother's menorrhagia, and his identification with his sister with regard to the incident of his weeping at Pushkin's grave. In 'Mourning and Melancholia' of course, he is constantly on the verge of it, in raising the question of who is really in pain: is it the ego berating the ego ideal or is it the ego ideal berating the ego?
>
> (Meltzer, p. 113)

Earlier in his discussion of the Wolf Man's phantasies, Meltzer remarks that psychoanalysts have been studying precisely 'the way in which infantile phantasies are related to the inside of the mother's body' (p. 111); then he brings the idea of identification with a child being copulated with inside the womb to his formulation of the masochistic phantasy, but the aim of this phantasy is, as in Freud's theory, the father's love. For Meltzer, 'a child being beaten' is a transformation of 'I am that child and I am being copulated with by my father in that painful beating way because he loves me' (p. 113). Thus, it can be concluded that Meltzer places masochism under the death instinct category and the economic principle of repetition compulsion, which can help to understand the destructiveness and 'repeatedness' of the perversion, but his analysis of 'A Child Is Being Beaten' shows that it is the *meaning* of the phantasy that is decisive in the experience of pain as pleasure.

Whether the masochistic phantasy originates in the conflict between separation and symbiosis with the mother, as in Studlar's formulation, or whether it goes back to an identification with someone inside her to attain the father's love, as in Meltzer's, my purpose here is only to establish the importance in conceiving of perversions as complex structures; to acknowledge their meaning, whatever it may be, as determining the pleasure experienced in pain; and to recognize the mother, her body and the interior of her body as playing a crucial role in phantasy.

Nevertheless, it is not only in masochistic phantasy that they are crucial; they are in fact of primary importance in what Melanie Klein calls the epistemophilic instinct. For Klein, an instinctual thirst for knowledge exists in the child's early relation to the mother, a desire to know about her body and her interior (Meltzer, II, p. 16). This desire to know and understand the mother's body is the prototype of all other thirst for knowledge: about the child's own body, other people and the world. Meltzer explains that, in Klein's view, the process of extending curiosity from the mother on to other objects takes place through symbol formation, which is a way to find meaning (p. 17). But Klein also notices that the epistemophilic instinct can be driven by persecutory or depressive anxiety, when the child explores in an intrusive and sadistic way the mother's body and its contents, and then needs to find out if they have not been damaged or if they can be repaired. The conflict between these destructive and reparative drives towards the mother is central to the developmental process. The depressive position brings the painful realization that the good mother and bad mother are one and the same person, it entails an integrated view of the object in its good and bad aspects, and this is what promotes development.

According to Meltzer, Freud's view of children's thirst for knowledge is substantially different. It is connected to the desire to know where babies come from (I, p. 67), and the desire to know about the sexual act (II, p. 16), and therefore it occurs later, at around three years of age, or at the time of the Oedipus complex. As Meltzer points out, Freud calls them the 'sexual researches' of children (I, p. 66). And whereas for Klein the process of extending the desire for knowledge on to other objects is made through symbol formation, Freud thinks that this process is a sublimation of the initial curiosity he identifies, because he sees it driven by anxiety. For this reason, Freud associates a strong thirst for knowledge with an unresolved Oedipus conflict and with sexual inhibition. In his paper on Leonardo, he relates Leonardo's genius with sublimation of homosexuality (II, p. 16). Freud believes that children's curiosity is ridden with anxiety because of the birth of a sibling, a rival which not only arouses jealousy, but also castration anxiety, as he considers the case of a male child who sees the genitals of his younger sister (I, p. 67). Therefore Freud does not distinguish, as Klein does, between a loving desire to understand, and an anxious and aggressive intrusiveness. Meltzer comments on how Freud's theory of the 'researches' of children, which presumably are aimed at discovering the truth, disagrees with his theories of repression and dream formation:

> Since Freud's idea seems to be that this curiosity is fundamentally driven by anxiety and hatred, it is very puzzling that he should think of it as something that should drive the child in the direction of wanting to discover the truth. For his whole theory of repression is based on the assumption that there is a certain necessity or desire to defend *against* knowing the truth (which is also true of his theory of dream formation). And his theory about defence against anxiety entails the defence being made by a distortion of the truth.
>
> (Meltzer, pp. 67–8)

In this idea that repressed memories and dreams can become conscious, but only do so in a censored, distorted form, Freud is implying that he conceives of the mind as an apparatus that is predisposed towards avoiding the emergence of painful truths. This is an issue that Joan and Neville Symington consider to be a major theoretical disjunction between Freud's thinking and that of Wilfred Bion. In their discussion of Freud's model of the mind, a model that they see as deterministic, they describe the formulation of the subject's acceptance of the reality principle as delayed gratification. But they identify a subtle, yet radical shift that can be made in the understanding of this delay:

> This implies the capacity to opt against pleasure at the present and the intervention of a judgement that it is better to renounce this present pleasure, with the further implication that the individual's action is not explicable by efficient causality but by a judgement motivated by desire for a future good. However, Bion implies that there is a shift from one motivational category – that determined by desire for pleasure and avoidance of pain – to another – one that is determined by the emergence of truth and desire for emotional growth.
>
> (Symington and Symington, 1996, pp. 6–7)

The subject's desire for understanding is, then, an intrinsic part of the developmental process, according to Bion; and this principle defies the determinism that underlies Freud's conceptualization of the mind. As the Symingtons explain, 'The idea that someone would choose pain rather than evade it is quite foreign to Freud's way of thinking, especially as Bion conceives that such an event can occur very early in life' (p. 7).

Already in his early papers collected in *Second Thoughts*, Bion makes a few short observations regarding curiosity and truth that he will continue to develop as major issues throughout his work. The first of these observations, made in an article titled 'On Arrogance', introduces, in a preliminary form, a different perspective on Freud's use of the Oedipus myth. Bion points to Oedipus's arrogant determination to find the truth, the discovery of which provokes his blindness and exile; to Tiresias's condemnation of Oedipus's pursuit; and to the Sphinx's destruction upon being answered (1957, p. 86). In a subsequent work, Bion postulates the three basic relationships that an emotional experience can establish: X loves Y, X hates Y and

X knows Y (1962, pp. 42–3); and so he places the epistemophilic instinct (the K link, or Knowledge link) alongside love and hate as an equally important motive force in mental life. Klein's love-hate dyad is not only extended with the K link, but also with the negatives of the Love, Hate and Knowledge links, as no-emotions or defences against emotion. −K is a defence against or envious hatred of the emotional experience of learning (pp. 95–8).

This model of links is brought to further considerations of the Oedipus myth in *Elements of Psycho-Analysis*. Bion states that Freud's theory of Oedipus focuses on the L and H links of the conflict, but that it is also useful to think of the myth in those features that reveal the K link and its negative: in the expression and suppression of curiosity (1963, pp. 48–9). And although here Bion refers to Oedipus in different terms from his previous formulation, by affirming that 'Oedipus represents the triumph of determined curiosity over intimidation and may thus be used as a symbol for scientific integrity' (p. 49), his preoccupation with hubris and omniscience as barriers to the emergence of truth remains. The relationship between Tiresias and Oedipus is representative of the conflict between K and −K, since it can be seen as stimulating and suppressing the pursuit of knowledge.[6] Bion identifies the condemnation of this pursuit in other myths also, that of Eden and of the Tower of Babel, in which 'the logical formulation of the problem points to a conflict between omniscience on the one hand and inquiry on the other' (1965, p. 58).

The second observation on the issue of curiosity appears in 'Attacks on Linking', in connection with the relationship between the infant and the breast. Bion writes that the denial of the use of projective identification, either on the mother's part or the infant's, 'leads to a destruction of the link between infant and breast and consequently to a severe disorder of the impulse to be curious on which all learning depends' (1959, pp. 106–7). Meltzer (III, pp. 32–3) notes that in this statement Bion is proposing that the epistemophilic impulse should be conceived as a motive in itself, which is an entirely distinct position from that of Freud and Klein; and also that Bion is elevating the function of the infant-breast relationship to that of learning. Klein conceives of the breast as an object that frustrates and gratifies, attacks and protects; Bion views the breast as the source of meaningful emotional experiences. For Bion (1965, p. 81), the breast supplies meaning, and this is what allows the development of the ability to learn. As Meltzer clarifies, 'Like Melanie Klein he sees the mind as developing in the context of the infant-mother relationship but for him it is a relationship whose essence is understanding rather than gratification, failure of such understanding rather than frustration' (III, p. 116).

In the last of Bion's early papers, titled 'A Theory of Thinking', he postulates how the subject achieves the experience of a sense of truth, and the implications of the deficiency of this process for psychical development. Bion writes that when different sets of sense-data conjoin and harmonize, a sense of truth is experienced (1961, p. 119). The modification of pain through omniscience is the failure of this process, and deterioration of the mind ensues, comparable to the deterioration of an organism that is deprived of food. Referring to primordial consciousness, Bion underlines the role of emotions in the growth of the psyche:

> The emotions fulfil a similar function for the psyche to that of the senses in relation to objects in space and time. [. . .] A sense of truth is experienced if the view of an object which is hated can be conjoined to a view of the same object when it is loved and the conjunction confirms that the object experienced by different emotions is the same object.
>
> (Ibid.)

Klein's legacy here is evident. But when Meltzer considers Bion's statement that a lack or deficiency in truth provokes debility of the mind, in view of Bion's preceding discussion of the arrogant pride of Oedipus in the pursuit of truth, he notes that for him Bion's model of the mind, at this stage, is yet unclear in formal terms (Meltzer, III, p. 36). It is only later that Bion develops his theory of thinking into the theory of container/contained, and formulates the idea that 'the truth does not require a thinker to exist, but rather that the thinker needs to find the truth as an idea which he can make grow in his mind' (ibid., p. 110). This is when Meltzer believes Bion brings together cogently what he implicitly or explicitly deals with in all his books: the transformation of container and contained through their ability to hold and make grow a new idea.

These introductory remarks on the work of Bion, which will be explored in more detail in what follows, serve to show that, with Bion, the thirst for knowledge is given a fundamental role in the functioning of the mind, and this is, in my view, the radical shift that can allow also a radically different way of thinking the cinematic apparatus. The conceptualizations of the apparatus that have been examined here neglect the existence of the epistemophilic impulse, and this is why they cannot incorporate unpleasure and pain in the experience of film, even when unpleasure and pain are clearly a part of this experience.

For Baudry, unpleasure in the cinema is in fact an exception, emerging with films that reveal the apparatus; Metz admits the existence of unpleasure in the cinema, but he construes it in quantitative measures of too little or too much pleasure, and sees pleasure as the main aim (and achievement) of cinema; and Studlar identifies the existence of pain in the cinema insofar as it is experienced as pleasure. Freud's thinking is ingrained in these film theories of the apparatus (even though Studlar purposefully departs from it), because pleasure in its various forms is the main point under discussion and criticism.

A central premise to my argument is that regardless of the film's form and content, and regardless of its social, economic, cultural and individual determinants, the presence of unpleasure in the cinema is much more significant than it has been acknowledged by theorists of the apparatus. Furthermore, I believe that films, or aspects of films, or moments in films, can cause anxiety and pain according to the *meaning* they have for the subject. If unpleasure, anxiety and pain can be given their proper place in a theory of the mind as well as in a theory of the cinema, cinema as retreat can begin to detach itself from the commonplace meanings of retreat that apparatus theory helps to sustain. The retreat in cinema is no longer seen to provide shelter from these emotions, and from the realities in which these emotions exist.

In the following section, I will argue that unpleasure can be imbricated in the experience of film in moments that are sometimes too subtle or ephemeral to be noticed as unpleasurable, but which nevertheless are intrinsic to the experience and its understanding. Bion's theory of thinking can contribute to the recognition of these moments, and towards thinking about absence in the cinema in a very different way than has been done so far in film theory.

Thoughts in search of a thinker

Bion's theory of thinking evolved over the course of several years, but here I will focus on its initial stage issued in the 1961 paper mentioned above, 'A Theory of Thinking', while using other material that will help to elucidate it.[7] This paper prefigures the idea of 'thoughts without a thinker', in that Bion proposes to consider the thinking apparatus as an entity subject to development by the pressure of pre-existing thoughts (pp. 110–11). 'Thoughts without a thinker' is a formulation that Bion finds useful to explain what happens when the link between analysand and analyst is being attacked, that is, when the analysand is trying to destroy both the analysand's and analyst's capacity to think and talk to each other (Bion, 1967, pp. 164–5). The link of verbal thought and verbal communication is attacked because the analysand feels that this link carries an emotion too powerful to be contained (Bion, 1959, p. 108). Bion will later articulate this idea as resistance:

> It is not often enough recognized that a patient in whom resistance is active can be reacting against what he feels to be a thought in search of a thinker. It is supposedly his own thought (classical resistance theory), but it does not have to be so.
>
> (1970, p. 117)

Bion believes it is helpful to be able to conceive of a personality without thought, and of already existent thoughts waiting for a personality to think them. A thought that is not necessarily produced by a thinker is a principle that Descartes would reject. Paulo Sandler, in his consideration of Bion's hypothesis, points out that Descartes formulates the idea of 'thoughts without a thinker' in *Discours sur le Méthode*, but only 'in its negative sense in order to discard it' (2005, p. 745). Sandler goes further by stating that to regard the idea of 'thoughts without a thinker' as an absurdity is comparable to finding the Copernican Revolution intolerable: 'The idea that the mind produces thoughts, exalted by Descartes, is clearly linked to omnipotence and is perhaps one of the manifestations assumed by the not-too-hidden idea that man is the centre of the universe' (p. 757). Bion only subscribes to Descartes's supposition if the thought is a lie. For Bion, the truth does not require a thinker, whereas the lie is a thought to which a thinker is necessary: 'It follows that all thought as it is ordinarily known, that is, as an attribute of the human being, is false, the problem associated with it being the degree and nature of the falsity' (1970, p. 117). Bion seems to be alluding here to the impossibility of knowledge of reality.

There is a certain Platonic idealism in 'A Theory of Thinking' when Bion states that his theory relates to observed occurrences in analysis in the same way a mathematical statement about a circle relates to a statement about a circle drawn on paper. Yet his theory of thinking in this article draws in a more explicit way from Kant's philosophy in that it conceives a primal structure of the mind constituted by *a priori* intuitions (1961, p. 111). According to Luigi Longhin and Mauro Mancia (2000, pp. 1197–8), Bion and other post-Kleinian thinkers are interested in the contribution that the philosophy of mind can make to their own investigations, because they consider this protomental structure, in which pure intuitions of time and space are operative, to allow the experience of the phenomenal world. They also see a fundamental divide between mind and brain, a view which is opposed to the causalism of the neurological sciences from which Freud's psychoanalysis originates. Longhin and Mancia argue that the neurosciences cannot account for the exponential cultural and technological developments of the last millennium:

> The thesis that mind is 'isomorphic' with brain seems untenable: a neural Darwinism [. . .] cannot be confused with a mental Darwinism because *cultural change* as the expression of the evolution of the mind is evidently out of phase with Darwinian evolution.[8]
>
> (p. 1201)

It is on this premise that Longhin and Mancia see the value of an intersection between psychoanalytic and philosophical debates, a value also recognized by Bion.[9] Longhin and Mancia identify in Bion's description of the gradual development of thoughts, a reference to Kant's well-known sentence: 'Thoughts without content are empty, intuitions without concepts are blind.' According to Bion's theory, first there are pre-conceptions, then conceptions or thoughts, and finally concepts, which are *named* conceptions or thoughts. The pre-conceptions are to be understood as a psychoanalytic equivalent of Kant's 'empty thoughts', and find an example in the infant's inborn expectation of the breast, or *a priori* intuition of the breast. The pre-conception conjoined with a realization that brings an emotional experience of satisfaction produces a conception, whereas a pre-conception conjoined with a frustration produces a thought (Bion, 1961, pp. 110–11). Thus, the presence of the breast results in a conception, while the absence of the breast, or internal 'no-breast', results in a thought. In *Learning from Experience*, which expands on the ideas delineated in the article, Bion clarifies the distinction:

> Sooner or later the 'wanted' breast is felt as an 'idea of a breast missing' and not as a bad breast present. We can see that the bad, that is to say wanted but absent, breast is much more likely to become recognized as an idea than the good breast which is associated with what a philosopher would call a thing-in-itself or a thing-in-actuality, in that the sense of a good breast depends on the existence of milk the infant has in fact taken.
>
> (1962, p. 34)

In the distinction made between a conception and a thought, Bion differentiates the psychical quality of the experience of a presence that satisfies hunger, from that of the painful experience of the absence of a wished-for breast. In this way, he is not only attempting to give precision to the thinking process in its germinal stages, but is also making a crucial step in placing its origins in emotions. It is important to emphasize that Bion considers the emotionally frustrating experience of absence to be the foundation for a thought. He asks:

> Is a 'thought' the same as an absence of a thing? If there is no 'thing', is 'no thing' a thought and is it by virtue of the fact that there is 'no thing' that one recognizes that 'it' must be thought?
>
> (p. 35)

These questions propose the hypothesis of a fundamentally dependent relation between absence and thought. And it is precisely this proposition that I believe makes it possible to rethink the idea of absence in the cinema. It has been discussed earlier that Metz and Studlar formulate absence as a fetish, the absence of objects covered over by the presence of light and shadow. But would not this absence be recognized at least when the film ends, or when the film is remembered, already outside the cinema? These moments are certainly integral parts of the experience of film in the cinema. Absence can also manifest itself during the film, in all that may exist in it that is not, in a restricted sense, articulated: for example, when there is an absence of sound or speech, or an absence of movement, or an unexpected absence of a character or object. A cut in the film can also make something present become absent, perhaps more obviously in a transition between different sequences. These moments may not be perceived as unpleasurable because they can be fleeting or too subtle, but, following Bion's formulation, they are thoughts in search of a thinker. It may be the intermittence between presence and absence intrinsic to the experience of film that enables its understanding.

Bion takes the function of the absent breast further by stating that it is the capacity for tolerating the frustrating experience of the 'no-breast' that develops the apparatus for thinking: the absence of a wanted breast has a formative function. He adds: 'A capacity for tolerating frustration thus enables the psyche to develop thought as a means by which the frustration that is tolerated is itself made more tolerable' (1961, p. 112). However, Bion points out that the absent breast is only turned into a thought if the infant is capable of tolerating frustration. If the infant is not able to do so, a decision must be made between modifying or evading frustration. The infant modifies the frustration when intolerance is not so strong as to induce evasion, but still strong enough that it precludes the acceptance of the reality principle. In this case, the personality develops omniscience and is unable to discern between true and false. This denial of reality is a function of the psychotic part of the personality (p. 114).

On the other hand, the infant can decide to evade frustration by expelling the bad object onto the mother through projective identification (p. 112). This bad object is a sense impression or emotion that is unassimilated, and is posited as an equivalent to Kant's noumenon or thing-in-itself; Bion names it beta-element. When the mother is receptive to the projected bad object and is able to transform it into an emotion that the infant can tolerate, the beta-element is converted into an alpha-element that can be re-introjected in a constructive way to the personality. This conjectural process that converts beta- into alpha-elements is called alpha-function (López-Corvo, 2003, pp. 26–7).

Still, as has been discussed very briefly in the preceding section, the use of projective identification can be denied by the mother or the infant. When the mother's response is inadequate, either by refusing the projection or by being prey to the infant's anxiety, or when the infant's hatred and envy is such that it will not allow the mother to exercise this function, the infant resorts to excessive use of projective identification. Denial and excessive use of this mechanism are detrimental to learning and development (Bion, 1959, pp. 106–7).

Thus the mother's role is vital in containing the unbearable emotions that the infant projects into her and in processing them into a tolerable form. This process of alpha-function is dependent on the mother's capacity for reverie. Maternal reverie 'refers to the mother's capacity to develop a psychological receptor organ capable of metabolizing the baby's conscious sensuous information and transform it into α-elements, which are in turn necessary to develop α-function [. . .] and a thinking apparatus' (López-Corvo, pp. 167–8). Joan and Neville Symington point to the origins of the word reverie:

> The etymological derivation of reverie is of interest as its present mild connotation of brown study or daydream has wilder origins. It derives from Latin *radix*, *root*, through *rabere*, *to be furiously angry*, presumably uprooted in the mind, to the Old French *reverie*, *rejoicing*, *wildness*, thence to *resverie*, *a state of delight*, *violent or rude language*, *delirium*, to *rever*, to dream.
>
> (Symington and Symington, p. 67)

With their interest in Bion's choice of the term, the Symingtons suggest that the mother's emotional state of mind in reverie can be wide-ranging. In fact, Bion considers the consequences of an exceedingly understanding mother: if she always accepts the projective identifications of the infant, fear and hatred of the loss of an idyllic state for a new situation associated with the 'no-breast' can engender a depressive state that is perpetuated, because the alternative, which is the thought that a perfect breast has been destroyed, is deemed to be worse (Bion, 1965, pp. 62–3).

Bion elaborates on his concept of maternal reverie, explaining that both mother and infant engage in a transformational process, that affects their relationship and their selves:

> Psychical quality will be imparted to the channels of communication, the links with the child. What happens will depend on the nature of these maternal

> psychical qualities and their impact on the psychical qualities of the infant, for the impact of the one upon the other is an emotional experience subject, from the point of view of the development of the couple and the individuals composing it, to transformation by alpha-function.
>
> (1962, p. 36)

The idea of container/contained transformed is already discernible in this passage. Projective identification processes in the cinema have been looked at suspiciously by Baudry and Metz, not completely without justification, but in their theories they reduce these processes to omnipotent operations, and thus charge them with a pathological meaning. Bion brings another perspective on this issue by underlining the importance of a balanced use of projective identification in communication, learning and growth (Sandler, p. 161). The impression of reality in the cinema is, in my view, closely connected with the strong emotional links that can be established between subject and film through projective and introjective identification; and it is by understanding the role of these mechanisms in communication and development that the impression of reality in the cinema can begin to lose its pejorative connotations.

Links are destroyed when the emotions they carry are too powerful to be contained, but if the working of reverie allows the subject to contain, investigate and assimilate these emotions, cinema could be seen as thoughts searching, and finding, a thinker. Thus, in the retreat in cinema could be found the meanings of investigation and assimilation of emotions. These processes of investigation and assimilation begin in the early relationship with the mother, building up the internal world through her presence and absence; and they continue to do so while traces of her presence and absence remain. It is in this way that I see a connection that is crucial in my argument: the connection between the retreat (here, the retreat in cinema) and the internal world.

The stage of Bion's theory of thinking described above gives a particular inflection to the retreat in cinema, linking it specifically with the development of a capacity for tolerating the unpleasurable or painful experience of absence, which is at the basis of thinking. I will now examine a more developed form of Bion's model of the mind, in which the significance of the element of pain will be revealed; Bion regards pain as an element of psychoanalysis, as a structuring element of the mind (1963, pp. 2, 61–2).[10]

The capacity to *suffer* pain, and container/contained transformed

Learning from Experience, published in 1962, follows 'A Theory of Thinking', and is the work in which Bion propounds his model of container and contained. This model continues to be developed until its culmination in 1970 with *Attention and Interpretation*, which will be my main point of reference in this section.

The model of container/contained is drawn from Klein's idea of projection of a split-off part of the infant's personality into the breast: the projected part is to be called the contained, and the container is that into which the contained is projected (Bion, 1962, p. 90). This theory is initially applied to investigate the mother-infant relationship, and the individual psyche, in their ability to retain and be receptive to emotions and ideas, and to grow, but later it becomes an observable underlying configuration in other instances, such as in the relationship between the mystic and the group. In *Attention and Interpretation*, Bion uses religion as an investigatory tool, hence the employment of terms like 'mystic' and 'messianic idea'.[11] The basic elements, and the nature of the links between the basic elements in this theory are formulated thus:

> In pictorial terms the container is represented by a mouth or vagina, the contained by breast or penis. The relationship between these objects, which I shall represent by the male and female signs ♂ and ♀, may be commensal, symbiotic, or parasitic.
>
> (Bion, 1970, p. 95)

A parasitic relationship between a thought and a thinker is established when the thought is known to be false but still is maintained as a defence against the true thought because the truth threatens to destroy the container (♀), or the ♀ threatens to destroy the truth (p. 118). The image of a (true) thought in search of a thinker as an instance of the activity of resistance could be recalled here. This relationship can also be observed in the social domain. The pre-conception in the domain of thought, or a stable aspect of the individual personality (p. 122), correspond to the Establishment or governing body in the society. The mystic is the 'exceptional individual' who claims to have direct contact with God. The Establishment, whose function is to incorporate the mystic and make the messianic idea available to the members of the society through dogmas and rules, can fail to do so either by a lack of judgement that will lead it to promote false views and lies, or by a rigid compliance with an existing scheme. This results in a parasitic relationship between mystic and group, or ♂ and ♀, because the vitality of the mystic will be subdued or the society will be disrupted (p. 111). The verbal expression of an idea can equally constitute a parasitic link:

> The more successfully the word and its use can be 'established', the more its precision becomes an obstructive rigidity; the more imprecise it is, the more it is a stumbling-block to comprehension. The new idea 'explodes' the formulation designed to express it.
>
> (p. 80)

But Bion makes a distinction between the use of a word as an expression of verbal communication and the use of the same word as a representation of a hallucination, because he is able to detect a difference in the emotional reaction of the analysand (p. 17). Bion remarks that 'hallucinations are *not* representations: they are things-in-themselves born of intolerance of frustration and desire. Their defects are due not to their failure to represent but to their failure to *be*' (p. 18). And so the emotional reaction to the 'no-thing' is replaced by a 'no-emotion', or by an emotion that is used to deny another emotion. Bion is trying to formulate a theory that can account for the difficulties of tolerating pain, and this includes a situation in which the subject experiences pain but is not *suffering* it. He states: 'people exist who are so intolerant of pain or frustration (or in whom pain or frustration is so intolerable) that they feel the pain but will not suffer it and so cannot be said to discover it' (p. 9). This involves what Sandler (p. 560), commenting on Bion's observation, designates by a 'quantum leap': from 'feeling pain' to 'suffering it'.

In *Elements of Psycho-Analysis*, Bion points to the importance of developing a capacity for suffering pain:

> The importance of pain can be dismissed as a secondary quality, something that is to disappear when conflicts are resolved; indeed most patients would take this view. Furthermore it can be supported by the fact that successful analysis does lead to diminution of suffering; nevertheless it obscures the need, more obvious in some cases than in others, for the analytic experience to increase the patient's *capacity* for suffering even though patient and analyst may hope to decrease pain itself.
>
> (p. 62)

Bion is concerned with the capacity to suffer pain because he recognizes the connection that exists between pain and growth. In relation to this he mentions the common use of the expression 'growing pains'. Sandler notes that in Bion's work there is a realization that no organism grows without an opposing force (p. 744), and further, that Bion's concept of growth should not be confused with something that happens from pathology to cure: it rather refers to 'a common-sensical harmony of the person with him(her)self, within him or herself' (p. 311).

There are several instances in *Attention and Interpretation* in which Bion tries to elucidate the conflicts that growth and maturation entail. The subject may be hostile to growth because it involves a change from the pleasure-pain principle to the reality principle, and this means that the subject is not able to control the proportion of pain to pleasure (1970, p. 53). Bion also remarks that an emotional situation in which the subject contributes a thought that is particular and unique to the subject's mind, and which for this reason approximates to the lie, is preferred because it is narcissistically gratifying. This emotional situation is contrasted with that in which the subject harbours a true thought, which requires no thinker, and which for that reason foregrounds the insignificance of the subject who thinks it (p. 105). Following the same line of ideas in an excerpt written in the form of a parable, Bion speaks of 'the spread of doctrines whose effect could only have been to induce a sense of helplessness and unimportance in the liars and their beneficiaries'

(p. 101). And in another instance, Bion considers the emotional turbulence in moments of catastrophic change, an idea that he will greatly elaborate on in later works with his concept of caesura:

> If we suppose now that the emotional upheaval against which the lie is mobilized is identical with catastrophic change it becomes easier to understand why investigation uncovers an ambiguous position which is capable of arousing strong feelings. These feelings relate to an outraged moral system; their strength derives from risk of change in the psyche.
>
> (p. 99)

Thus Bion arrives at a conception of how and why parasitism is established, in which both parties of the relationship and their product are destroyed, in a manner of anti-growth. This is the delusional world of lies and omnipotence, instituted and perpetuated in order to avoid a catastrophic change, and a sense of helplessness and unimportance.

Nevertheless, catastrophic changes are not always avoided. The commensal relationship is present when the two sides coexist, ♂ and ♀, mystic and group, true thought and thinker, but have no impact on each other (p. 78). The truth exists but it has not yet been discovered. This relationship changes when a 'critical situation' emerges, induced by the threat of a discovery. In this critical situation, thought and thinker approximate, and become susceptible of correspondence in a symbiotic relationship, in which they modify each other: 'The thought proliferates and the thinker develops' (p. 118). In a symbiotic relationship, the container (or thinker, or group) needs to remain integrated, in order to avoid being fragmented by the contained; but at the same time the container must lose rigidity and expand, in order not to destroy or reduce the meaningfulness of the contained (or messianic idea, or mystic) (Meltzer, III, p. 110).

Bion's model of the mind, in which 'the objects are many but the relationships are not' (Bion, 1970, p. 122), can help to understand the relationships that exist between film institutions and filmmakers; film institutions and audiences; filmmakers and their films, and their audiences; a film, or an idea in a film, and a subject. In the theories of the cinematic apparatus that have been explored here, there are no symbiotic relationships between these elements because the existence of pain and growth is not recognized in them. In Studlar's argument, the symbiotic attachment to the mother pursued by the subject in the cinema is never fully achieved, and if it were, it would have no transformational value.

After this exposition of Bion's theory of thinking, and returning to the question of regression that issued from my reading of Baudry's article, posed in the beginning of this first chapter: Could the cinematic apparatus still be seen to engender an artificial regressive state to a primordial moment of satisfaction in the subject's relationship with the breast? In my view, the relationship of the subject with the cinema does bear traces of the early relationship with a maternal figure, but since the experience of film is never without moments of unpleasure, and often involves moments of anxiety and pain, this relationship has to be considered in its Love, Hate and Knowledge aspects, which have been there from its inception. The negatives of LHK exist in a parasitic relationship, where subject and cinema are destroyed through denial of emotions, lies and resistance to change. But in symbiosis, subject and cinema can be seen as a growing entity linked by emotion and the thought developed from it, an entity in which each party is able to retain knowledge and yet be receptive to new ideas.

The distinction that Bion makes between feeling pain and suffering pain, and the relation he draws between suffering pain and growth, are of paramount importance to the recognition and understanding of growth in the retreat. Growth in the retreat and the retreat as growth are recurrent ideas in this book.

'Won from the void and formless infinite'

One of the other points in Baudry's argument that needs to be addressed is the understanding of the cinematic apparatus as a representation of the unconscious. It has already been discussed that Baudry mentions Freud's description of how the unconscious is represented in dreams: in underground places, symbolic of the woman's body or womb. It is this idea that Baudry employs to suggest a parallel between dreams' succession of images, with their close rapport with the unconscious, and film, projected in the cavernous space of the cinema. Nevertheless, earlier in his article, Baudry includes a rather long passage from *The Interpretation of Dreams*, in which Freud proposes to consider the psychical apparatus as resembling the photographic apparatus in its functioning. In a segment of that passage, Freud writes that 'psychical locality will correspond to a point inside the apparatus at which one of the preliminary stages of an image comes into being' (Baudry, 1975, p. 300). This optical metaphor illustrates Freud's conception of mental functioning, whereby an unconscious image is formed as a negative image, which may or may not be developed into its positive, or into consciousness. And even though Baudry does not quite pursue a comparison between the cinema and an optical apparatus that produces a static image, the idea of the cinema as representing that which has not yet been understood in the full light of consciousness is still explicit in the closing statement of his article:

> The presence of the unconscious also makes itself felt through the pressure it exerts in seeking to get itself represented by a subject who is still unaware of the fact that he is representing to himself the very scene of the unconscious where he is.
>
> (p. 317)

Baudry concludes that the subject in the cinema is in the dark chamber of the unconscious. The unconscious may be present in the cinema, but it is what this means in the context of Freud's metapsychology, especially when he uses the metaphor of the photographic apparatus to describe it, that I find problematic.

In order to understand what the implications are when this apparatus is used as a model, I now turn to the work of Sarah Kofman, who examines this issue in a chapter of her book *Camera Obscura: Of Ideology* (1973).

As outlined before, and as Kofman explains, Freud adopts the photographic analogy to express the idea that psychic occurrences first pass through an unconscious stage before being admitted to consciousness, in the same way the (analogue) photographic apparatus first produces a chemical impression in the form of a negative before it is processed into a positive image (p. 22). Freud notes that 'Not every negative, however, necessarily becomes a positive' (p. 23), because he is aware (as Baudry also is) that in this process there exists a selection, a censorship. Here the metaphor reveals its crudeness, as Freud himself admits, despite the fact that he returns to it in several of his writings. In 'A Note on the Unconscious' and in 'General Theory of the Neuroses: Resistance and Repression', the idea of the censored negative is used in order to establish the operation of repressive forces; in 'Moses and Monotheism: The Return of the Repressed', the idea of the negative is used to convey the restraining character of the unconscious, which will be repeated, duplicated in the image of the positive, or control behaviour and emotions (pp. 22–4). Kofman considers the usage of the metaphor to be ambivalent in these two instances; and when Freud affirms, in the last text, that past experiences may only come to be known through psychoanalytic treatment, she argues that the analytic procedure merely provides the construction of a hypothesis, not the realization of something that necessarily was originary (pp. 27–8).

Kofman further denounces the inadequacy of the photographic metaphor by pointing out that it cannot account for the conflicting force of the death instinct (p. 27), but it is her recognition of the exclusion of the process of development as a determining factor, in the passage from negative to positive, that I want to underline: 'The positive image, the double of the negative, implies that "what is at the end is already there in the beginning." Development adds nothing: it only enables the darkness to be made light' (ibid.). Indeed, it does seem inadequate to use such a mechanical apparatus as a metaphor when the obscure processes of repression and manifestation of the repressed are in operation, not only because these processes are themselves integral to a developing personality, but also because, as a consequence of this development, what comes to light cannot be simply a double of what was repressed at a previous stage. Thus, it is not so much that Freud is giving here another example of his mechanistic way of thinking, but rather that his use of the metaphor is another example of his wish to formulate a model of the mind that can fit into mechanical and deterministic parameters. And it is this aspect of Freud's project that subtends Baudry's argument, when for him the subject in the cinema is imprisoned in a system of immutable and inscrutable unconscious relations.

For Bion, the unconscious is not a locality in the psyche, nor essentially opposed to consciousness, or awareness: it is formless, in the same way the infinite has no form or number (Symington and Symington, p. 8). Bion quotes the English poet John Milton to describe the procedure by which something passes from infinite to finite grasp: 'The rising world of waters dark and deep | Won from the void and formless infinite' (1965, p. 151). This is the process by which Bion believes knowledge is gained, 'won from the void and formless infinite', it is the binding process of K. Bion replaces the opposition conscious-unconscious with finite-infinite. Thus the experience of film could be seen as a process that binds infinity into the finite, and cinema as an infinity of thoughts seeking a thinker.

Conclusion

I have completed the first part of my study of the retreat in cinema. To have theorized the existence of unpleasure in the cinema through a model of the mind that recognizes the significance of the epistemophilic instinct, which drives the subject in the search for truth even if it is painful, is important not only to establish the notion of cinema as a thinking space, but to begin opening up the notion of retreat to more positive meanings.

Despite the strong points of disagreement between my theory of the cinema and the theories of the apparatus that I engaged with, the links that the latter draw between the cinematic situation and the early maternal relationship, between cinema and absence, and between cinema and the unconscious, have contributed to my own conceptualization of the retreat in cinema, and of the retreat in connection to the internal world. In the following chapter I will continue to explore the retreat in cinema with a particular focus on mental growth.

Notes

1 For a discussion of the limited, flawed use of Lacan's mirror in film theory, and an investigation of the use that can be made of Winnicott's insight into the mirror-role of the mother and family in a theorization of the visual field, see Vicky Lebeau (2015).
2 This and subsequent quotations from *The Kleinian Development* are reproduced by permission of Meg Harris Williams.
3 As will be discussed later, the problem of identification with an object in pain is not restricted to the identification processes that occur in mourning and melancholia, but the questions raised by Freud's work on these states give an indication of its complexity. Meltzer phrases these questions: '"Who is in pain?" – is it the ego or its object that is in pain; and "Who is the one that is being reviled?" – is the person truly reviling himself or is he reviling the part of himself that is identified with an object that, at another level, he is really accusing' (p. 85). In the tendency of melancholia to give way to mania, and of mania to relapse into melancholia, is discerned a destructive cyclical process of attacking the object while identifying with it (p. 86).
4 *Secondary cinematic identification* denotes identification with characters and actors.
5 Laura Mulvey's 'Visual Pleasure and Narrative Cinema' (1975) is a renowned critique of the apparatus grounded in Freud's and Lacan's theories of castration and the mirror phase that reveals a patriarchal order of pleasure produced in Hollywood cinema. Studlar argues that such feminist readings of the apparatus fail to recognize masochism among the pleasures of cinema, female scopophilia and fetishism, and bisexual desire. For a reconsideration of Mulvey's critique and of queer theories of the apparatus see Carole-Anne Tyler's 'Desiring Machines? Queer Re-visions of Feminist Film Theory' (1998). Homi K. Bhabha addresses issues of racial difference in 'The Other Question: The Stereotype and Colonial Discourse' (1983).

6 See also Chapter 4 in Part II for Bion's development of the theory of Oedipus.
7 Reference to the year in which 'A Theory of Thinking' was presented can be found in Paulo C. Sandler (2005, p. 743).
8 Longhin, L. and Mancia, M. (2000). Kant's philosophy and its relationship with the thought of Bion and Money-Kyrle. *International Journal of Psychoanalysis*, 81 (6), p. 1201. Copyright © Institute of Psychoanalysis, London, 2000. Reprinted with permission of John Wiley & Sons Ltd.
9 For a list of philosophical sources in Bion's work see Sandler, pp. 570–5. See also the collection of articles edited by Nuno Torres and R.D. Hinshelwood (2013).
10 See also Sandler, p. 559.
11 Meltzer (III, p. 104) clarifies: 'While this seems to put psycho-analysis on a grand scale, and to place Bion in a self-aggrandizing position as the new Messiah, this would be a gross misunderstanding of his method of exposition. [. . .] Words like "messianic", "God", "establishment", "explode", etc., carry what he would call the penumbra of bigness, importance. To understand him one must put this aside and think of little messiahs, little gods, little explosions as well. The question of size in cosmic terms is irrelevant.'

References

Baudry, J-L. (1970). Ideological effects of the basic cinematographic apparatus. In: Rosen, P. (ed.) *Narrative, Apparatus, Ideology: A Film Theory Reader.* New York: Columbia University Press, 1986.

Baudry, J-L. (1975). The apparatus: Metapsychological approaches to the impression of reality in the cinema. In: Rosen, P. (ed.) *Narrative, Apparatus, Ideology: A Film Theory Reader.* New York: Columbia University Press, 1986.

Bhabha, H.K. (1983). The other question: The stereotype and colonial discourse. In: Merck, M. (ed.) *The Sexual Subject: A Screen Reader in Sexuality*. London: Routledge, 1992.

Bion, W.R. (1957). On arrogance. In: *Second Thoughts: Selected Papers on Psychoanalysis.* London: Karnac, 2007.

Bion, W.R. (1959). Attacks on linking. In: *Second Thoughts: Selected Papers on Psychoanalysis.* London: Karnac, 2007.

Bion, W.R. (1961). A theory of thinking. In: *Second Thoughts: Selected Papers on Psychoanalysis.* London: Karnac, 2007.

Bion, W.R. (1962). *Learning from Experience*. London: Karnac, 1991.

Bion, W.R. (1963). *Elements of Psycho-Analysis*. London: Karnac, 1989.

Bion, W.R. (1965). *Transformations*. London: Karnac, 1984.

Bion, W.R. (1967). Commentary. In: *Second Thoughts: Selected Papers on Psychoanalysis.* London: Karnac, 2007.

Bion, W.R. (1970). *Attention and Interpretation*. London: Karnac, 2007.

Klein, M. (1946). Notes on some schizoid mechanisms. In: *Envy and Gratitude and Other Works: 1946–1963.* London: Hogarth Press and the Institute of Psychoanalysis, 1987.

Klein, M. (1952). Some theoretical conclusions regarding the emotional life of the infant. In: *Envy and Gratitude and Other Works: 1946–1963.* London: Hogarth Press and the Institute of Psychoanalysis, 1987.

Klein, M. (1955). On identification. In: *Envy* and *Gratitude and Other Works: 1946–1963.* London: Hogarth Press and the Institute of Psychoanalysis, 1987.

Klein, M. (1957). Envy and gratitude. In: *Envy* and *Gratitude and Other Works: 1946–1963.* London: Hogarth Press and the Institute of Psychoanalysis, 1987.

Klein, M. (1958). On the development of mental functioning. In: *Envy* and *Gratitude and Other Works: 1946–1963.* London: Hogarth Press and the Institute of Psychoanalysis, 1987.

Kofman, S. (1973). *Camera Obscura: Of Ideology*. Translated by W. Straw. New York: Cornell University Press, 1999.

Lebeau, V. (2015). *Mirror* images: D.W. Winnicott in the visual field. In: Piotrowska, A. (ed.) *Embodied Encounters: New Approaches to Psychoanalysis and Cinema*. Hove, East Sussex: Routledge.

Longhin, L. and Mancia, M. (2000). Kant's philosophy and its relationship with the thought of Bion and Money-Kyrle. *International Journal of Psychoanalysis*, 81 (6), pp. 1197–211.

López-Corvo, R.E. (2003). *The Dictionary of the Work of W.R. Bion*. London: Karnac.

Meltzer, D. (1978). *The Kleinian Development*. Strath Tay: Clunie Press, 1985.

Metz, C. (1975a). The imaginary signifier. In: *Psychoanalysis and Cinema: The Imaginary Signifier*. Edited by S. Heath and C. MacCabe. Translated by B. Brewster. London: Macmillan Press, 2001.

Metz, C. (1975b). The fiction film and its spectator: A metapsychological study. In: *Psychoanalysis* and *Cinema: The Imaginary Signifier*. Translated by A. Guzzetti. Edited by S. Heath and C. MacCabe. London: Macmillan Press, 2001.

Mulvey, L. (1975). Visual pleasure and narrative cinema. In: Rosen, P. (ed.) *Narrative, Apparatus, Ideology: A Film Theory Reader*. New York: Columbia University Press, 1986.

Sandler, P.C. (2005). *The Language of Bion: A Dictionary of Concepts*. London: Karnac.

Segal, H. (1964). *Introduction to the Work of Melanie Klein*. London: Karnac and the Institute of Psycho-Analysis, 1988.

Sobchack, V. (2004). *Carnal Thoughts: Embodiment and Moving Image Culture*. Berkeley: University of California Press.

Studlar, G. (1988). *In the Realm of Pleasure: von Sternberg, Dietrich, and the Masochistic Aesthetic*. Urbana: University of Illinois Press.

Symington, J. and Symington, N. (1996). *The Clinical Thinking of Wilfred Bion*. London: Routledge, 2008.

Torres, N. and Hinshelwood, R.D. (eds.) (2013). *Bion's Sources: The Shaping of his Paradigms*. Hove, East Sussex: Routledge.

Tyler, C-A. (1998). Desiring machines? Queer re-visions of feminist film theory. In: Merck, M., Segal, N. and Wright, E. (eds.) *Coming Out of Feminism?* Oxford: Blackwell.

2

RETHINKING THE CINEMATIC APPARATUS WITH BION'S CONCEPT OF O

Introduction

In the previous chapter Bion's theory of thinking inspired a conceptualization of the cinema as a space of retreat in which, through an intimate engagement with the film, the binding process of K (knowledge) could take place, whereby thoughts that were based on the symbiotic projection and assimilation of emotional experiences were able to find a thinker to think them. It was important also to have shown the significance of the operation of the epistemophilic instinct in the development of the mind, and to recognize the role of this instinct in the capacity to tolerate unpleasure and pain. But as Bion developed his theory, he was able to address with more rigour the problem that he was already aware of when he conceived of the idea of thoughts without a thinker, an idea that could suggest the activity of resistance. In this second chapter I intend to take the work on the cinematic apparatus begun in the first chapter further, as well as to pursue more fully the issue of mental growth, by drawing on a relatively late aspect of Bion's investigations: the concept of O. The exploration of this aspect of his work will contribute a critical response to the parallel that Jean-Louis Baudry draws between the cinema and Plato's cave, in answer to the question that was posed early in Chapter 1: how can psychoanalysis further expose the implications and inadequacy of the analogy between Plato's scheme and the cinema?

Cinema and Plato's cave: an exhausted analogy

As stated earlier, Bion's theory of thinking was first outlined in a 1961 presentation, and subsequently developed in *Learning from Experience* (1962), *Elements of Psycho-Analysis* (1963), *Transformations* (1965), and *Attention and Interpretation* (1970). Among the general and underlying epistemological concerns concomitant with the whole of Bion's project, an important issue emerges at the time of *Transformations*, which is the first book to mention his concept of O. The issue that Bion addresses with the formulation of this concept is apparent for example in a situation in which an interpretation is known by both analyst and analysand and yet no change seems to be taking place. O is an attempt to address the question of being or becoming or not being able to be or become, which is a question, according to Bion, that is separate from the realm of knowledge (K). He writes:

> Any interpretation may be accepted in K but rejected in O; acceptance in O means that acceptance of an interpretation enabling the patient to 'know' that part of himself to which attention has been drawn is felt to involve 'being' or 'becoming' that person.
>
> (Bion, 1965, p. 164)

O is first referred to as 'the absolute facts of the [analytic] session' (p. 17), and as 'a thing-in-itself and unknowable (in Kant's sense)' (pp. 12–13). But this is just the beginning of Bion's long endeavour to describe what he means by O, throughout which he will have recourse to the philosophy of Kant and Plato, and the Christian mysticism of Meister Eckhart and St John of the Cross – two mystics considered to have been influenced by Neoplatonism (Bléandonu, 1990, pp. 211–12). After *Transformations*, in 1967, Bion writes an article titled 'Notes on Memory and Desire' which introduces ideas that will be of vital importance to the later elaborations on the concept of O in *Attention and Interpretation*. All of this will be discussed in detail, and as I hope will become evident, my conceptualization of the cinematic apparatus as a space of retreat would be incomplete without this aspect of Bion's work.

In my view, it is also the case that Bion's concept of O is capable of exposing a certain rigidness in the analogy drawn between the cinema and Plato's cave, and in Plato's allegory itself, as I will argue. Within the field of film theory, Elsaesser and Hagener present an overview of the critiques that take issue with theories of the apparatus that compare the subject's 'arrested' position in the cinema to that of the prisoners in Plato's cave, of which, again, the most influential proponent is Baudry. Apparatus theory is seen to rely on a historical view of cinema as having its origins in an early Renaissance monocular perspective, which overlooks, for example, the relevance of stereoscopy (Elsaesser and Hagener, 2010, p. 196, n. 35).[1] Elsaesser and Hagener write:

> While the genealogy of cinema deriving from monocular perspective was challenged by the art historian Jonathan Crary, historians of early cinema and pre-cinema also cast doubt on the idea that the moving images' first spectators were even metaphorically 'chained' to their seats. Instead, the ranked auditorium seating as we know it from classical movie houses resulted from an intriguingly protracted process of 'disciplining' the audience, transforming them from a noisy and often unruly collectivity into the individualized, silenced and captivated spectator.
>
> (p. 69)

The authors cite the work of Tom Gunning which explores precisely a mode of address in the cinema that elicited a self-conscious reaction from the subject, characteristic of what he called 'cinema of attractions' (p. 70). Gunning identifies early films that ruptured cinema's reality effect by directly confronting the subject who experienced them. As I have already pointed out, Baudry (1970, pp. 297–8) also believes that certain films are able to do this, though these are considered by him as exceptions to the rule. Nevertheless, Elsaesser and Hagener (p. 69) note that Constance Penley criticized apparatus theories' validation of films that reveal cinema's instrumentation: from a feminist perspective, Penley argued that 'the filmic avant-garde was still caught in its own imaginary, constructing a kind of "bachelor machine" (Marcel Duchamp) of failed male control'. Both the critiques developed by Gunning and Penley consider specific historical contexts and the content and formal qualities of the films; however, continuing with the approach I adopted in Chapter 1, such specific considerations are not part of my theory of the cinematic apparatus; furthermore, my theory does not see the immobility of the subject in the cinema as a problem, nor indeed cinema's reality effect: the immobility of the subject is in fact an advantage to a focused engagement with the film. But this does not mean that, to my mind, the recurrent analogy between the cinema and Plato's cave does not present difficulties; I believe it does so, in points that I will proceed to outline below, and that I will develop more fully in the subsequent sections of my argument.

It is interesting to note that not only Plato's allegory has been used many times in theories of the cinema, but the cinema itself has been used to understand the allegory: in a comment on the relevant section of *The Republic of Plato*, Francis Cornford writes that 'a modern Plato would compare his Cave to an underground cinema, where the audience watch the play of shadows thrown by the film passing before a light at their backs' (Plato and Cornford, 1941, p. 223). The analogy appears to disregard the fact that the cinema is not a space in which the subject was born and has lived since, it is a space the subject goes to sometimes, or sometimes 'creates' at home or in other spaces; whereas Plato believed most subjects have always lived in the cave and only the philosophers can go outside.[2] To conceive of the cinema as a space of retreat implies the existence of an 'outside world' from which it is separated. In this scheme each locality can be put into perspective from each standpoint. But in Plato's scheme only very few have access to such 'binocular vision', to use another of Bion's concepts. This concept of binocular vision will be looked at in more detail in Chapter 4, but for now, it can be said that Bion (1962, p. 54) formulates it in his investigations on the perception of psychic quality, when he states that the conscious and the unconscious are capable of correlation and self-observation: they are capable of binocular vision (as opposed to monocular vision), in a similar way to two eyes that are able to correlate two different views of an object.

For Baudry, the *impression of reality* that both the apparatus of the cave and the apparatus of the cinema create is the crux of the problem.[3] And this, he argues, is less dependent on the apparatuses' capacity to credibly reproduce the real, than on the reproduction of a specific condition for the reception of that reproduction of the real. The passage in which Baudry makes this point in relation to Plato's cave, quoted below, occurs after he has commented on the artificiality of the set-up, in that the projected shadows are not of real people and animals, but of figures that resemble them made of materials such as wood or stone. Baudry writes:

> It seems that Plato ingeniously attempts and succeeds in fixing up a machine capable of reproducing 'something' that he must have known, and that has less to do with its capacity for repeating the real (and this is where the Idealist is of great help to us by sufficiently emphasizing the artifice he employs to make his machine work) than with reproduction and repetition of a particular condition, and the representation of a particular place on which this condition depends.
>
> (1975, p. 306)

The condition and the place alluded to can be inferred from the beginning of the paragraph, which reads: 'Cave, grotto, "sort of cavernous chamber underground", people have not failed to see in it a representation of the maternal womb, of the matrix into which we are supposed to wish to return' (ibid.).[4] As his argument develops, the intra-uterine condition becomes associated with the physical and mental torpor of the subject who dreams or hallucinates a good, feeding breast; and the womb becomes associated with the unconscious. I have already responded to these contentions in Chapter 1, but what I want to highlight here is that in his conceptualization of the cinematic apparatus, Baudry is less concerned with the level of success in providing credible copies of the real, or indeed, as he notes elsewhere, with the content of the films, but rather with what he sees as an incapacity of the subject, created by the apparatus, to form 'proper' judgements on the subject's experience in the cinema.

Elsaesser and Hagener see Baudry's stance as a typical example within the strand of film theory that draws on psychoanalysis, and which has found opposition among film theorists that draw instead on cognitivism. They write:

> Psychoanalytic film theories tend to treat the relationship between spectator and the screen as if it were based on a perceptual 'illusion' (i.e. as if spectators believed that the objects seen on the screen were really present), when it is equally plausible to argue that what one sees are representations, i.e. symbolic constructions or culturally determined images. This has been the line of reasoning among many theorists inspired by cognitive theories of perception and comprehension, when discussing 'identification' and spectatorship.
>
> (Elsaesser and Hagener, p. 100)

As suggested in the previous chapter, the impression of reality in the cinema is connected with the emotional links established through processes of projective and introjective identification, which can be extremely complex and nuanced. I also underlined in that first chapter that with Bion, these processes of identification are seen to have a fundamental role in communication and growth. The impression of reality seems to be dependent on a certain receptiveness of the container (both film and subject acting as containers vis-à-vis each other due to the reciprocity of the container/contained relationship). As I will argue here, contact with O can be made in and through the cinema, as well as at a certain distance from it.

If Baudry is more concerned with the subject's incapacity to exercise clear judgements in the cinema rather than with the content of the films, classics scholar Desmond Lee offers a different assessment of the analogy:

> As Cornford pointed out, the best way to understand the simile is to replace 'the clumsier apparatus' of the cave by the cinema, though today television is an even better comparison. It is the moral and intellectual condition of the average man from which Plato starts; and though clearly the ordinary man knows the difference between substance and shadow in the physical world, the simile suggests that his moral and intellectual opinions often bear as little relation to the truth as the average film or television programme does to real life.
>
> (Plato and Lee, 1955, p. 240)

Leaving aside Lee's juxtaposition of cinema and television, his statement serves as a reminder that in the Platonic view a lack of judgement affects any 'average' subject, not just, and in particular – as Baudry suggests – the subject in the cinema. However, for Lee, the cinema happens to be a good comparison because the 'average' film has little relation to real life. Here the issue seems to reside precisely in the content of the films, or in their tenuous connection to real life. But Lee's analogy implies judgements of value, so that it is not clear, for example, whether the 'real life' that he values could be that of an 'average' subject, or if it has to be that of an 'extraordinary' subject. For if the opinions of an 'average' subject bear little relation to 'the truth', an 'extraordinary' film could never have any connection to the real life of an 'average' subject. Following the same line of ideas, perhaps even less could an 'extraordinary' film have any connection to an 'average' subject's fantasies.

Lee's use of the term 'the truth' is less ambiguous, as it must refer to the ultimate reality in the Platonic sense: the realm of the Platonic forms. Bion refers to the Platonic form in his formulation of the concept of O, but O and the Platonic form are not the same. My reading of the cinematic apparatus through Bion's concept of O will be largely grounded in the differences and similarities between these concepts, so that an understanding of the cinema that departs from the Platonic scheme of oppositions will be possible. With the above, I have begun to show that the terms of the analogy do not sit easily together in several aspects. Plato's audiovisual construct is, in my view, too rigid to contain the cinema, it is divesting it of its possible meanings, of its evolving meanings. It could be that at the same time Plato's allegory is also having its meaning reduced through its long and close association with a construct such as the cinema – even when the cinema is not a static construct – by potentially making different forms of human activity less open to scrutiny through its lens.

If there is a certain idealism that runs throughout Bion's work, as he posits the existence of an ultimate reality from which only corresponding phenomena can be known, there are also points where Plato's thought and Bion's diverge. Plato's idea of justice – debated extensively in *The Republic* – as 'doing the job for which one is naturally fitted and not interfering with other people' (p. 130) is seen by Bion as an example of how certain classical philosophical views need to be extended by an acknowledgement of the existence of the unconscious and of unconscious motives (Bion, 1974, p. 205). And Bion's use of poetry in his investigations, such as in the example already mentioned of his dissatisfaction with the concept of the unconscious in favour of Milton's image of 'the void and formless infinite', also attests to a fundamental disagreement with one aspect of Plato's ideal society. Plato's dismissal of the work of poets and artists as having a corrupting effect by appealing to the emotions (or what Plato calls 'the lower elements in the mind' [Plato and Lee, p. 348])[5] rather than to reason, disagrees not only with the value Bion attributes to poetry in his work but also with the place emotions have in his conceptualization of mental life, in that the growth of the mind is seen to be dependent on the capacity to think about emotional experiences.[6]

The ensuing discussion of the concept of O will be interwoven with reflections on how the cinematic apparatus might be rethought in the light of that concept.

Cinema with no memory, desire or understanding

In the course of postulating O as ultimate reality or truth, Bion discusses examples of similar configurations that can help in the understanding of his theory. He refers to the Platonic theory that phenomena can 'remind' the subject of the existence of something (the form) that is no longer known, but used to be. Bion writes that 'the significance of O derives from and inheres in the Platonic Form' (1965, p. 138). He then provides a different example of a similar configuration in the distinction that Meister Eckhart makes between God and Godhead. 'God' is used to designate the God of the Trinity, described within the limitations of human thinking (Bléandonu, p. 211), whereas 'Godhead' is the absolute origin of divine power, about which nothing can be said (Bion, 1965, p. 139). Bion explains that 'Eckhart considers Godhead to contain all distinctions as yet undeveloped and to be Darkness and Formlessness. It cannot be the object of Knowledge until there flows out from it Trinity and the Trinity *can* be known' (p. 162). In this configuration, rather than 'reminding' the subject of the form, phenomena enable the subject to achieve union with an incarnate part of the Godhead. This is how Bion brings both configurations together:

> In both there is a suggestion that there is an ultimate reality with which it is possible to have direct contact although in both it appears that each direct contact is possible only after submission to an exacting discipline of

> relationships with phenomena, in one configuration, and incarnate Godhead in the other.
>
> (p. 139)

What this exacting discipline of relationships is that makes possible contact with O, in the analytic setting, will only be formulated in *Attention and Interpretation*. Here Bion introduces the idea that contact with O is only attainable in a state in which there is no memory, desire or understanding. The prelude to this idea can be found in the already mentioned article 'Notes on Memory and Desire', in which there is in fact no mention of the concept of O. It is a short and controversial article that aims to advise analysts to eschew memory and desire in the analytic sessions; the element of understanding as something to be eschewed appears here as *desire for understanding*.

In 'Notes on Memory and Desire', Bion begins by pointing out that memory is distorted by unconscious forces, and desires have a similar detrimental effect on judgement by selecting and suppressing parts of what is being judged. Memory and desire, Bion defends, accentuate the aspects of the mind that proceed from sensuous experience; however, psychoanalysis is concerned with psychic reality, which differs from the reality available to the senses. Moreover, memory is concerned with what has already happened, and desire, with what has not happened yet; whereas psychoanalysis, or more precisely psychoanalytic observation, is concerned with what *is* happening. Bion further notes:

> The only point of importance in any session is the unknown. Nothing must be allowed to distract from intuiting that. In any session, evolution takes place. Out of the darkness and formlessness something evolves. That evolution can bear a superficial resemblance to memory, but once it has been experienced it can never be confounded with memory. It shares with dreams the quality of being wholly present or unaccountably and suddenly absent.
>
> (1967, pp. 136–7)

In this passage Bion refers to a distinction between two different phenomena that are commonly known as 'memory'. He recognizes a difference between an idea that presents itself from a deliberate attempt at recall, which is what he considers to be related predominantly to experience derived from sensuous impressions (a memory), and 'the experience where some idea or pictorial impression floats into the mind unbidden and as a whole' (an evolution) (p. 147).[7] Evolution in this context will also be referred to as 'dream-like memory', again considered to be a part of psychic or psychoanalytic reality rather than sensuous reality. Bion clarifies: 'The emotional tone of this experience is not peculiar to the dream: thoughts also come unbidden, sharply, distinctly, with what appears to be unforgettable clarity, and then disappear leaving no trace by which they can be recaptured' (1970, p. 70). It can be said that here there is an allusion to an important aspect of O, which is that O is evolving continuously. I will come back to this.

As Gérard Bléandonu notes, the idea that the analyst should seek a state of mind empty of memory and desire is one of the facets of Bion's work that was met with most scepticism by the psychoanalytic institution (p. 221), and this is evident already in most of the commentaries written by a group of analysts who were invited to respond to Bion's article at the time of its original publication.[8] They could not understand how the analyst should strive not to remember the analysand's history and the work done on previous sessions; and how the analyst should not desire 'analytic progress' or the analysand's 'cure'. Thus a great part of *Attention and Interpretation* seems to be dedicated to elaborating on what was meant with the ideas outlined in the earlier article. Making use of terms from his theory of thinking with which his readers are already familiar, Bion remarks that memories and desires interfere with pre-conceptions because they saturate a space that should be left unsaturated (1970, p. 41). He suggests that in a sense memories can be seen as possessions, and desires as possessing the mind; and that this can have a harmful effect on the rapport between analyst and analysand:

> A certain class of patient feels 'possessed' by or imprisoned 'in' the mind of the analyst if he considers the analyst desires something relative to him – his presence, or his cure, or his welfare. [. . .] If the psycho-analyst has not deliberately divested himself of memory and desire the patient can 'feel' this and is dominated by the 'feeling' that he is possessed by and contained in the analyst's state of mind, namely, the state represented by the term 'desire'.[9]
>
> (p. 42)

Desire can possess the minds of analyst and analysand, hindering their openness to the perception of the emotional experience of the present. The reasons to cast aside memory in the analytic situation can be equally, perhaps deceptively, simple. Bion illustrates this point when he considers why he should not strive to remember whether his analysand is married or not:

> An analyst may feel, to take a common example, that his married patient is unmarried; if so, it means that psycho-analytically his patient *is* unmarried [. . .]. [E]rror is more likely to arise through inability to *divest* oneself of memory than through forgetfulness. If the analyst does not remember that his patient is married, the fact that he *is* is irrelevant until the patient says something that reminds the analyst of this fact.
>
> (p. 49)

Dwelling on what is known obstructs contact with the unknown, and again it is the unknown that is the point at issue in analysis. Similarly, the attempt to understand can interfere with this 'exacting discipline of relationships'. For Bion, the aim to understand as an aim of analysis can become so obvious that it obscures the dangers of prematurity. Bion (1977, p. 12) believes Darwin was aware of this problem when he quotes him writing that 'it is fatal to reason whilst observing, though so necessary beforehand and so useful afterwards'. The attempt to understand can also become associated with possessiveness, contrary to what John Keats defined as 'Negative Capability': the capability of 'being in uncertainties, mysteries, doubts, without any irritable reaching after fact and reason'. It is significant that Bion cites Keats's definition of 'Negative Capability' in the beginning of the last chapter of *Attention and Interpretation* (1970, p. 125).

The elements of the theory discussed so far can be used to begin thinking about what cinema with no memory, desire or understanding might be. It is a cinema in which the subject's experience of the film is divested of deliberate attempts at remembering (anything in particular), but is still open to thoughts unbidden, that is, evolutions. The subject's experience in the cinema is also divested of projections of desire, insofar as they may interfere with the emotional experience of the present; though this emotional experience could be desire. Similarly, it is divested of any struggle to understand. It is a state of complete receptiveness to the emotional experience of the present, which could then lead to contact with the ultimately real.

In Bion's thought there are subtle yet radical distinctions to be made: for example, between the wish to know on which all learning depends, the wish to know as arrogant, omniscient impulse, and the wish to know as obstructing contact with O. Eschewing memory and desire because they proceed from sensuous experience rather than psychic reality may also seem paradoxical when observation is at stake, especially when thinking about the cinema, which relies on sensuous experience. But again there is a distinction between sensorial perception that obstructs contact with O (dwelling on memories and desires) and a sharpening of sensorial perception in order to establish that contact.

Bion explains that the state of mind needed for contact with O can be compared to a hallucinatory or psychotic state. The psychotic seems to 'know' the thing-in-itself because in order to 'think' something, the situation needs to be acted out or the thing needs to be present (or appear) in external reality (1965, p. 40). But whereas the psychotic seems to be imprisoned in this state of mind – that is, the psychotic cannot know primary and secondary qualities, but only the thing-in-itself – Bion advocates a partial, deliberate, participation in this state, so a constructive contact with its depth and creativeness can be made. The state is similar, but the purpose is different: the psychotic aims to destroy links, severing contact with sensuous and psychic reality; Bion wishes to establish links, and 'diminish' sensuous perception so psychic reality can emerge (1970, p. 69).

This diminution of sensuous perception is also compared to a situation, already referred to in my introduction to this book, in which a diminution of light is needed so the features of something dark and obscure can be revealed. The metaphor comes from a letter that Freud wrote to Lou Andreas-Salomé, in which he states: 'I know that I have artificially blinded myself at my work in order to concentrate all the light on the one dark passage' (Freud quoted in Bion, 1967, p. 148). To be without memory, desire and understanding is to be 'artificially blinded' so a beam of penetrating darkness can be directed towards the dark object of investigation.

Thus, in analysis, attention to the emotional experience of the moment is what can allow contact with O, and its acceptance in O determines the possibility of mental growth. On this change from knowing to being (K→O), Bion writes:

> The transformation of the emotional experience into mental growth of analyst and analysand contributes to the difficulty of both to 'remember' what took place; in so far as the experience contributes to growth it ceases to be recognizable; if it does not become assimilated it adds to those elements that are remembered and forgotten. Desire obstructs the transformation from knowing and understanding to being, K→O.
>
> (1970, p. 71)

As his writings on catastrophic change and the caesura suggest, which will be considered in detail in Part II, for Bion 'mental evolution or growth is catastrophic and timeless' (p. 108), growth is turbulent; and as will be discussed, even the analyst's resistance is implicated in the process of being or becoming the real self – what Donald Meltzer interprets to be due to 'the potential explosiveness of the truth' (1978, III, p. 91).[10] But in the above citation there is a sense in which there is a stage in the process of growth that is manifested in subtle, or imperceptible ways. In the earlier *Elements of Psycho-Analysis* Bion already alludes to this idea by stating that 'growth is a phenomenon that appears to present peculiar difficulties to perception either by the growing object or the object that stimulates it, for its relationship with precedent phenomena is obscure and separated in time' (p. 63). But later the imperceptibility of growth gains a new depth when Bion postulates that the realm of O is separate, or inappropriate to the realm of K, L and H (1965, p. 140). He explains:

> It is not knowledge of reality that is at stake, nor yet the human equipment for knowing. The belief that reality is or could be known is mistaken because reality is not something which lends itself to being known. It is impossible to know reality for the same reason that makes it impossible to sing potatoes; they may be grown, or pulled, or eaten, but not sung. Reality has to be 'been': there should be a transitive verb 'to be' expressly for use with the term 'reality'.
>
> (Bion, p. 148)

For Bion, the subject cannot 'know' reality, the subject can only 'be' reality, 'be' or 'become' reality, or real. And here is, to my mind, where Bion's thought radically diverges from Plato's as it is expounded in the simile of the cave.

According to Plato's simile, the prisoner who is released is first able to look at shadows and reflections of the objects outside, then at the objects themselves, and finally at the sun (Plato and Lee, pp. 242–3). Thus, in the Platonic view the ultimate source of truth *can be perceived* in the intelligible region (p. 244). This means that for Plato it is possible to have knowledge of the ultimate reality, of the Platonic forms, even though only with difficulty and after much effort. But Bion posits that the most, and the least that the subject can do is to *be* O (1965, p. 140). Again, O is unknowable because O is inappropriate to the realm of knowledge. Knowledge is appropriate to transformations of O, not to O itself.

There are other points in which the disjunction between the two theories can be discerned. Plato believes that the sensible domain is in a constant state of flux, whereas the forms are intelligible *immutable* principles. The forms are what is ultimately real, and the ultimately real is unchanging (Plato and Lee, pp. 193–4). However, Bion posits that O is continuously becoming, continuously evolving. The O of one moment is no longer the O of the moment that follows (1970, p. 103).[11] Bion points out that in the analytic session the emotional experience can be perceived to be in constantly changing patterns, comparable to kaleidoscopic changes (1977, p. 11).

Another distinction that should be made is between Plato's and Bion's conceptions of the *value* of the ultimate reality. In his exposition of the simile of the cave, Socrates states that the sun corresponds to 'the form of the *good*; once seen, it is inferred to be responsible for whatever is right and valuable in anything, [. . .] and being in the intelligible region itself controlling source of truth and intelligence' (Plato and Lee, p. 244 [my italics]). For Plato, the Good occupies the highest position in his scheme, because the Good is considered to be the ultimate source of knowledge and truth.[12] But Bion posits that O is not good or evil (1965, p. 139). He reflects on the case of a man who commits a suicidal act but believes he will survive uninjured. The O of the belief that he will be uninjured and the O of the belief that he will be killed can both be regarded as valuable. Bion considers John Ruskin's definition of 'valuable' as life-giving, but then he observes that 'if value is to be the criterion, difficulty arises because there is no *absolute* value: the individual does not necessarily believe it is better to create than to destroy; a suicidal patient may seem to embrace the opposite view' (1970, p. 101). This aspect of O, to be neither good nor evil, evokes Bion's interest in Meister Eckhart's conception of the Godhead as containing all distinctions still undeveloped.

What are, then, the implications of these differences towards rethinking the cinematic apparatus? Perhaps the most fundamental shift that occurs if Plato and Bion were to consider the subject in the cinema is that Plato would be concerned with the subject's capacity to apprehend the forms through the acquisition (or reminiscence) of knowledge and use of reason, whereas Bion would be concerned instead with the subject's experiential capacity to be or become the real self (more on the real self will be said later).

Furthermore, to conceive of the ultimate reality as continuously evolving rather than unchanging, is to conceive of the possibility of contact with it at a given realization of an emotional experience, at a given moment of a given film for a given subject, but that does not necessarily have to be rigidly inscribed in an instance that is the same to all subjects, which, to my mind, makes it all the more elusive.

Also, to not restrict a conception of the ultimate reality to the Good is to accept the possibility that a realization of evil in the cinema may be the establishment of contact with the ultimate reality, which in a sense is to accept the reality of evil; however, ultimately, it is to conceive of O as divested of such distinctions that belong to the realm of K. The example that Bion gives of the suicidal analysand is already a transformation of O into K (O→K), as it has been conceptualized, but it is still able to give the sense of how the reality of an emotional experience of destructiveness can be shared between analysand and analyst to the extent of at-one-ment with the O of that emotion, though the recognition of that emotion as 'destructiveness' would already be a transformation of O into K.

In his consideration of Bion's turn to the mystics in order to learn from their experience of the ineffable, the Brazilian psychoanalyst Antonio Muniz de Rezende makes an important point that can be one way of synthesizing how Bion's theory contrasts with Plato's. Rezende remarks that the experience with which the mystics, and Bion, are concerned, is of an *affective* order, rather than *intellective*. He writes: 'The mystical model in Bion has an epistemological thrust: it is not through religious but through epistemological necessity that the mystical model is introduced. I cannot name the mind. I cannot name the ineffable. So, how to experience? Affectively' (1994, p. 89).[13] This is, I believe, a crucial point towards rethinking the cinema in the light of the concept of O. While in Plato's scheme the subject has to strive to get out of the cave (and the cinema) through knowledge of reality, Bion's theory of O is rather interested in the subject's realization of the emotional experiences that connect the subject to the internal and external worlds, a realization that happens both inside and outside the cave – if the cave is thought to be the place in which both analyst and analysand share an experience of the unknown; and this intimate relation that may allow contact with the ultimate reality (and allow real change, or growth) could be that between subject and film, in the cinema.

Being or becoming *real* in and through the cinema

The survey of the differences between the Platonic form and O helps to illustrate what Bion means by O but it is important to remember that 'O is by definition [. . .] not subject to, circumscribed by, beginnings and ends, rules, laws of nature or any construct of the human mind' (Bion, 1975, p. 88).[14] This statement can be found in *A Memoir of the Future*, an epic work of fiction about psychoanalysis, or a psychoanalytic work in the form of fiction, that Bion wrote in the last four years of his life. In it can also be found another passage that conveys this sense of difficulty in grasping what O is, and the sense of a certain fluidity of the concept:

> From O = zero to O which is O = oh! to O which is a picture which is a picture of a hole or greedy mouth or vagina which offers perfect freedom which is death which is perfect freedom which is perfect pitch or absolute colour or Eternal Life or Eternal Death or Perpetual Motion or Perpetual Inertia or Absolute Space or space like mental space in which there exist objects

> so compact that they are like white dwarfs or so sparse and rare that they can only be grasped by finite means like Poisson's law governing exceedingly infrequent events or so absolute a space that your mental life is itself destroyed as in a body which is anaemic because mind is lost like blood in a body whose capillaries are so greedy that there is not enough blood to be shared.
>
> (pp. 36–7)

Rezende comments on how the form of Bion's writing in this passage conveys the oneiric quality of the realm of O, and the attempt to communicate what is ineffable (p. 112). It is perhaps this passage that Bléandonu has in mind when he suggests that O is related to the mathematical use of zero as a point of origin; when he mentions the erotic text *The Story of O* in order to establish a connection between the roundness of the vowel and the female genitals (p. 283, n. 36); and when he draws an analogy between a space in analysis and a pause or silence in music (p. 284, n. 40).[15] The ineffable nature of O is also considered by Chris Mawson, who sees this notion

> as representing the dimension of real life which lies behind what we can articulate in language and to which Wittgenstein was referring in the final proposition (7) of his *Tractatus Logico Philosophicus* (1922) when he wrote: 'Whereof one cannot speak, thereof one must be silent'.
>
> (2011, p. 28)

A space that opens in the analytic setting, 'which offers perfect freedom': a space in which to effect the transition from knowing about the real self, to being or becoming the real self. But how can the real self be known, if the real is unknowable? It cannot be known; however, Bion contends that during the psychoanalytic procedure this problem seems to arise in the form of resistance: 'Resistance is only manifest when the threat is contact with what is believed to be real. There is no resistance to anything because it is believed to be false' (1965, p. 147). It is perhaps fair to say that Bion is aware that the situation cannot be as unequivocal as he puts it in these statements, nevertheless the idea is to be taken seriously as a guiding principle. And a few pages later in the text, it becomes clear that Bion considers the analyst's resistance too to play an important role in the unfolding of the analytic procedure:

> In terms of analytic theory it is approximately correct, but only approximately, to say that the conditions for an interpretation have arrived when the patient's statements provide evidence that resistance is operating: the conditions are complete when the analyst feels aware of resistance in himself – not countertransference which must be dealt with by analysis of the analyst, but resistance to the reaction he anticipates from the analysand if he gives the interpretation.
>
> (p. 168)

The last section of this statement is quoted and commented on by Meltzer, who recognizes in it a crucial idea that goes well beyond any familiar notions on the timing of an interpretation. In Meltzer's understanding of Bion's 'approximately correct' theory, the communication of what the analyst thinks, truthfully, of the analysand's material, involves courage. Meltzer writes:

> The courage required relates to the potential explosiveness of the truth, which may certainly, as Bion asserts again and again, be the food of the mind but also threatens the person, really analyst and patient alike, with the catastrophic change of becoming a different person.
>
> (III, p. 91)

It may be recalled pertinently at this point that Bion considers the capacity to suffer pain to be fundamental in the process of mental growth, and that he identifies a need to increase this capacity in the analytic experience. But from a theory that posits the real self as unknowable, it follows that, as Meltzer puts it, 'the analyst is reduced to offering his opinion' (p. 93). As it is apparent particularly in the idea of giving up memories, desires and understanding, Bion regards the achievement of any possible knowledge of the real self (O→K) as relatively passive, in contrast with the more active or omnipotent use of lies. Meltzer explains that 'Bion sees the manufacture of lies as an employment of positive ingenuity, while the achievement of truth is more passive, requiring submission to the operation of container and contained' (p. 107). The process of being or becoming the real self involves giving up resistances, it involves a certain passive receptiveness towards the potential explosiveness of the truth.

Thus, my conceptualization of the space of retreat as bearing a relation to the internal world is developed here more specifically into a conceptualization of the cinema as a privileged space for the recognition and working through of resistances. It seems to me that the cinema is able to do this in a way that other spaces do not, because the cinema is separated from the outside world – both spatially and temporally – while being a space and time that opens to something else, which has the potential to be contact with O. The cinema as retreat allows a certain engagement that is not dissimilar in some aspects to the rapport with which Bion is preoccupied and which his theory of O reflects: the opening up of a space in which the analysand, and the analyst, can be or become their real selves by sharing the emotional experience of the present, while being separated from the relationships, responsibilities and circumstances of their selves in the outside world (a separation that happens to both analysand and analyst in the transformation K→O). This separation is not an evasion (active or passive) of those circumstances because the retreat can lead precisely to an encounter with them, yet, and crucially, from a different vertex.

The idea that the outside world constrains the subject, or that the self of the outside world is a 'less real' self could be seen to be implied, but this is not my suggestion. Neither am I suggesting that the film has to deeply involve the subject emotionally for a resistance to be recognized and for contact with O to be established (potentially). Nevertheless, Bion speaks of the 'perfect freedom' of O; he speaks of memories, desires and understanding as possessions or things that possess; and he writes that he may forget that his analysand is married if he is not reminded of the fact. The cinema as retreat, because of its separation from the outside world, and its relation to the internal world, is a privileged space for the emergence of an awareness of resistances to being or becoming the real self, and a privileged space for working through those resistances, regardless of how small or great they are, and regardless of how small or great a role they play in a small or catastrophic change.

The space of retreat can allow growth, in particular; however, the retreat and the outside world do not exist independently of each other, and thus the process of growth has ultimately to be considered in terms of how the two have an impact on each other. Meltzer conveys the sense of this relation between internal and external in a passage on the growth of thought according to Bion:

> This growth, which proceeds in sophistication, complexity and level of abstraction by being put to different uses, depends on the operation, either internally or with an external object, by which the disordered *and painful* thought finds a container that can modify it by means of a shift in value system, or vertex, or view-of-the-world.
>
> (pp. 92–3)

There needs to be a correlation between 'the understanding derived from more than one vertex' (p. 93) in order to discern between truth and lies; and the cinema as retreat – that is, as something that exists also in relation to the outside world – enables that correlation to be made. This is the transformation O→K, the understanding of an emotional experience and its truth value through testing it from different vertices. It is the reality testing enabled by a binocular vision. And while in Plato's scheme, the cave/cinema is the realm of lies, and the outside world, that of truth, with Bion no such distinction can be made.

It has already been discussed that on close analysis Plato's scheme is based on acquisition of knowledge and use of reason to apprehend reality, whereas Bion demonstrates not only that knowledge and use of reason are impossible if emotions cannot be assimilated, but also that knowledge is insufficient in the process of growth (i.e., the process of being or becoming real) because he observes that an interpretation can be accepted in K, but rejected in O. Thought has an emotional basis, it has an emotion at its basis; it is generated from, or found in, an emotional state that is assimilated, and it is completely dependent on this assimilation.[16]

To rethink the cinematic apparatus with Bion's concept of O is, then, to conceive that all possible knowledge that can be used and acquired in the cinema *is only possible through* the subject's experiential capacity to assimilate emotions, and that all possible knowledge *does not suffice* in the process of mental growth: the subject has to be or become real, in and through reality, or O (which includes the reality of the cinema).

In Chapter 1 I showed how Freud influenced the theory of the cinematic apparatus in its pleasure-centredness, and its neglect of the thirst for knowledge as an instinct; in this chapter I contend that Plato influenced not only apparatus theory but much of the whole of western thought in their giving supremacy to knowledge and reason with little or no regard for the emotional and experiential capacities that indeed make knowledge and reason possible. With such influences, these theories of the cinematic apparatus have not only succeeded in removing knowledge with any truth value from the cinema, they have also dismissed the value of emotions in the cinema. Rethinking the cinematic apparatus with Bion means recognizing the value of knowledge and emotions in and through the cinema, which means recognizing cinema's role in the growth of the mind.

This concludes my exploration of the retreat in cinema; in the following part of this book, I will consider representations of retreat in film, as I strengthen and develop in my argument the relation between the space of retreat and the internal world – more specifically, the retreat and the internal world at times of dramatic psychical change, of caesura. The films that I have chosen to examine demonstrate the significance of the retreat during those turbulent stages of growth.

Notes

1 The influence of *quattrocento* painting in spatial representation was already mentioned in Chapter 1 in the context of Metz's definition of *primary cinematic identification*.

2 A recent book by Nathan Andersen, dedicated to the study of the analogy from the perspective of film-philosophy, makes a similar point:

> Modern readers of the *Republic* often consider Plato to have anticipated cinema in his description of the rightly famous allegory of the cave. There are, yet, important differences. Moviegoers can leave their seats, exit the theater, into the light. They arrive at the theater with memories drawn from outside, and compare what they see there with what they've seen and encountered elsewhere. In Plato's cave, by contrast, the prisoners have no access to any other kind of experience than the shadows they witness and echoes that appear to them to emanate from the cavern wall, until, that is, they are released from the shackles and educated.
>
> (2014, p. 37)

3 The issue of the impression of reality in the cinema also preoccupies Christian Metz in an article written prior to the articles discussed in this book, in which his approach is phenomenological (Metz, 1965).

4 For a philosophical critique of Plato's simile of the cave from a gendered perspective, see Luce Irigaray (1974).

5 It can be said that Plato would have shared Baudry and Metz's suspicion of projective mechanisms in relation to the cinema (see 'The Effects of Poetry and Drama' in Plato and Lee, pp. 349–53).

6 For Bion's relatively implicit remarks on this divergence see for example *Attention and Interpretation*, p. 60 and *Brazilian Lectures*, p. 26.

7 'Evolution' according to Bion might call to mind Proust's involuntary memory.

8 The scepticism and controversy surrounding Bion's later writings continues to this date. See O'Shaughnessy, de Bianchedi and Ferro (2005), and the more recent discussion by Blass, Vermote and Taylor (2011).

9 Donald Meltzer (III, p. 101) comments on this point, noting that Bion is concerned with the unhindered evolution of the transference.

10 In the films that will be examined in Part II there are striking visual and aural examples of the 'explosiveness' of the truth.
11 See also López-Corvo (2003, p. 197).
12 Shortly before introducing the simile of the sun, Socrates states that 'the highest form of knowledge is knowledge of the form of the good, from which things that are just and so on derive their usefulness and value' (Plato and Lee, p. 229).
13 (My translation).
14 For a comparison between Bion's and Lacan's notions of the real and unknowable see Michael Eigen (1993, pp. 130–1).
15 Here Bléandonu could possibly be referring to Bion's idea of 'perfect pitch'. Hoping not to confuse matters, it is perhaps interesting to note that a pause or silence could be thought of as the absence of a thing (a thought) (see Chapter 1), and that in poetry and music the term 'caesura' denotes a silent pause (see Part II). A silent pause could also evoke an image of retreat.
16 Longhin and Mancia, the authors of an article on the relationship between Kant and Bion already cited in Chapter 1, point out that this is one of the ways in which recent developments in object relations psychoanalysis can contribute to the philosophy of mind. They argue that '[Kant's] conception proves to be incomplete, because the emotional and affective component is now [with recent psychoanalytic theory] deemed to be part of the "protomental" structure of *a priori* or transcendental forms, so that it possesses characteristics of universality and necessity. [. . .] For this reason, Kant was not justified in excluding the psychological aspect on the grounds that it was merely *empirical* and hence not necessary or universal. Bion, after all, held that the emotions perform the same function as sense impressions do in the objective knowledge of objects situated in time and space, and have a universal and necessary function.' Longhin, L. and Mancia, M. (2000). Kant's philosophy and its relationship with the thought of Bion and Money-Kyrle. *International Journal of Psychoanalysis*, 81 (6), pp. 1202–3. Copyright © Institute of Psychoanalysis, London, 2000. Reprinted with permission of John Wiley & Sons Ltd.

References

Andersen, N. (2014). *Shadow Philosophy: Plato's Cave and Cinema*. Oxon: Routledge.

Baudry, J-L. (1970). Ideological effects of the basic cinematographic apparatus. In: Rosen, P. (ed.) *Narrative, Apparatus, Ideology: A Film Theory Reader*. New York: Columbia University Press, 1986.

Baudry, J-L. (1975). The apparatus: Metapsychological approaches to the impression of reality in the cinema. In: Rosen, P. (ed.) *Narrative, Apparatus, Ideology: A Film Theory Reader*. New York: Columbia University Press, 1986.

Bion, W.R. (1961). A theory of thinking. In: *Second Thoughts: Selected Papers on Psychoanalysis*. London: Karnac, 2007.

Bion, W.R. (1962). *Learning from Experience*. London: Karnac, 1991.

Bion, W.R. (1963). *Elements of Psycho-Analysis*. London: Karnac, 1989.

Bion, W.R. (1965). *Transformations*. London: Karnac, 1984.

Bion, W.R. (1967). Notes on memory and desire. In: Aguayo, J. and Malin, B. (eds.) *Wilfred Bion: Los Angeles Seminars and Supervision*. London: Karnac, 2013.

Bion, W.R. (1970). *Attention and Interpretation*. London: Karnac, 2007.

Bion, W.R. (1974). *Brazilian Lectures*. London: Karnac, 1990.

Bion, W.R. (1975). *A Memoir of the Future Book 1 – The Dream*. London: Karnac, 1991.

Bion, W.R. (1977). The grid. In: *Two Papers: The Grid and the Caesura*. London: Karnac, 1989.

Blass, R.B., Vermote, R. and Taylor, D. (2011). Psychoanalytic controversies: On the value of 'late Bion' to analytic theory and practice. *International Journal of Psychoanalysis*, 92 (5), pp. 1081–116.

Bléandonu, G. (1990). *Wilfred Bion: His Life and Works 1897–1979*. Translated by C. Pajaczkowska. London: Free Association Books, 1994.
Eigen, M. (1993). *The Electrified Tightrope*. Edited by A. Phillips. Northvale, NJ: Jason Aronson.
Elsaesser, T. and Hagener, M. (2010). *Film Theory: An Introduction through the Senses*. New York: Routledge.
Irigaray, L. (1974). Plato's *hystera*. In: *Speculum of the Other Woman*. Translated by G.C. Gill. Ithaca: Cornell University Press, 1985.
Longhin, L. and Mancia, M. (2000). Kant's philosophy and its relationship with the thought of Bion and Money-Kyrle. *International Journal of Psychoanalysis*, 81 (6), pp. 1197–211.
López-Corvo, R.E. (2003). *The Dictionary of the Work of W.R. Bion*. London: Karnac.
Mawson, C. (2011). Introduction: Bion today – thinking in the field. In: Mawson, C. (ed.) *Bion Today*. Hove, East Sussex: Routledge.
Meltzer, D. (1978). *The Kleinian Development*. Strath Tay: Clunie Press, 1985.
Metz, C. (1965). On the impression of reality in the cinema. In: *Film Language: A Semiotics of the Cinema*. Translated by M. Taylor. New York: Oxford University Press, 1974.
O'Shaughnessy, E., de Bianchedi, E.T. and Ferro, A. (2005). Psychoanalytic controversies: Whose Bion? *International Journal of Psychoanalysis*, 86 (6), pp. 1523–42.
Plato and Cornford, F.M. (1941). *The Republic of Plato*. Translated by F.M. Cornford. Oxford: Clarendon Press.
Plato and Lee, D. (1955). *The Republic*. Translated by D. Lee. London: Penguin, 2003.
de Rezende, A.M. (1994). *A Metapsicanálise de Bion: além dos modelos*. Campinas, SP: Papirus.

PART II

The retreat in film

Introduction to part II

The films considered in the chapters that follow are concerned with a stage of dramatic psychical change in the lives of their protagonists. This difficult stage of growth involves a gesture of retreat, a circumscribed space and time. It is my claim that this space and time of retreat is closely connected with the protagonists' internal world, and that in it can be recognized traces of the early maternal relationship. It is noteworthy that the mother as a character is absent in most of these films; but, if I can put it this way, her absence is felt as a presence. The mother's presence is felt through these traces that pertain to a prenatal or a preverbal relationship with her. The mother's absence in relation to the development of thinking was considered in Chapter 1, and in Chapter 2 psychical growth was discussed in relation to a state of complete receptiveness to the emotional experience of the present moment. In this second part of the book, the conceptualization of 'retreat as caesura' requires some important distinctions to be made. The thinking and becoming activity that was explored in previous chapters can certainly be found in these films, but some aspects of the caesura and of the struggles that emotionally turbulent growth more generally can entail will bring to the fore other situations and phenomena. The caesura is linked to a prenatal stage in which physical and mental life are not yet differentiated, to certain feelings or physical impulses for which there is not yet an appropriate mental representation. There is thus a difficulty in translating or communicating these feelings. At certain points in these films the struggles of dramatic growth involve hallucinations, catatonic states, omnipotent narcissism or intrusive processes of identification; but I aim to show that at the basis of the protagonists' gesture of retreat can be discerned the activity of the epistemophilic instinct, that there is a sense of the protagonists' wish to engage with both the external and the internal worlds, and that through the experience of the retreat they eventually achieve a more integrated view of these worlds.

A psychoanalytic reading of a film text, like the psychoanalytic process itself, can be seen as an aesthetic process of symbolization. It is a process of bringing together different discourses in meaningful ways, in an attempt to understand how different elements can be brought together to create meaning. Of course my readings of these films coexist among many possible alternatives. I have focused on textual analysis, and tended to move away from the biographies of the authors of the films, thinking they may hinder the open-endedness of interpretative work. The film analyses that I conduct in the following chapters establish close relations between the psychoanalytic (and sometimes the clinical) and the filmic, but this aesthetic process understands meaning as infinitely evolving.

3

THE CAESURAS IN *THROUGH A GLASS DARKLY*

Introduction

Through a Glass Darkly (Ingmar Bergman, 1961) is set on an island, and its aquatic surroundings, during the time between two consecutive sunsets. Although some of the four characters in the film travel from or to places beyond this outside enclosure, these places are never actually seen, an aspect which further delimits the film's other circumscribed spaces: the various rooms of an isolated house, boats and a stranded shipwreck. The significance of these enclosures is reinforced by the insistent framing of the liminal spaces between them. Images of window and door panes, half-open windows and doors, stairs and ladders, piers, the hatchway on the deck of the ship, and a dark opening in the wallpaper of an empty room, recur throughout the film, linking and separating the spaces on either side. By this means, Ingmar Bergman is not only able to project the idea of God in an invisible, or darkly seen, beyond, but also to convey the idea that his characters stand at critical junctures in their lives.

The cast is composed of Karin (Harriet Andersson), her brother Minus (Lars Passgård), their father David (Gunnar Björnstrand) and Karin's husband, Martin (Max von Sydow). Bergman refers to this cast as a string quartet, alluding to the 'chamber play' quality of the film (1994, p. 256). As Frank Gado notes, this quality is drawn from August Strindberg's expressive dramas, played in intimate settings bared to their essentials (1986, p. 260). Part of the film's ensemble of family members, but only referred to in the script, is Karin's and Minus's deceased mother. The absence of her figure, in my view, does not imply the absence of her role. She is, albeit in different degrees, omnipresent, in all the spaces inhabited by this family, particularly in relation to some of the events that take place in them.

Minus asks his sister: 'I wonder if everyone is caged in? You in yours, I in mine. Each in their cubicle . . . Everybody.'[1] This cubicle that Minus refers to seems to be connected with the internal world; and the characters' internal worlds seem to be projected into and penetrated by, contained by and containing, the circumscribed spaces of the film. As I will attempt to show in this and the other three chapters of Part II, spaces of retreat are brought into play when the subject faces the challenge of psychical change. Wilfred Bion provides a clue for why this should be so:

> It is in course of transit, in the course of changing from one position to another, that these people seem to be most vulnerable [. . .]. At the same time they are vulnerable to the observation of others who cannot tolerate the totality of the human personality, and therefore cannot tolerate someone who is so 'mad', so 'curious', so 'eccentric', or so 'sane'.
>
> (1977, p. 53)

Vulnerability in the course of change could thus be seen as a possible factor at the origin of the gesture of retreat. The people Bion mostly refers to in the article from which the above passage is taken are the analysands, though he does sometimes seem to be referring to people in general. He stresses the problem of whether to regard obstacles in psychical development as pathological or non-pathological. He writes: 'We need to re-view commonplace formulations – psychotic, neurotic, psycho-somatic, soma-psychotic and so forth – to consider, from our own experience, what we think those things are when we meet them' (p. 51). These passages are quoted from an article first published in 1977, but based on a talk given in 1975, titled 'Caesura'. The word 'caesura' can be found in a statement written by Freud in *Inhibitions, Symptoms and Anxiety*, which inspired Bion to develop a concept, around ideas that had been preoccupying him for some time. Freud's statement is the opening citation in 'Caesura': 'There is much more continuity between intrauterine life and earliest infancy than the impressive caesura of the act of birth allows us to believe' (p. 37). Gérard Bléandonu provides its original context: 'Freud meant that the mother's early "psychological" care is an equivalent of the biological environment before birth' (1990, p. 239). How Bion developed the meaning of caesura will become progressively clearer throughout the chapter, but I will begin by drawing attention to its paradoxical aspect, namely that the caesura is a break, an interruption, but also implies a continuity. Bion refers to it not only as a 'barrier', 'obstacle', 'layer', but also as a 'link' or 'synapse'. Suggesting that there is such a continuity, Bion conjectures how much of what the foetus thinks or feels is carried over to life after birth.

Bion's conjecture appears to stem from his awareness in his consulting room of feelings that seem to have 'an intense and unformed character' (1977, pp. 42–3). He intuits that there are feelings faintly expressed, or disguised, because they are of such magnitude and intensity that the analysand fears to express them, or is not able to express them any better than in a faint or disguised form:

> I can imagine that there may be ideas which cannot be more powerfully expressed because they are buried in the future which has not happened, or

> buried in the past which is forgotten, and which can hardly be said to belong to what we call 'thought'.
>
> (p. 43)

Here, two important points are made: the problem of translation or articulation of ideas that are not known as such; and a present situation seen to bear a relation to the past or the future. Bion points out that there is a misleading tendency to think that the analysand is only referring to past events (p. 47). Analyst and analysand should be seen as two personalities that are constantly changing. Nevertheless, and this is a crucial point in Bion's notion of caesura, there are times when psychical change is dramatic, times or events like birth, adolescence, the onset of senility, or death; they are periods of emotional turmoil. Bion evokes Leonardo's drawings of swirling water and hair as an example of images that may come to mind when thinking about emotional turmoil, but he advises his listeners to recall their own images and experiences of mental or emotional turbulence (1976a, p. 296). When thinking about whether an example of such images can be found in *Through a Glass Darkly*, the swirling patterns of foliage on the wallpaper of the room to which Karin retreats may come to mind.

Thus, the caesura becomes a model with which these dramatic moments in mental life can be investigated. And because in these moments the past and the future can be inscribed in some way, there is a need to penetrate the caesura in both directions, a need to look at it from both sides. And again, in the course of development, in the course of attempting to transcend the caesura in both directions, the problem of articulation arises:

> In the psycho-analytic experience we are concerned both with the translation in the direction of what we do not know into something which we do know or which we can communicate, and also from what we do know and can communicate to what we do not know and are not aware of because it is unconscious and which may even be pre-natal, or pre-birth of a psyche or a mental life, but is part of a physical life in which at some stage a physical impulse is immediately translated into a physical action.
>
> (Bion, 1977, pp. 53–4)

The caesura can find a form of articulation in a physical impulse, an action or a gesture. In what follows, I will examine the articulation of the caesuras in *Through a Glass Darkly*, by considering some of the gestures that the characters perform, and the various spaces they use and move through; this will be done by following closely the film's narrative development, also because its pivotal moments are interrelated and arranged in sequential structures in such a way as to communicate more than a present event or situation. In my analysis, such formal aspects of the narrative are also part of the ways in which the caesuras in this film are articulated. The importance of gestures and spaces of retreat during these pivotal moments will be apparent.

The problem of containing, in Bion's words, the 'messianic hope', could be seen as an overarching theme in *Through a Glass Darkly*, a theme that Bergman continues to explore in the other two films of the 'trilogy of faith'. I will now look at some writing on this trilogy, as *Through a Glass Darkly* is generally considered in its context, and note some distinguishing aspects of my approach.

The 'trilogy of faith'

The monumental reference guide that Birgitta Steene compiled with existing literature and other sources of information on Ingmar Bergman gives a good picture of the vastness of the critical interest that his work has raised. According to Steene, religious approaches by Protestant or Catholic authors exceed in volume any other groupings that draw on other fields (2005, p. 905). Perhaps this is not surprising, as several of his films deal explicitly with religious questions, though it could be argued that even those films invite psychoanalytic, or psychological, readings. This view may be supported by the fact that there seems to be a recurrent preoccupation with the characters' psychological journeys, often lived through intimate relationships.

Although *Through a Glass Darkly* was not initially intended to be the first of the 'trilogy of faith', it subsequently became so, followed by *Winter Light* (1963) and *The Silence* (1963). On the occasion of the publication of the films' scripts, Bergman provides the following introductory note: 'These three films deal with reduction. *Through a Glass Darkly* – conquered certainty. *Winter Light* – penetrated certainty. *The Silence* – God's silence – the negative imprint' (1994, p. 245). In studies of the trilogy, it is common to find a reference to the function of the last two films as being one of undoing the 'conquered certainty' of the ending of *Through a Glass Darkly*, an ending that not only displeased Bergman but also several of his critics (p. 243). Steene's summarized view of the trilogy comments on the collapse of the figure of God, but emphasizes the collapse of the father figure:

> Bergman's so-called trilogy [. . .] depicts the eventual demise of the providential god of Bergman's religious heritage but also exposes the failure of the earthly father. David in *Såsom i en spegel* is so absorbed in his own frustrated efforts to write that he is tempted to use his own daughter's mental illness as an object of study. Tomas, the pastor in *Nattvardsgästerna*, fails to be the father of his flock that his congregation has a right to expect. In *Tystnaden*, the father of the child Johan is conspicuously absent and the substitute father figure, the old waiter in the foreign hotel where the action takes place, is a kind but doddering fool.[2]
>
> (Steene, p. 145)

As already noted, so is the mother conspicuously 'absent' in *Through a Glass Darkly*. The representation of mother figures as opposed to father figures in Bergman's films is a complex issue, an issue that the film under consideration does raise. Marilyn Johns Blackwell (1997) has written the most thorough critique of his films from a gender perspective, attentive to the representation of the maternal. I will engage with some of her views towards the end of my study.

Psychoanalytic approaches to Bergman's work understandably draw on Freud, a lesser number on Lacan, but notably on Jung as well, particularly on his concept of 'shadow'.[3] Other works are perhaps situated in a more psychological rather than psychoanalytic strand, such as Robin Wood's monograph (1969). Wood makes pertinent remarks on some general characteristics of Bergman's films, the first mentioned being the fact that his characters are rarely seen in their permanent homes. This leads him to consider that these characters are in a state of suspension, 'in the process of movement not only from place to place but from one condition to another' (p. 10). The journey then becomes a recurring narrative, 'during which present events and memories of the past combine to steer the protagonist to a point of self-confrontation, provoking in him or her a radical change in attitude to life, a new orientation with regard to the future' (ibid.). Other motifs that Wood identifies are that the narratives and their turning points often occur within a 24-hour period, and that there is a general movement 'from sickness and imprisonment towards a health and freedom not necessarily reached but passionately sought' (p. 13). Wood's observations resonate with the situations and events depicted in *Through a Glass Darkly*, and I would highlight the relation that he draws between the characters' psychical experiences and their physical surroundings.

Firmly located in the psychoanalytic strand is Daniel Dervin's book *Through a Freudian Lens Deeply: A Psychoanalysis of Cinema* (1985). In the chapter dedicated to the study of Bergman, Dervin defends the prominence of primal scene material in several of his films, but especially in *The Silence* and *Through a Glass Darkly*. On the latter film, Dervin argues that 'every character is drawn into his most dreaded encounter' (p. 118), and further, that 'the poisonous inner dimensions of all the relationships is [sic] governed by the invisible malignant spider, just as each individual is trapped either by witnessing or by producing a primal scene' (p. 119). Dervin's argument is partly supported with references to scenes in the printed version of the script that have not been included in the film.[4] I will not refer to this version of the script because I would like to focus on the film itself as object; also, it is the film rather than the printed script that is mostly known.

Dervin's study poses another question in relation to my approach, one that is also present in all the literature on Bergman that I have referred to so far, which is the use of what Bergman himself has written or said about his films, to the extent that they relate to his own personal experiences. Examples of frequently cited sources are the autobiographical works *The Magic Lantern* (1988) and *Images: My Life in Film*, and also interviews, of which perhaps the most used are those collected in the book *Bergman on Bergman* (1973). Bergman encourages biographical approaches to his work by giving accounts of his dreams, childhood, relationships, and by affirming that one of his reasons to make films is that it is a form of self-therapy (Steene, p. 838). In the introduction that preceded this chapter I have already stated that I will not incorporate biographical details in my studies of the films. Specifically in the case of Bergman there is already a very considerable amount of research that adopts a biographical perspective,[5] and I believe that to repeat the gesture would begin to inhibit the exploration of meaning in his films.

Frank Gado's comprehensive analysis of Bergman's oeuvre, up until *Fanny and Alexander* (1982), is no exception in the biographical vein, drawing frequently on a diary written by Vilgot Sjöman, a director who also collaborated with Bergman. The recurring themes of God, art, women, apocalyptic situations, and the values of the bourgeoisie, are recognized in Gado's investigation 'as surrogates for conflicts lodged deep in Bergman's personal history' (p. xv). This personal history, in Gado's view, is inscribed in the films in a symbolic language related to dreams, hence his following a psychoanalytic method in order to understand them (pp. xvi-xvii). He also points out, referring to Sjöman's diary, that Bergman revealed a sudden interest in psychoanalysis around the time of the trilogy's conception (p. 264).

The 'trilogy of faith' is regarded by Gado as dealing with such fundamental issues that a purely theological interpretation would be too narrow; one of his comments on *Winter Light* defends the view that the film articulates its existential or religious concerns as issues that pertain to the psychology of its main protagonist, the pastor Tomas (Gunnar Björnstrand).[6] Gado writes: 'the film rejects theology as an answer to the humanistic question it poses about life's purpose – a question which takes form in the context of a specifically psychological problem' (p. 294). This problem is seen to be the pastor's relationship to his parents, his sense of guilt for not having fulfilled their expectations, his anger at their insufficient love towards him, and his subsequent search for substitutes: God as a substitute for his father, and his wife for his mother. The protagonist's conviction that his wife's death and his suffering are God's punishment is meant to destroy the idea of God as love, proffered at the end of *Through a Glass Darkly* (p. 285); and for Gado, the open-endedness of the film's epilogue further unmasks the certainty, when the pastor decides to celebrate the mass despite his doubts and despair, and despite the fact that his mistress, whom he spurns, is the only person attending. In *Winter Light*, 'there is no truth to believe in except the truth created by belief' (p. 292).

If even in its form *Winter Light* discards certainty, *The Silence* is considered to be still more resolute in its refusal to halt meaning (pp. 294–5).[7] Gado's interpretation of *The Silence* underlines the importance of the boy's character, insofar as it is through his perception that the film can be read as a dream, and *The Dream* was its working title (p. 296). It is to a description of the boy's actions and experiences in the hotel, as occurrences that more or less explicitly relate to his psychosexual development, that Gado dedicates most of his study of *The Silence*. But he also remarks that the dead father of the two sisters is an 'obvious symbol of God' (ibid.), and thus the Oedipal motif reappears, as it does, though in different forms, in all the films of the trilogy. This is Gado's thesis on the significance of the trilogy, that whether or not love can redeem, whether or not the father's forgiveness is sought, the father is the one who ultimately determines the movement of the films; and *The Silence* is the work that marks the end of that movement: 'From this point on, the quest for father that had taken the guise of a quest for God disappears from Bergman's films' (p. 307).

In the dialogue that I will establish between Bion's psychoanalytic theory and *Through a Glass Darkly*, it will be seen how the film, in its preoccupation with the problem of containing the messianic idea – a problem of growth, according to Bion – actually unsettles the contention that its quest for God conceals a quest for the father. The analysis of the trilogy's two other films is beyond the scope of this chapter, but it can still be observed that in *Winter Light*, if it is the idea of God as love that is rejected, it is also the mistress's unconditional love that the pastor rejects; and in *The Silence*, it is towards the mother that her son and her sister manifest utter dependence and devotion. The films of the trilogy seem to be particularly open to unresolved meanings, or opposing interpretations; and, considering the elusiveness of the matter with which they deal, it is perhaps reasonable to think that they *are* open – notwithstanding all that Bergman has said or written about them – and that they will remain so.

Gesture and space of retreat as caesura

Through a Glass Darkly begins with three short consecutive shots of the sky reflected on the dark surface of undulating water. This trinity of shots could be seen to introduce the film's religious theme, as well as announce the course of the film's narrative, and establish its formal structuring principle. The contrast between the light of the sun and the darkness of the clouds becomes sharper as the sequence progresses, and this dramatic development delineates the tragic course that the narrative will take. The division of this sequence into three separate fragments resonates with the way the film is structured: the film's decisive moments are tripartite sequences of interrelated, but separate, events, which lead the narrative to its culminating point. One of these sequences of decisive moments is marked by the deep sound of the island's foghorn, heard repeatedly on three occasions; and the other, of the three crucial events that determine Karin's separation from her family, is immediately followed by non-diegetic music: excluding the opening credits, the opening notes of Bach's sarabande for cello are inserted three times in the soundtrack.

The religious theme implicit in this introductory sequence alludes to the biblical passage from which the film's title is taken, as the water appears as a reflective surface.[8] The glass or mirror of the title and its original context have not been disregarded in studies of the film. Peter Cowie writes that 'In *Through a Glass Darkly*, Bergman subjects his characters to the most ruthless scrutiny. Each one is forced to study himself and his attitudes as reflected in the others' (1963, p. 116). Gado pursues a similar idea: 'In the course of twenty-four hours, the characters progress from self-delusion to self-recognition, a process in which each character first sees himself as he is seen by others and then sees in others a mirror of himself' (p. 267). In my interpretation, the images of water in the beginning of the film function as a metaphor for the film's formal structure: as the water can show the textures of the movement of its surface, its stillness reflect the sky above, and its transparency reveal what lies under it, each of the crucial moments of the film can be seen as present events in which traces of the past and the future can be found. Bion provides the following image of the caesura: 'There is a contact through this permeable membrane in both directions; the caesura is a transparent mirror' (1980, p. 108). A transparent mirror like still water, but also a membrane if the water surface is turbulent.

The last in the sequence of those initial images of water, which is still accompanied by Bach's music, dissolves into a shot of the four characters, who are in high spirits, emerging from the sea where they were bathing. Soon after, while David and Martin go off on a boat to set the fishing nets, Karin and Minus walk to the farm to get some milk. Karin stops suddenly and asks her brother whether he just heard the sound of a cuckoo. As the answer is negative, Karin observes that the electric shock treatments she had may have caused her unusual acute hearing. Moments later, Karin is amused by Minus's expectations of their father's success as a novelist, and so she kisses and teases him: 'Seventeen and nearly ten feet tall! Where's your girlfriend?' to which Minus, annoyed, replies: 'No one wants to be with me!' Meanwhile, on the boat, Martin reveals to David that Karin's psychiatrist diagnosed her illness as 'relatively incurable', but that Karin is unaware of this.

The next scene shows Karin and Minus returning from the farm, but the landscape around them is very different. They had made their way in daylight, among the shrubs, but now it is dark, and they walk on the watery surface of the rock along the shore. The faint beam of a lighthouse in the distance, and the distant sound of the foghorn, punctuate the film's first critical moment.

Minus drops the milk container in an abrupt gesture, spilling some of it, and when Karin comes close to him he warns her to stay away, to stop her provocative behaviour, as he is disgusted by women. Karin eventually calms her brother's emotional turmoil, but a sense of foreboding remains.

During the evening, the behaviour of the family oscillates between the peaks of excitement, sheer disappointment, feigned jubilation and despair. When the four sit in the front yard for dinner, the atmosphere is cheerful, until David makes known he is only staying for a month since he has accepted some work abroad. Minus points out to his father that he had promised to stay at home once he was back from Switzerland. The silence that follows Minus's reproach is interrupted by Karin: 'Listen . . . We were going to have a nice evening – and instead we're on the verge of tears!' after which David exclaims: 'I've got presents for you all from Switzerland!' While they unwrap the presents, which turn out to be unsuitable, David excuses himself to get some tobacco from his room, where he sobs. On his return, he is greeted with exalted expressions of gratitude, and informed that a surprise has been prepared for him. They lead him blindfolded to the front of a small hut where Minus and Karin perform a play. Written by Minus, it is intended to impress his father, but also to confront him with his obsession with work and consequent negligence towards his family. Despite being visibly hurt by his son's indirect criticism while the play unfolds, David leaps from his chair and applauds enthusiastically at the end. In an uncanny way, this play also foreshadows what will happen between the two siblings inside the shipwreck. The artist (Minus), referring to the princess (Karin), declares: 'Here I shall meet her, my bride-elect. Here, by this tomb redolent with the smell of death.'

Night time, in their bedroom, Karin gently turns away from Martin's caresses. Later, she wakes up with the cry of a bird. Unable to sleep, she gets up and walks towards the bedroom door, but before reaching it, she pauses to listen: the foghorn sounds, for the second time, now more distinctly. The foghorn continues to be heard throughout the following scene. Karin walks upstairs into an empty room, where the light of dawn reflected on water is projected on the wall, surrounding a dark opening on the patterned wallpaper. Voices whisper through this opening, and Karin enters a hallucinated world where she joins people who are waiting for God. She falls to her knees in ecstasy.

At this point, it will be useful to return to Bion's thoughts on the caesura, particularly those concerned with the life of the foetus, and with what might surface from this life after the 'impressive caesura of birth':

> The embryologist speaks about 'optic pits' and 'auditory pits'. Is it possible for us, as psycho-analysts, to think that there may still be vestiges in the human being which would suggest a survival in the human mind, analogous to that in the human body, of evidence in the field of optics that once there were optic pits, or in the field of hearing that once there were auditory pits? Is there any part of the human mind which still betrays signs of an 'embriological' intuition, either visual or auditory?
>
> (Bion, 1977, p. 42)

In other articles on the caesura, Bion comes back to these conjectures, that a foetus may see light and hear sounds caused by variations of pressure in the amniotic fluid, and that such experiences may survive in some form in the adult mind (1976a, p. 300; 1976b, p. 310).[9]

Karin's gesture of retreat to the room upstairs and her hallucination seem to suggest that such experiences do survive. The only object in the room is a chair that evokes the presence of her mother. Yet this chair is not the only element that connects this space with the past, or with a maternal space. The shimmering light projected on the wallpaper, the voices that Karin hears and tries to understand, her sense that a pivotal moment is approaching, could be seen as traces of an embryonic intuition.

It is only later in the film that her experience is described in words, when Karin takes Minus to this room and tells him that once someone called her from behind the wallpaper. She continues: 'So I pressed myself against the wall, and it gave, like foliage – and then I was inside.' Inside is a peaceful, big room, where people are waiting for someone to come through a door. When Minus asks her who this person is, she explains: 'No one has said for certain. But I think it's God who shall reveal himself to us.'

In Karin's distant past, the God she was expecting, and who revealed herself to her, was of course her mother. But why this sense of helplessness and expectation now? Why does this emotional turmoil occur at this point in her life? The film gives several indications of what Karin's present situation is: that her relationship with her husband is unfulfilling, that her father continues to put his work before his family, that her mother died, and that she inherited her illness, for which she has spent some time in hospital. But another incident must also be connected to her hallucinatory episode, and one of the elements that establishes this connection is the sound of the foghorn. When the foghorn is heard for the first time, it is its sound, Minus's words, and the spilling of the milk that symbolically stands as an attack on the mother's breast, which can be regarded as having become embedded in Karin's conscience, as something that concerns her relationship with her brother, and their relationship with their mother. When the sound of the foghorn returns during the night, so does the maternal space, but here they may be seen to be associated with Karin's wish to be reborn into an idealized world.

Nevertheless, the creation of this idealized world is not only born out of the past and the present. It is also born out of her future, a future of separation that she fears may happen soon. The shadow of this future could have been cast since the beginning of her life, according to Bion. He writes:

> I don't suppose there will ever be any chance of knowing, so to speak, what a foetus thinks, but [. . .] I suggest that there is no reason why it shouldn't *feel*. I think it would be quite useful to consider that some stages of fear, of intense fear, are more easily visualized or imagined by us if we think of them as thalamic fear, or as some sort of glandular manifestation such as something to do with the adrenals, or what later on turn out to be the genital structures. You can look at this as you like, say as memory traces, but these same memory traces can also be considered as a shadow which the future casts before.
>
> (Bion, 1976, p. 309)

Memory traces or a shadow of the future, contained in Karin's experience of the present. Her present is emotionally turbulent, as she seems to experience a conflict between a wish for a world in which she does not hurt and is not hurt by her family (which would entail to be separated from it) and the fear of being separated from the family she loves. The wish for separation, and the fear of separation, could be regarded as memory traces of a distant past, or a shadow of a distant future.

The sound of the foghorn in this scene is part of a recent past, and part of a near future, as it will occur for a third and last time, on the same day. Karin's hallucination will also have its sequel, in the same room. These impending moments will reflect the devastating effect of a discovery still to happen, but in some ways they are already foreshadowed by their previous counterparts. Therefore, even when these previous counterparts have aspects of a past that goes as far as intrauterine life and the early relationship with the mother inscribed in them, they also have an unequivocal orientation towards the future. They are articulations of Karin's and Minus's caesuras, in so far as in their emotional turmoil something that belongs to other times and spaces is striving to be articulated. Karin's gesture of retreat to the upstairs room is an attempt to make sense of her past, present and future, in articulations that contain all of these dimensions in some form, even if those articulations exist in different degrees of consciousness. Thus, at a particular moment in time, a gesture of retreat, and a space of retreat, as caesura.

Past, present and future

Karin's disheartening discovery happens a short while after her hallucinatory state subsides. Alone in her father's room, she searches through the drawers of his desk, and, appearing to have found the object she was looking for – her father's diary – she begins to read. She reads that there is no cure for her illness, though there are temporary improvements; that this certainty is unbearable to her father; and that he is horrified by his own curiosity, by his wish to record the course of her gradual disintegration so he can use it in his writing. If Karin was already anticipating a future separated from her family, this is the pivotal moment that draws that future near. As she closes the diary, the sombre music of the cello marks the beginning of the tripartite sequence mentioned earlier.

Karin then reveals to Martin what she read, but when he and David set off on the boat for the day, she bids them farewell as if nothing had happened. Having returned from the pier, she surprises Minus looking through pictures of naked women in a magazine, over the Latin book he is supposed to study. Minus's irritation at his sister's intrusion quickly dissipates, almost as quickly as they get bored of studying together. Eventually, Karin decides to take her brother to the upstairs room and share with him her experience there. As she runs towards the house, Minus follows, but halfway along his path, he takes a stone from the ground, turns towards the sea, and throws it far into the distance.

The significance of this gesture is subtly emphasized by a short interruption of the camera pan that follows the movement of the two characters towards the house. Its significance can also be recognized if the character who performs it is considered more closely. Minus finds himself at the juncture between adolescence and adulthood, an emotionally turbulent stage in itself, complicated by his suffering with his sister's illness, and by the difficult relationship with his father. With this gesture, Minus projects his turbulence beyond the containment of his physical boundaries,[10] but also seems to project it beyond the present, in either direction: as if challenging a troublesome past and its effect, or challenging an unknown future. His emotional turbulence is apparent in his physical actions in other scenes: for example, when his father is clearing up the dinner table just after the play, Minus is seen in the background fighting an invisible enemy, still wearing the cloak and sword.

In one of Bergman's earlier films, *Summer with Monika* (1953), the two main protagonists also stand at a similar juncture in their lives. Harry and Monika, about to turn into young adults, flee from their oppressive families and jobs in the city, to spend the summer together on an island. The discovery of each other and of their emerging new selves is echoed in images of both of them looking at their reflections on the surface of the placid water of ponds. In one of these scenes, Harry throws a stone into the pond, as if to test the depth of the water. Or is this gesture aimed at testing the reality of their blissful present? Or perhaps aimed at sinking their past, out of sight? Or aimed at testing the water of their future? This moment is followed by a cloudy sky, the sound of thunder, a bolt of lightning; and then, the rain falling on the surface of the pond. This sequence, in that it recalls the frustrations of their past, and foreshadows their unhappiness and separation some time after they return to the city, suggests that they penetrated the barrier of the present, of the caesura, even if momentarily; and it affirms the meaningfulness of their interaction with the landscape, of their gestures, as ways in which they articulate the process of change that they are going through, in the circumscribed space of the island.

In a similar way to Harry and Monika during their retreat, Minus translates his caesura into a physical action, from what he does not know into something which he can communicate, and from what he knows and can communicate to what he does not know. What he does not know or is not aware of, belongs to a past that has been forgotten, or a future that has not happened, but emerges, thus, in gestures that are not thoughts yet: gestures of caesura.

While Karin confides in Minus, Martin confronts David with what he wrote in his diary, once again in the privacy of a journey on the boat. David's response is drawn-out. He asks: 'Can you control your innermost thoughts?'; then he continues with another question, whether Martin has wished Karin's death, since his and her suffering are pointless; and concludes with a story about his failed suicide attempt in Switzerland that awakened a love for the three of them. He also says, 'I want to tell you that I no longer have any front to protect. The truth won't bring a catastrophe.'

But it does. The effect of her father's words comes after this scene, when Karin, seeing that a storm is approaching, and hearing the foghorn, takes refuge inside a shipwreck not far from the house. The foghorn sounds never as intensely, and accompanies Minus's search for her. Finally he finds her lying down inside the hulk, and when she sees him, she pulls him tightly close to her, while her expression conveys something between anger and disgust. The film cuts to the floorboards of the hulk, where it now rains; the implicit incestuous act that happened between them stands as a symbolic attack on the mother's womb, but more than that, is Karin's self-destructive attack and an attack on her family.

Minus runs home to get some covers for the rain, as Karin seems unable to move. In his room, he falls on his knees and bends forward in pain, then stares through the window, and utters the word 'God', as if wondering about its meaning. A close-up of Karin's and Minus's faces follows, looking transformed, which cuts to a long shot of both, sitting still in the darkness and wetness of the hulk. Bach's theme reinforces once more the exposure to a painful reality.

Then the rain stops, and Martin and David can be heard arriving at the pier. Karin asks to be left alone with her father so they can talk, and so Martin leaves, and calls an ambulance. Their dialogue begins with Karin saying that she cannot go on living in two worlds and that she wants to stay at the hospital; and ends with David apologizing for having turned to his work when Karin first got ill, as he could not bear the thought of her having the same illness as her mother.

Back in the house, in the middle of packing, Karin returns to the upstairs room. David and Martin find her, speaking towards the wall with the opening in the wallpaper, in a calm voice: 'Yes, I understand. I know it won't be long now. It's a great comfort to know. But our waiting has been one of joy.' While David stands by the door, paralysed with fear, Martin comes close and tries to persuade her, unsuccessfully, that she is having visions. She kneels, expectantly.

Soon comes the noise of the ambulance helicopter, and its black shape is seen through the window. It is apparent that the helicopter casts its shadow into the room, and at the same time Karin is seen to be suddenly aware of something terrifying; she recoils from it, screaming and contorting with horror. Now both David and Martin try to intervene, but she frees herself from them and runs down the stairs, at the bottom of which Minus stands looking at her. The three men succeed at holding her down, Martin gives her an injection, and a few moments later she is able to describe what she saw:

> I was frightened. The door opened . . . but the god was a spider. He came up to me . . . and I saw his face. It was a terrible, stony face. He scrambled up and tried to penetrate me – but I defended myself. All along I saw his eyes. They were cold and calm. When he couldn't penetrate me . . . he continued up my chest . . . up into my face and onto the wall. I have seen God.

These are Karin's last words in the film. She leaves in silence, her eyes behind dark glasses. As Minus opens the door of the house to see the helicopter taking off, the notes of the cello underline the film's tragic ending. The image of the helicopter in the air dissolves into an image of the sunset and the sea, the same sunset that can be seen through the window in David's room throughout the film's epilogue.

The epilogue consists of Minus turning to his father for advice on how to face the harsh reality in which he now lives, and David replying that the thought of love and God being the same fills his life with hope. Minus observes: 'If it is as you say – then Karin is surrounded by God, since we love her. Could that help her?' David answers, 'I believe so.' Before the image fades to black, Minus, already alone, whispers in amazement: 'Dad talked to me.'

The messianic hope

What the spider represents is largely the focus of Daniel Dervin's study, which, as I have already mentioned, is also concerned with identifying the primal scene in Bergman's films. He begins by associating the spider's legs with the riddle of the

Sphinx, a mythical character whose ambiguity stands as the combined parental image (p. 110). Other psychoanalytic interpretations of spider symbols that Dervin finds, supported by clinical data, include 'female genitalia with concomitant fears of engulfment' and the 'fearful, pregenital, orally incorporating mother' (ibid., n. 8). For Dervin, spiders are sexually ambiguous. He writes that 'setting a trap, strangling, devouring, sound feminine; striking with a poisonous fluid, masculine' (p. 111); but the particular image of the spider-god with its forbidding facets 'stems from the father image as it was distorted by childhood fantasies and fears and before it has been partially mastered through identification' (pp. 115–16). In the end, Dervin gathers all these interpretations and leaves the question open:

> The spider apparently represents the combined parents, but perhaps also the figure conspicuously missing from the family. It is quite possible that behind the explicitly masculine spider-god is the more primitive and dreaded Medusa-like representation of female genitalia [. . .]. In like manner within the image of the Sphinx (literally the Strangler) is the terrifying mother of the oral sadistic stage: one line of interpretation does not exclude the others.
> (pp. 119–20)

Another interesting image Dervin brings to his comments on *Through a Glass Darkly*, one that he calls a 'crude visualization' and does not pursue very far, is that the three men can be seen as a spider that subdues and imprisons Karin: 'What literally happens is that in escaping from her terrors, Karin hurls herself at the three men who compositely form a six-legged beast which traps her and subdues her with the hypodermic needle's venom' (p. 111). It can be said, then, that the three men compose an image of God that Karin can see but that none of the four characters seem to recognize.

Excluding Minus from this visualization, Frank Gado also considers the idea, but for him the spider-god is in fact the apotheosis of the father's emptiness: 'As Karin waits for her God of love to appear through the half-open closet door, David, whose failure to love has stimulated the religious fantasy, stands in the room's doorway. The parallel's meaning is unmistakable' (p. 277). However, after stating that Karin's father is the figure who has stimulated her religious expectation and who stands behind the image of the spider-god, Gado goes on to conclude: 'Regression to the womb, which had represented a dream of refuge, now represents a dangerous delusion, a surrender to the spider-God' (p. 278). Surrendering to the spider-god now means returning to the maternal space of the womb. Gado also argues that the father and son undergo a transformation, are redeemed by love, and have the courage to embrace the future; whereas the mother, whom he sees represented in the figure of Karin, stands for a withdrawal from life, 'tantamount to death' (ibid.).

Not only does Gado set David's and Minus's attitudes towards life completely apart from Karin's, he also gives them precisely the opposite orientations. This is his interpretation of Karin's first hallucinatory episode:

> Beyond this terrifying surface she imagines a 'still and silent' universe of timeless innocence that suggests the womb. A slit in the wallpaper resembles a vagina, and when Karin describes her movement from reality to her world of voices, her language unmistakably implies a reversal of birth.
>
> (Gado, pp. 276–7)

Karin's language, which Gado subsequently quotes, is her account of how the foliage of the wallpaper opened up and she found herself *inside*. In Gado's view, her actions and her illness 'plainly indicate a desire to regress to her younger self' (p. 276); and when he compares Minus's and Karin's roles, she is 'the antagonist whose retreat represents the counter-motion against which he strives' (ibid.). Thus it can be understood that Gado considers Karin's gesture of retreat to be a merely regressive movement. In my view, however, the film's crucial moments can be seen not as simply regressive but as articulations of the caesura.

I have already suggested how the film's first critical moment, in which the foghorn sounds for the first time, is connected with Karin's first hallucination. This hallucination of an idealized world, created when she hears the foghorn for the second time, is also related to a fear of future separation from her family, and so it contains the shadow of her future experience in the same room, which is realized in the form of the spider. But this particular image of the spider is also the culmination of a series of attacks. After the reading of the diary, the sound of the foghorn returns for the last time not as part of the idealized world, but as part of the cold, dark, wet landscape, the maternal space that was attacked by the spilling of the milk, and that has been further attacked by the father: the decayed womb-like space of the shipwreck. And it is here that the incest will happen as the ultimate destructive attack on Karin and her family.

It could be argued that the sound of the foghorn in *Through a Glass Darkly*, in that it foreshadows a future event, is nothing but a formal device employed to give formal coherence to the diegesis. But as I have been suggesting since the introduction to this study of the film, the circumscribed spaces that the characters inhabit are connected with their internal worlds, in such ways as to penetrate those internal worlds, as well as receive their projections. Thus, Karin's internal world can be said to be penetrated, and to contain, the sound of the foghorn in those moments, but it can also be said that those sounds act as containers for her projected emotions. The same applies to other qualities of the circumscribed spaces in the film – such as light, or water – which sometimes remain similar across different spaces, and other times change within the same space at different moments. Moreover, the moments in the tripartite sequences divide the film into three segments of time and are themselves 'divided' three times: past, present and future. The film integrates forms that go beyond being mere film forms; they are part of the characters' caesuras, they are forms of caesura.

Accordingly, what happens in the shipwreck is also implicated in Karin's vision of the spider. When she talks to her father, she already seems to be suffering terribly from feelings of guilt. Referring to the incest, she says: 'I didn't do it of my own free will. A voice told me what to do.' David, in the beginning, thinks she is referring to her reading his diary, and her telling Martin what she had read. Then Karin admits she has done worse. Although David apologizes for his neglect in the end, his remarks do not help to ameliorate Karin's guilt for her intrusion and her subsequent vengeful act. And it is this terrible feeling of guilt that suggests the possibility that the image of the spider is a self-reflection. But Karin's destructiveness and vengefulness can only be partly inherent, for they have been undoubtedly provoked by the father's cruel words.

It is, then, interesting to note that the idea of God as a reflection of the self emerges in the film, in so far as the four characters either see a mirror reflection of the spider, or embody the image of the spider. However, despite the several possible interpretations of this image that have been discussed so far, studies of the film maintain God's affiliation to a patriarchal system. Marilyn Johns Blackwell's examination of the film is an example. Blackwell argues that the nurturing, loving figure of the mother is absent, and that the father's power, which stands for God's power, is absolute and malevolent. She writes:

> While the collapse of Bergman's religious ideology also precipitates a collapse of the male ideological system with which it is complicit, he seems to find it difficult completely to jettison male values, for the female protagonist in *Through a Glass Darkly*, however accurate her imaginative vision may be, achieves this vision through mental illness.
>
> (Blackwell, p. 203)

Blackwell follows this statement with a reference to R. D. Laing, who defends that the illness is in society itself, therefore those who will not or cannot partake in it are in fact healthy. But for Blackwell, Karin does not escape a 'traditional male stereotype of women's mental activities, closely aligned with the image of women as hysterics' (ibid.). In the end, the father is indeed the one who shares his wisdom with his son only, whereas Karin and her mother might be seen to be confined to mental illness and oblivion. But this would be, in my view, a facile theory of the film. The film is really a tragic story that aims to convey the difficulty of intimate relationships, the difficulty of growing, and the elusiveness of religious belief, in which Bergman seems to have felt the need to include a glimmer of hope and certainty in an ending that he later regretted. And even though Karin sees things that none of the other characters see, Bergman shows very clearly why she sees them; and the reasons are certainly not only because of who she is, or who her mother was. Her hallucinated worlds, at times idealized, at other times persecutory and vengeful, are also, as I have argued, inextricable from the past, present and future realities that concern her and her family.

Blackwell's premise that God stands for the patriarchy, and Gado's claim that behind the quest for God stands a quest for the father, become unsettled once the film begins to be seen through Bion's psychoanalytic theory. I return to Dervin's statement, 'It is quite possible that *behind* the explicitly masculine spider-god is the more primitive and dreaded Medusa-like representation of female genitalia' (pp. 119–20),[11] to highlight the word 'behind'. Gado himself affirms that the father has unmistakably stimulated the religious fantasy, but then he also states that Karin's dream of refuge is a fantasy of regression to the womb. The mother's image can then be discerned, but it seems that it is often behind something else, secondary; silent or invisible, as she is in the film. However, I have argued that her figure might be invisible and silent (absent), but her presence is not. Her presence, like the caesura, can sometimes only be articulated in gestures, or actions; or the sound of the foghorn – which, interestingly, provides guidance in difficult conditions of visibility – or the cry of a bird that causes fear, or the soothing voices that give a sense that a pivotal moment is approaching; or spilt milk, or water that reflects shimmering light.

In the beginning of the film, Bergman introduces three images that can be said to carry a millennial signification, but literally, they are images of water. Like in water, images of God in *Through a Glass Darkly* seem to become slowly discernible in something more or less transparent, at other times suddenly clearly reflected, and still at other times just turbulent and indecipherable. The three introductory images are a form of caesura, proposing an investigation of what they meant in the past, what they mean now, and what they will mean in the future. And it is precisely this process of investigation that Ingmar Bergman undertakes not only in this film, but in the whole 'trilogy of faith'.

This process presents the problem of containing a new idea, in this context, the problem of containing the 'messianic hope'. There is a passage in *A Memoir of the Future* in which Bion suggests how the 'messianic hope' can be seen as a model of mental growth. The following is extracted from the musings of a character called Myself:

> God [. . .], though unknown or perhaps because unknown, or perhaps because of being respected, remains as an Invariant clothed in no matter how many variables and under whatever vertex. He is a 'constant' which is an 'unknown' and the centre of a human discipline served by a mathematics which must be capable of manipulation, by a mathematics in which the constant is unknown and whose place is taken by an infinity of variables.
>
> (Bion, 1975, p. 142)

This passage brings to mind that in Bion's theory of the process of mental growth, the problem is not of arriving at a particular idea, but of the process whereby a new idea becomes susceptible to being contained, and which will at some point be replaced by another idea. It is a question of whether a new idea is able to be contained in a symbiotic relationship, in a manner that promotes growth, regardless of the levels of anxiety and pain that might be involved (an 'unknown' that must be capable of manipulation). And, crucially, *Through a Glass Darkly* approaches this question of growth through a certain articulation of retreat: it articulates retreat as caesura.

Notes

1 I quote from the English subtitled version of a 2001 DVD release of the film by Tartan Video, part of 'The Bergman Collection'.
2 *Såsom i en spegel* literally means 'as in a mirror', referring to the same biblical passage translated in English as 'through a glass darkly'. I will come back to this. *Nattvardsgästterna* is the original title of *Winter Light*, of which the literal translation, sometimes used, is *The Communicants*.
3 Bergman's film *Wild Strawberries* (1957) has been of particular interest in individual case studies that adopt a psychoanalytic perspective, perhaps because of its notable dream sequences. See for example Elizabeth Cowie (2003).
4 See Ingmar Bergman (1963) for the publication of the script.
5 Examples of such research include Peter Cowie (1982) and Geoffrey Macnab (2009).
6 *Winter Light* follows Tomas, plagued by ill health and religious doubt, and involved, after his wife's death, with the local school teacher (Ingrid Thulin); Tomas fails to provide reassurance to one of the members of his congregation (Max von Sydow), who eventually commits suicide.
7 In *The Silence*, the two sisters Ester (Ingrid Thulin) and Anna (Gunnel Lindblom), and Anna's son Johan (Jorgen Lidstrom), stay at a hotel in a foreign city threatened by imminent war. Ester is gravely ill, and consumed with jealousy when Anna pursues sex with a waiter. In his mother's absence, Johan encounters throughout the hotel people and objects that communicate in a foreign or symbolic language.
8 Gado provides the relevant excerpt from I Corinthians 13: 'For now we see through a glass, darkly; but then face to face; now I know in part; but then I shall know even as I am known' (p. 267).
9 In one of the talks in New York, Bion also conjectures that the foetus may have olfactory capacity (1980, p. 50).
10 Referring to the latency period, Bion speaks of an emotional upheaval that ceases to be bound by the corporeal frame (1976a, p. 295).
11 (My italics).

References

Bergman, I. (1963). *A Film Trilogy: Through a Glass Darkly, The Communicants (Winter Light), The Silence*. Translated by P.B. Austin. New York: Marion Boyars, 1967.
Bergman, I. (1988). *The Magic Lantern: An Autobiography about Ingmar Bergman*. London: Penguin.
Bergman, I. (1994). *Images: My Life in Film*. Translated by M. Ruuth. London: Bloomsbury.
Bergman, I. (1973). *Bergman on Bergman: Interviews with Ingmar Bergman by Stig Björkman, Torsten Manns and Jonas Sima*. Translated by P.B. Austin. London: Secker and Warburg.
Bion, W.R. (1975). *A Memoir of the Future. Book 1 – The Dream*. London: Karnac, 1991.
Bion, W.R. (1976a). Emotional turbulence. In: *Clinical Seminars and Other Works*. London: Karnac, 1994.
Bion, W.R. (1976b). On a quotation from Freud. In: *Clinical Seminars and Other Works*. London: Karnac, 1994.
Bion, W.R. (1977). Caesura. In: *Two Papers: The Grid and the Caesura*. London: Karnac, 1989.
Bion, W.R. (1980). *Bion in New York and São Paulo*. Perthshire: Clunie Press.
Blackwell, M.J. (1997). *Gender and Representation in the Films of Ingmar Bergman*. Columbia, SC: Camden House.
Bléandonu, G. (1990). *Wilfred Bion: His Life and Works 1897–1979*. Translated by C. Pajaczkowska. London: Free Association Books, 1994.

Cowie, E. (2003). The cinematic dream-work of Ingmar Bergman's *Wild Strawberries* (1957). In: Sabbadini, A. (ed.) *The Couch and the Silver Screen: Psychoanalytic Reflections on European Cinema*. Hove, East Sussex: Brunner-Routledge.

Cowie, P. (1963). *Antonioni, Bergman, Resnais*. London: Tantivy Press.

Cowie, P. (1982). *Ingmar Bergman: A Critical Biography*. London: Secker & Warburg.

Dervin, D. (1985). *Through a Freudian Lens Deeply: A Psychoanalysis of Cinema*. New Jersey: Analytic Press.

Gado, F. (1986). *The Passion of Ingmar Bergman*. Durham: Duke University Press.

Macnab, G. (2009). *Ingmar Bergman: The Life and Films of the Last Great European Director*. London: I.B. Tauris.

Steene, B. (2005). *Ingmar Bergman: A Reference Guide*. Amsterdam: Amsterdam University Press.

Wood, R. (1969). *Ingmar Bergman*. London: Studio Vista.

Filmography

Fanny and Alexander (1982). Directed by Ingmar Bergman. [DVD] Sweden: Cinematograph AB/Svenska Filminstitutet/Gaumont/Personafilm/SVT Drama/Tobis Filmkunst.

The Silence (1963). Directed by Ingmar Bergman. [DVD] Sweden: Svensk Filmindustri.

Summer with Monika (1953). Directed by Ingmar Bergman. [DVD] Sweden: Svensk Filmindustri.

Through a Glass Darkly (1961). Directed by Ingmar Bergman. [DVD] Sweden: Svensk Filmindustri.

Wild Strawberries (1957). Directed by Ingmar Bergman. [DVD] Sweden: Svensk Filmindustri.

Winter Light (1963). Directed by Ingmar Bergman. [DVD] Sweden: Svensk Filmindustri.

4

CAESURA AND BINOCULAR VISION IN *PIGSTY*

Introduction

Pigsty (1969)[1] is the third film in a group of four that is referred to as the 'mythical cycle' in Pier Paolo Pasolini's filmic oeuvre.[2] The four films of the cycle reflect a preoccupation with the survival of a mythical or mythicized past. The Oedipus myth, for example, is interpreted in the cycle's first work, *Oedipus Rex* (1967), and recurs in *Pigsty*, even if in a significantly different form. *Pigsty*'s treatment of the Oedipus situation will be the focus of the present chapter, as it is the emergence of this situation for its main protagonist that is closely connected with his retreat.

The film is composed of two intertwined narratives that unfold in very different settings. One of the narratives occurs some time during the late 1960s in a palatial mansion located in Germany, where a young man named Julian (Jean-Pierre Léaud) lives, largely indifferent to his parents and their business, and to his girlfriend Ida (Anne Wiazemsky) who occasionally visits. Throughout a considerable length of the film – while other events take place in the mansion and in the other setting – Julian is seen in his bedroom, to which he has retreated, and in which he lies immobile and silent, with his eyes open. The other narrative follows another young man (Pierre Clémenti) wandering in a volcanic landscape, in the surroundings of what appears to be a medieval village. In my view, some of the events taking place in these two parallel narratives and the way they come together as a whole can be understood through the reading of one of Bion's early articles entitled 'The Imaginary Twin' (1950). Here Bion further develops his concept of 'binocular vision' as a process of unisensual investigation aimed at reality testing, in connection with his consideration of the emergence of the Oedipal conflict. In *Pigsty*, Julian's binocular vision could be seen to coincide with the camera's vision: the camera alternates between an observation of Julian's present in his parents' mansion and, what is in my interpretation, Julian's phantasy of his imaginary twin personified by the nameless character roaming the volcanic landscape. But this alternating process, with its disrupted continuity and its ambiguity with regard to the time of events, is also, arguably, an articulation of Julian's emotional turbulence at a transitional stage in his life: an articulation of his caesura, of a stage of psychical growth in which can be found in some form his past, present and future. Thus, as I will show, the form of the film – 'form' in the restricted sense of the way the film is shaped or constructed through editing – is given by Julian's binocular vision, and his caesura.

The binocular dynamic of investigation in *Pigsty* foregrounds the distance, spatial and temporal, between the worlds of Julian and his twin. Julian's home is far from the volcanic land, both in space and time. But does this distance really exist if the volcanic land is thought to be a representation of Julian's internal world? What system of coordinates could be used for mental space and time? In one of the seminars held by Bion in Italy, one of the participants poses a question on the problem of distance and time in analysis, and Bion responds with the following:

> What is the distance between 'there' and 'here'? What is the distance between the state of mind which is repressed and the state of mind which has done the repressing? The same thing, put in a different way: what is the distance between the person, awake and conscious, who says, 'I had a dream last night', and the person who, in a different state of mind, experienced the dream?
>
> (2005, pp. 38–9)

There seems to be a distance between the person who dreams and the person who remembers a dream or gives the account of a dream, yet a distance that is difficult to measure. From a different vertex, there would be no distance between these persons, if they are seen to exist in the same body. An act of cannibalism could be seen to obliterate the distance between two bodies. *Pigsty* produces a tension between being very much distant from objects and being terribly close to them, so close that the characters end up by eating or being eaten by these objects. The distance between bodies, their state of being separate, is on occasions obliterated to such a degree as to entail the actual incorporation of the other.

Yet mostly the film insists on distance, as bodies hardly ever touch. The only visible examples of corporeal proximity are given in the pigsty scenes, among the pigs; in the copulation between the twin's companion and one of the prisoners; and among the servants who announce Julian's death.[3] Otherwise, distance is either kept or its traversal is significant. In the volcanic scenes, the twin has to traverse the distance between himself and his victims; and before eating them, he decapitates their bodies and carries their heads all the way to a smoking crater, into which he throws them. In the mansion setting, Julian traverses the distance between the mansion and the pigsty, but keeps that between himself and Ida. While the former movement breaks the rigorous symmetry that continually frames the imposing villa, the latter situation repeats and reinforces that symmetry, as epitomized in the scene in which the two walk along either side of the reflecting pool, in parallel lines that are far apart. Distance is emphasized through the predominant use of extreme long shots, and through the duration of these shots, which last the whole length of time it takes very small figures in a vast landscape to move between distant points.

Early in the film, Ida asks Julian: 'What blocked you here, stunned you forever?' Ida's question is one of her several attempts to understand his indifference to her love (only later does it become apparent that Julian has a secret passion for pigs), his 'neither obedience, nor disobedience' to his parents, and his scepticism of political interventions. Julian replies: 'Oh, in this vast, Italianate villa . . . surely a trifle . . . a lost leaf . . . a creaking door . . . a distant grunt.' Julian's reply may seem absurd or disconnected, but if *Pigsty* is seen in some way to continue the work of *Oedipus Rex* (a film that actually stages a child's encounter with the primal scene), it may also invite a psychoanalytic exegesis: a trifle (or an overwhelming encounter?), a lost leaf (that uncovers the genital organs), a creaking door (that opens, revealing the primal scene), a distant grunt (that signals the sexual act). This early passage in the script establishes the relationship to the parents and to the parental relationship as the theme of the film. As I will show, *Pigsty* traces a relationship between sexuality and Oedipus that is turbulent, but nevertheless epistemophilic: it is an epistemophilic impulse that drives Julian to his retreat; and, as has been outlined in Chapter 1, in Bion's subsequent work the epistemophilic impulse is of central importance in his conceptualization of the Oedipus myth. I will look at this development of the myth in more detail in the last section of my study of this film. However, in 'The Imaginary Twin', Bion focuses on two aspects of the emergence of the Oedipal situation that recur in three of his analyses: the appearance of ocular elements in the material, and the personification of splittings of the analysands' personality in a twin or twins whose real existence is uncertain. Towards the end of his article, Bion wonders whether the ability to personify splittings of the personality could be analogous to the capacity for symbol-formation that Melanie Klein (1930) expounds in 'The Importance of Symbol-Formation in the Development of the Ego'. The examination of this article will also be useful in my reading of film.

There is material in both narratives that can be considered to make references to Freud's exposition of the Wolf Man case – as has been identified previously by Maurizio Viano (1993, pp. 231–2) – and these correspondences will be traced in the course of my study. But I will begin with some comments on existing texts on Pasolini, and readings of *Pigsty*, which often consider this work in conjunction with the other films of the mythical cycle.

Transgression, ambivalence, martyrdom . . . and epistemophilia

In her book *Pier Paolo Pasolini: Cinema as Heresy*, Naomi Greene begins her survey of the mythical cycle by considering Pasolini's interest in archaic civilizations. These archaic worlds are contrasted with the corrupted and corrupting bourgeois ideologies that preside over modern societies (1990, p. 129). The past is seen to have a stronger connection to the sacred, but this past is also outside history: it is recreated, invented, mythicized; it symbolizes an ideal moment of humankind. Greene (p. 129) identifies a dichotomy between past and present already in *Hawks and Sparrows* (1966) – the film that precedes the mythical quartet – a dichotomy that becomes increasingly foregrounded in the films of the quartet up until *Medea* (1969), its last work. Nevertheless, it could be argued that in Pasolini's preoccupation with forms of the past that return in the present, there is an implicit preoccupation with how or whether these forms will survive in the future. In fact, Sam Rohdie finds a future of the past written in most of Pasolini's films, a future that wants to go beyond the films themselves:

> What he sought in Palestine, India, Calabria or the *borgate* of Rome are these analogies from a past for a future ideal use, just as his idea of reality was in and of a past, and film and text the future of this past, its writing, with which he could criticise the present.
>
> (1995, p. 59)

The present is criticized with something in view, something to follow it. The future is also inscribed in the past and the present of Pasolini's films in other ways, and *Oedipus Rex*, for example, shows this. In the prologue of *Oedipus Rex*, there is a sequence set in a meadow where the mother (Silvana Mangano) is holding her child, still an infant, in her arms. The camera, from below, pans rapidly over the foliage of the trees that surround them, so that the image becomes blurred. This could be a metaphor for Oedipus's vision, still unformed or formless, and later for a vision that Oedipus (Franco Citti) destroys with his own blinding. But what Oedipus cannot yet see, or later cannot bear to see, is visible already in the mother's worried expression, at a certain moment, while she breast-feeds him; and is visible in Oedipus's expression, in the mythical episode, as he tries to remember a bad dream, before deciding to visit the oracle in order to discover its meaning. Something in his memory of the dream makes him bite his hand suddenly, and this same gesture is repeated by the blind Oedipus in the film's epilogue, before he is led to the place of his childhood. It is the meadow of the prologue, and in it he speaks these words: 'Life ends where it begins.' He speaks of the end of his life before dying, but also as if the end of his life has already occurred. The prologue, the past of the mythical episode and the epilogue, could be seen to follow each other as they are presented; but in them there are forms, at once barriers and links, to what happened in a distant past and to what is still to happen. Thus the complex temporalities of the caesura can also be discerned in *Oedipus Rex*.

Greene's brief incursions into psychoanalytic theory are restricted to her study of *Oedipus Rex* and of *Medea*, though in a reference she does make a connection between the cannibalism in *Pigsty* and the oral stage. She quotes a passage from the *Three Essays on the Theory of Sexuality*, in which Freud writes on the oral, or cannibalistic (as he also proposes to call it), pregenital sexual organization. The aim of this stage is seen to be the *incorporation* of the object, which Freud considers to be the prototype of identification. Greene comments:

> A number of Freud's observations concerning the oral stage (which signals the beginning of libidinal or sexual development) are of interest not only for *Edipo Re* [Oedipus Rex] but for *Porcile* [Pigsty], where Pasolini's preoccupation with cannibalism, with eating and being eaten, reaches its apogee. One thinks particularly of the scene where the young cannibal looks amorously at his first victim before killing and eating him.
>
> (p. 157)

Cannibalism figures subsequently in Greene's argument, next to bestiality, incest and Medea's passion, as one of the 'scandalous' loves of the mythical cycle; and considering the homoeroticism in *Medea*, when Medea's brother exchanges glances with Jason, and the camera frames Jason as an object of desire, Greene suggests that all of these 'scandalous' loves have homosexual passion at their basis (p. 163), a passion that 'breaks the law':

> Homosexual passion is an archetypal moment in a worldview that conceives of Eros only in relationship to transgression and the law, to guilt and atonement. Pasolini's heroes *must transgress and must be punished for their transgression*: otherwise they will not go through the 'purification,' as Pasolini remarked of Oedipus, that permits them to reach the sacred, 'the domain of heroism or poetry.' As in the case of Oedipus, too, this process of 'purification' must etch itself, painfully and agonizingly, upon every fiber of their bodies.
>
> (p. 164)

Greene quotes from an interview conducted by Jean Duflot, in which Pasolini refers to Oedipus's self-punishing act of blinding himself as a certain form of purification through which he can access the domain of heroism or poetry (Duflot, 1970, pp. 107–8). Greene argues that the protagonists of the mythical cycle suffer punishment and death for their transgression, and that at the same time they become consecrated, they become martyrs. Homosexuality is, then, in Greene's interpretation of the cycle, (the basis of) a transgressive act that must be punished if the subject is to become 'purified' of having transgressed the law. But if in this view the 'contamination' arises from the transgression of the law, in subsequent additions to the interview with Duflot, given a few years after the first publication, Pasolini (1981, p. 198) puts forward the idea that 'contamination' arises from the reproduction of the law:

> Respect for the sanctity of the mother predisposes him [the homosexual] to a particular identification with her; I would say, in fact, that at the core of the homosexual there is, unconsciously, a reassertion of chastity: the desire for purity. In a rather obscure way the homosexual seeks himself in the other (the other-same), a partner with whom he does not risk reproducing the terrible power of the father, of the profaner.
>
> (Rohdie, p. 70)

The above English translation is provided by Rohdie, who considers Pasolini's myth about homosexuality to have 'the same degree of falsity as his parable about the maharaja and the tiger, and therefore the same force of emotional truth' (p. 69). The parable Rohdie refers to is an idea that Pasolini wanted to turn into a film, for which he made the preliminary *Notes for a Film on India* (1968), and which purported to tell the story of a maharaja who lets himself be devoured by hungry tiger cubs, out of compassion, while consequently his family starves to death; the film would have juxtaposed fiction with documentary images, contrasting an ancient with a modern India, in which the truth of a magical world was being destroyed (pp. 64, 66).

Before I turn to the theme of martyrdom, notably recurrent in Pasolini's work and its study, I will consider briefly the object of Julian's love, which seems to be connected with the ideas of purification and contamination referred to above. In Duflot's interview, Pasolini (1981, p. 115) explains that Julian's love for the pigs is symbolic, analogous to cannibalism; and further on, that 'metaphorically, the pigsty is society, Julian's family, his father, his mother and Herdhitze; on the other hand, the animals themselves are the nicest characters in the film' (p. 132).[4] It is interesting to find this ambivalence in Pasolini's statement, and then to find among the Wolf Man's clinical material, the associations 'God-shit' and 'God-swine' (Freud, 1918, p. 66). These associations resonate with Rohdie's observation that the banquets often depicted in Pasolini's films, such as the banquet of shit in *Salò, or the 120 Days of Sodom* (1975), or the devouring of Julian by the pigs in *Pigsty*, are at once parody and utopia:

> At these banquets everything was reversed. The sacred was not found in a celestial heaven, but in terrestrial shit. Pasolini reversed the conventional order of the sacred and in so doing offered a criticism of the existing order, and of order itself, especially that of the authorities, of power. He countered power with shit and in a language often composed of it.
>
> (Rohdie, p. 122)

Contaminating substances are then a source of celestial pleasures and that with which the existing order can be countered. Rohdie suggests that 'many of the things Pasolini thought valuable were ambiguous, contaminated, hybrid in their nature' (p. 58). This is perhaps one way of thinking about Julian's love for the pigs. The compound 'God-swine' is implicit in Julian's attempt to speak of his love as 'a grace that has struck me like the plague'; and, in the film's opening, the voice of his father Mr Klotz (Alberto Lionello) is heard reading a text carved on slabs of stone: 'Having closely questioned our conscience we have decided to devour you for your disobedience. [. . .] I, affectionate mother, have this son neither obedient nor disobedient.' Thus, the opening of the film not only foreshadows the ending in which Julian will be devoured by the pigs, it also creates a hybrid figure compounded of father, mother, God and pigs.

Julian's love devours him; and Julian's twin is sentenced to death for his cannibalism. Julian, it seems, voluntarily makes his way to the pigsty before being devoured, and the twin does not resist his arrest and his punishment. Pasolini writes, in an essay titled 'The Unpopular Cinema', that freedom is 'freedom to choose death', and that 'freedom cannot be manifested other than through a great or small martyrdom' (1970, p. 267). This essay is referred to by two authors who draw on Lacan in their analyses of Pasolini's films, in two articles that I will now consider in order to bring out some differences of interpretation and approach.

In 'Liberation Hurts: Violence, Masochism and Anti-Capitalism According to Pasolini', Fabio Vighi (2007, p. 63) defends that all of the mythical films aim to establish a dialectic between the Lacanian Real and the Symbolic with a view to launching an attack on the existing socio-symbolic structure. This transgressive act involves the staging of a self-inflicted act of violence. For Vighi, in 'The Unpopular Cinema', Pasolini makes the ideas of martyrdom and masochism coalesce. Through the staging of masochism, the subject is able to break his or her attachment to a libidinal subjection to the law, which is the first step towards being liberated from it; and the subject is also able to bring into visibility the law as the Sadian figure of the executioner, and thus to expose its inconsistency. An example of such staging is found in Julian's 'mode of enjoyment':

> [In Julian] we have masochism as a domain beyond the pleasure principle, where pleasure turns into 'pleasure in displeasure', reiteration of a gesture that paradoxically finds satisfaction in *missing its object*. [. . .] The repetition that qualifies the masochistic act circumscribes the domain of *jouissance* as the destabilizing force at work in death-drive.
>
> (Vighi, 2007, p. 68)

Vighi finds support for his argument in one of Julian's statements during a dialogue with Ida. Julian says, about himself: 'The whole is immobile . . . enjoying . . . the infinite repetition of the same thing.' This compulsion is interpreted to imply an endlessly sought encounter with the traumatic Real of desire, or the Real of *jouissance* (p. 68, n. 19).

But this interpretation is refuted by Viola Brisolin, in an article titled 'Martyrdom Postponed: The Subject Between Law and Transgression and Beyond. Reading Pasolini's *Porcile* with Lacan' (2010, pp. 121–2). Brisolin argues that Julian's passion is complicated by an identification with the powers it is trying to subvert, since the parents are identified with pigs; and so *jouissance* in this film fails to establish eros and subjectivity beyond symbolic exchange (p. 119). By focusing on a passage from 'The Unpopular Cinema', in which Pasolini affirms that 'the essential thing is to remain alive',[5] and by examining Lacan's reading of *Antigone*, Brisolin locates a suspended moment between life and death that guards the limit between the law and its alienating or annihilating transgression. This suspended moment is the ethical position of the author/artist who postpones martyrdom, yet one which Julian does not fulfil. Brisolin writes that 'Julian is completely absorbed in a compulsive repetition from which he stubbornly refuses reflexive detachment' (pp. 121–2), appending to this statement a reference with an excerpt from the script in which Ida asks Julian whether he wants to know himself, a question he replies to negatively.

However, in my view, Julian's evasive or cryptic communication with Ida is not sufficient to undo the evidence that the twin's acts and experiences are Julian's visions of, and efforts at, self-reflection. Moreover, Julian's epistemophilia can also be found in the script when, in the last meeting with Ida, after relating to her a dream he had, Julian wonders: 'Who knows the truth of dreams, beyond that of making us eager for the truth.'[6]

Vighi combines the notion of death drive and repetition compulsion to define Julian's desire as masochistic; Brisolin defines it as blind, or mindless, repetition. Repetition compulsion can also be found in Maurizio Viano's psychoanalytic reading of *Pigsty*, already referred to, which considers the twin to be Julian's unconscious: 'PC [the character played by Pierre Clémenti] is Julian's unconscious – an unconscious that is depicted rather conventionally as the seething space where the compulsion to repeat reigns supreme' (p. 224).

Two excerpts from Paulo Sandler's consideration of Bion's model of 'binocular vision' can begin to suggest ways in which my reading of this film differs from the above psychoanalytic approaches. Sandler writes:

> [The model of binocular vision] sheds light on some general epistemological issues, to the extent that it can constitute a step forward from what is called 'dialectics' in philosophy. Rather than dealing with a pair of competing opposites, under the aegis of Death instincts, it elucidates by operating with a creative couple.
>
> (Sandler, 2005, p. 82)

An example of the creative couple is the analyst and analysand, and I would add here, Julian and his twin. The idea of an eroticized death drive is indeed present in some of Pasolini's texts, but I disagree with Vighi when he writes, elsewhere, that 'the rebellious core of *Porcile*, as with most of Pasolini's films, is firmly situated in the self-destructive nature of its split protagonist, in the overwhelming and scandalous emphasis accorded to his death-drive' (2006, p. 54). I disagree with the emphasis that the studies mentioned above attribute to repetition compulsion and the death instinct in their conceptions of Julian's impulses. Instead, I believe that Julian's epistemophilic impulse, realized in the creative couple he forms with his twin, is the main drive of the film, because the film's movement is a movement towards an understanding, an awareness in the process of growth, not towards death. Death in this film, in my view, is something that happens *after* the achievement of this awareness.

Sandler also remarks the following: 'When functioning intra-psychically, binocular vision means learning from experience and self-observation. It cannot be done without the help of others; in the first instance, from mother' (p. 83).

The mother helps to initiate the capacity to observe the intra-psychic tensions of the self, to observe the internal world, and thus the internal world is configured in ways that are very close to a conception of the mother's body. The mother is absent from the Lacanian studies discussed, as it is the relation to the father that is seen to subtend the film's symbolic structure. It is also absent from Viano's study, in which 'slaying the father, cannibalism, and pleasure sum up "the other scene" as the exclusive locus of Freudian discourse' (p. 234), a discourse employed in such a way that it only acknowledges the relation to the father (pp. 231–2).

Colleen Ryan-Scheutz structures the main body of her work on Pasolini's use of female characters in his films according to specific types, and her study of *Pigsty* falls into the 'Daughters' chapter, focusing on the role of Ida as a representation of the student generation of the time, as a 'daughter of the bourgeoisie' (2007, pp. 115–16).[7] Her brief consideration of the character of Mrs Klotz (Margarita Lozano) describes her as 'far removed from any life-giving qualities' (p. 119), a character that, like Mr Klotz, has been completely absorbed by capitalism: 'Mrs Klotz is [. . .] an unthinking, unfeeling, inanimate object, a stiff and shapeless human subject'(pp. 120–1).

It is unquestionable that Julian's mother in the mansion setting has no proper, autonomous existence. She follows Julian's statement on how he would own half of Germany if he were to marry Ida with a comment that fully expresses her position in relation to what stands for the father: 'A marvelous complicity!' Her complicity is further emphasized in the merger celebration – which happens, presumably, after Julian's secret has been revealed to her – where she appears to be wearing men's clothes. The mother's absence or insignificance in studies of *Pigsty* is therefore not without justification, but only if the twin's narrative is disregarded. Turning for a moment to the work of Melanie Klein, I propose that the twin is in Julian's internal world, which is very much a maternal space.

Symbol-formation

The phase of mental development with which Klein is concerned in 'The Importance of Symbol-Formation in the Development of the Ego' pertains to the early stages of the Oedipus conflict, more precisely a phase that is initiated with oral sadism and is brought to an end with the culmination of anal sadism (p. 219). Klein's core thesis in this article is that the predominance of sadism in relation to the mother's body and its contents, characteristic of this phase, gives rise to anxiety; and anxiety, she argues, is necessary for the processes of identification and symbol-formation to be set in motion (pp. 219–20). The weight and quality that Klein attributes to sadism and anxiety, respectively, at this point in time, have to be considered in the context of the clinical work done with a four-year-old boy named Dick, which she describes in the article; moreover, her argument has to be understood in the wider context of the development of her work. Donald Meltzer (1978, II, pp. 16–17) points out that when Klein wrote the article under discussion (in 1930), she had not yet formulated the depressive position, so she had not yet made a distinction between persecutory anxiety and depressive anxiety as different motivations for the curiosity about the mother's body; this curiosity was extended to other objects through symbol-formation, and the latter was conceived of as a search for meaning. In this article, however, Klein brings libidinal, sadistic and epistemophilic impulses directed at the mother's body to bear on the process of symbol-formation, but it is sadism and the resulting anxiety (with no distinction between different kinds of anxiety) that she underlines if the development of a symbolic relation to the internal and external worlds is not to be suspended.

Klein observes in Dick's behaviour an almost absolute indifference to his environment, a 'complete absence of affect and anxiety, a very considerable degree of withdrawal from reality, and of inaccessibility, a lack of emotional *rapport*, negativistic behaviour alternating with signs of automatic obedience, indifference to pain' (Klein, p. 230) and difficulties in coordinating certain movements. For example, he was not able to grip knives or scissors, but could easily handle a spoon to feed himself (p. 222). Klein argues that, in Dick's case, an incapacity to tolerate anxiety and a premature empathy led to an *excessive* defence against the sadistic appropriation of the mother's body, and consequently to a suspension of the establishment of a symbolic relation to its contents, and thus to the objects of external reality (p. 227).

Even if succinctly, it will be useful to follow her line of argument, which, again, is founded on the premise that the early stages of the Oedipus conflict are concurrent with the eruption of oral sadism. She writes:

> The child expects to find within the mother (*a*) the father's penis, (*b*) excrement, and (*c*) children, and these things it equates with edible substances. According to the child's earliest phantasies (or 'sexual theories') of parental coitus, the father's penis (or his whole body) becomes incorporated in the mother during the act. Thus the child's sadistic attacks have for their object both father and mother, who are in phantasy bitten, torn, cut or stamped to bits.
>
> (Klein, p. 219)

These sadistic attacks that aim to appropriate and destroy the mother's body and the objects it contains, generate what Klein regards as an overwhelming anxiety, a fear of punishment by the parental couple, a fear of retaliation from the attacked objects. Anxiety will in its turn mobilize defence mechanisms, which are violent, and opposed to subsequent mechanisms of repression: 'In relation to the subject's own sadism the defence implies expulsion, whereas in relation to the object it implies destruction' (p. 220). This point is important and I will come back to it.

Klein formulates her theory of identification – which she sees as the precursor of symbol-formation – in the following passage:

> Side by side with the libidinal interest, it is the anxiety arising in the phase that I have described which sets going the mechanism of identification. Since the child desires to destroy the organs (penis, vagina, breasts) which stand

> for the objects, he conceives a dread of the latter. This anxiety contributes to make him equate the organs in question with other things; owing to this equation these in their turn become objects of anxiety, and so he is impelled constantly to make other and new equations, which form the basis of his interest in the new objects and of symbolism.
>
> (Ibid.)

Thus, symbol-formation is dependent on libidinal and destructive impulses, anxiety, *and* desire for knowledge: Klein adds shortly after the above statement that a desire to know the mother's body and its contents is concurrent with the sadism of this phase (p. 221). Symbol-formation is 'the foundation of all phantasy and sublimation but, more than that, it is the basis of the subject's relation to the outside world and to reality in general' (ibid.).

With the above in mind, I can proceed to consider the imaginary twin's acts and experiences in Pasolini's work. The first object that the twin kills and eats is a butterfly that almost poisons him, as he is seen curled up in pain in the following scene. The second object, subjected to violent and successive attacks with big stones, and subsequently devoured, is a serpent. He then sees people walking in the distance and anxiously hides from them. Later he comes upon what must have been a battle scene, as he finds human bone remains, armour and swords. The twin looks apprehensively, then sadly at the objects, but soon avails himself of weapons. Up to this point the landscape was arid, but next the twin is seen running towards a vast expanse colonized by plants, from which he eats. This is perhaps the most untroubled moment in the whole of the twin's narrative. The volcanic landscape, sinuous, alive, at times barren, at others fertile, populated with nurturing objects and dangerous objects, suggests a representation of the internal world, 'when the mother is still the "world"' (Meltzer, II, p. 16). Thus, the butterfly could be seen as an object that is attacked and then retaliates; the serpent could be seen as the father's penis; the people seen at a distance, perhaps as children; the human remains, as children attacked; the plants, as the mother's good breast.

In his study of the film, Viano recalls that the Wolf Man was once running after a big and beautiful butterfly, though he does not consider the specific meaning that the butterfly acquires in Freud's exposition of the material:

> The patient remarked that the opening and shutting of the butterfly's wings while it was settled on the flower had given him an uncanny feeling. It had looked, so he said, like a woman opening her legs, and the legs then made the shape of a Roman V, which, as we know, was the hour at which, in his boyhood, and even up to the time of the treatment, he used to fall into a depressed state of mind.
>
> (Freud, p. 90)

The association of the butterfly with the female sex could inform a possible interpretation of the first two objects that the twin attacks – the butterfly and the serpent – as the female and male sexes, or indeed as mother and father still at the level of part-objects.

The sequence that follows is long, which arguably attests its importance. The twin encounters a man, and for a few moments they stare at each other. Suddenly the man turns around and runs away, but the twin chases him, over a long distance. They shoot their guns, and they fight with swords; but eventually the man kneels, defeated, and is killed and decapitated. Carrying the man's head, the twin climbs to the top of the volcanoes where craters expel smoke with a threatening force, and throws the head into one of the craters. A while later, the twin is seen eating by a small fire; and the two static images that follow, one of the dead man's foot, and another of his hand, suggest that the twin is eating the dead man's flesh.

Another nameless character (played by Franco Citti) joins the twin in his meal, and becomes his companion in future wanderings. Others will take part in their nomadic life, such as a group of women prisoners whom they release by killing their escorts. These murders immediately precede the copulation between the twin's companion and one of the women, a scene that the twin watches at a distance with apparent impassivity.

In a subsequent sequence, the group attacks a woman who passes near their camp. The man she was travelling with is too late and powerless to save her, and only witnesses her decapitation from a distance, while remaining unnoticed by the group.[8] Again, before the cannibalistic ritual, the twin takes the victim's head to the top of the volcanoes, and throws it into a crater.

There is an image in the clinical material with which Klein supports her findings in her article that I connect with the twin's expulsions into the crater. I believe the twin's expulsions bring together the three crucial events described above: the attack on the man, the sight of the copulation, and the attack on the woman. The image taken from Dick's play therapy relates to the point already made about the defence mechanisms that are mobilized against the object, and against the destructive impulses towards the object. In the initial stages of the therapy, Dick's defences were excessive, but gradually he began to manifest not only his aggression, but his defence against it. Dick took a toy cart (a representation of his mother) that he had damaged in a previous session and some pieces of coal that it had contained, and put them in the space between the two doors of the consulting room. Klein interprets:

> It became clear that in thus throwing them out of the room he was indicating an expulsion, both of the damaged object and of his own sadism (or the means employed by it), which was in this manner projected into the external world.
>
> (p. 226)

When the twin decapitates the bodies of the man and the woman, and throws their heads into the crater, the crater is comparable to an anus through which the damaged objects and the sadism can be expelled into the external world. The twin performs the decapitations in a state of turmoil, but once he expels the heads and his own sadism into the crater, he eats the bodies in relative peace.

Among other killings carried out by the twin, these two are the only ones that involve the expulsion into the crater, and this leads me to suggest that they represent the killing of the father, and later of the mother, now as whole objects. It is interesting to note that the killing of the mother happens after the twin's witnessing of the primal scene, which can be considered as the first sign of the mother's complicity with the father in this narrative.

Both narratives have now reached a turning point. In the mansion episode this point is marked by the visit of Mr Herdhitze, whom Julian's father believes is an ex-colleague he will be able to manipulate as he knows of Mr Herdhitze's criminal deeds as a former Nazi. The result of their long conversation turns unexpectedly for Mr Klotz, as Mr Herdhitze knows of Julian's secret passion and uses this knowledge to his own advantage, forcing Mr Klotz into a business partnership. In the volcanic episode, the turning point is reached by the denunciation of the twin's crimes to the authorities in the nearby village, and the plan they devise to capture him and his group, which involves the use of a naked man and woman as bait. The encounter between the twin and this naked couple differs substantially from his previous ones. Up to this moment the twin's explorations have been read as pertaining to the early stages of the Oedipus conflict, in which the relation to objects happens primarily on an oral and anal level. I will now consider Bion's article in order to introduce the ocular level to the emergence of the Oedipal situation – as well as provide insight into the concept of the 'imaginary twin' – which will enable me to examine the development of the narrative from this point onwards, and to comment further on the form of the film with regard to Julian's retreat.

The imaginary twin: caesura and binocular vision

'The Imaginary Twin' is largely composed of an exposition of clinical material, derived from the analytical work conducted separately with three adults, that Bion brings together on account of its recurrent themes and common attendant issues. In all three cases the analysands refer to a twin, or twins, who at times become personified in the analyst or in some other acquaintance, and who are in some way connected to the emergence of the Oedipal situation and of genital sexuality; furthermore, this process seems to have a concomitant concern with vision.

The article focuses on the case of the analysand whom Bion calls 'A', in which the change from a superficial to an emotionally charged Oedipus situation is, according to Bion, very marked. At a point in the analysis, because of a peculiarity in A's speech, Bion begins to form an intuition: some of the conversations A claimed to have had with certain people could no longer be said with certitude to have really happened (p. 6). This ambiguity between real and imaginary then began to be extended to the actual characters to whom A referred: a man of the same age and profession as his own, but who was able to travel freely, unlike himself; a homosexual brother-in-law who was attracted to A's wife; a man with whom he played tennis; some of A's students who were 'psychological cases'; and a colleague whom he did not like but who had on occasions acted for him as a locum (pp. 6–7).

These potential personifications of splittings of the analysand's personality can perhaps evoke different images and functions; they could also evoke or be evoked by some images in Pasolini's film. For example, even though Julian's imaginary twin seems to be under the permanent threat of being caught for his crimes, it is through him that Julian is able to 'travel' in his internal world, while lying immobile in bed; and a tennis player could be seen as someone with whom to maintain a dialogue without using words, just as Julian seems to maintain a silent dialogue with his twin.

On one occasion during A's analysis, Bion voices his belief that he himself is a twin of A who supports him in evading interpretations, thus lessening A's resentment. A reacts dramatically to this interpretation, as if he has just introjected a poisonous object. In the following session he recounts a terrifying dream which involved a man of similar build as himself blocking the exit from his car (p. 8). Bion concludes that the function of the imaginary twin at this stage in the analysis is that of denying external reality; and, with this denial, Bion also observes that there is an intolerance or a fear of the internal world and its mechanisms (p. 19). However, some time after, a change begins to occur:

> Only when I had been able to demonstrate how bad I was on all levels of his mind did it become possible for him first to recognize his mechanisms of splitting and personification and then to employ them, as it were in reverse, to establish the contact which they had originally been used to break.
>
> (Bion, pp. 19–20)

The initial manifestation of this reversal of the process is an association that involves an eye infection of one of A's female students, and consultations with two eye specialists. One specialist believes it is not worth trying to treat the infection, but the other believes it is; A complains of having to mediate between the two, and having to send the girl to be tested for syphilis. It is important to note that in this process there is a tension produced by opposing impulses, the suppression and expression of curiosity (−K, K), in which a threatening genital situation emerges, with its theme of contamination. Among several other possible meanings, the two eye specialists are interpreted to be twins who need to be brought together into cooperation, then they are seen as a parental couple, and finally as part-objects:

> I could consider the two eye men as parts of his body, possibly his two eyes that were to be harmonized into binocular vision. The injured girl was some object, recovered from his inside, which was to be subjected to the scrutiny of both his eyes and a developing intellect, a scrutiny thus exercised on an externalized object.
>
> (Bion, p. 14)

Here, an existing internal damaged object – which had already been explored orally, according to Bion (p. 15) – is externalized and investigated by means of an ocular method. Again, the method is binocular because the investigating instrument is binary, able to correlate different views of the object or situation under scrutiny.

The Oedipus conflict that is thus revealed is intolerable to A and results in oscillations between oral and ocular stages. Bion believes these oscillations are a means of testing reality and testing the instruments with which to test reality; and this permits a strengthening of the ego, and consequently the ability to tolerate the Oedipus situation that has become emotionally powerful (pp. 15–16). This oscillatory pattern is also observed in material from the other two analyses. For example, analysand B personifies his real twin in the man whose therapy session is before his, and feels that the speech he leaves behind is poisonous. Eventually, however, Bion notes that he himself has taken the role of the twin, as the twin becomes someone who makes things difficult, but who has psychoanalytic insight. B provides associations that involve the use of a binocular microscope, which he admits is difficult to use initially; later Bion realizes that his lack of confidence in using the binocular instrument was due to 'his fear that it might make a very small twin look like a very big father' (p. 19). Perhaps this threatening image of the father could also be an externalization of an internal injured object.

Are there any such externalizations to be found in *Pigsty*? The beautiful naked man and woman that Julian's imaginary twin first sees from a very long distance might not be, at first sight, a prototypical externalized injured object; in fact, they could appear to be quite the opposite, perhaps a vision of innocent Adam and Eve before biting into the apple: an idealized parental couple, standing and lying down at a certain distance from each other. The emotional reaction of the twin to this sight deserves attention, no less because he is transfixed by it for a long time.

From a lateral view of the twin's companions, who seem to be waiting for him to act, the camera pans over the volcanic rock, and stops behind the twin. This image is almost a point-of-view shot, so the camera sees the twin lying down, looking from the edge of the rocks, at a very hazy landscape.[9] A subsequent close-up of his face reveals him looking with suspicion, perhaps fear, but also curiosity. Then the landscape appears again, this time in full point of view, and its previous opacity and flatness are replaced by a clearer image that zooms in on the naked figures. This zoom is extremely long, almost telescopic; but even so it culminates in an image in which the figures are virtually microscopic. With an expressive use of shallow focus that conveys the twin's blurred vision in the initial moments of his observation, and later with the use of an immense zoom that nevertheless only achieves an extreme long shot view of the couple, this sequence is, to my mind, an ocular investigation of an object when the instruments of investigation are still being tested.

For Bion, Julian's Oedipus situation would have now become emotionally charged; referring back to Klein's article, the twin's emotional state and hesitancy could perhaps be interpreted as a defence against libidinal impulses, in contrast with the earlier defences against sadism and the destroyed object. Klein writes that 'it is only in the later stages of the Oedipus conflict that the defence against the libidinal impulses makes its appearance' (p. 232), while the earlier defences are directed against destructiveness.

The end of the conversation between Mr Klotz and Mr Herdhitze is marked by a cut to the volcanic setting, and the thunderous sound of an explosive eruption.[10] It is then that the twin gives up his defences and walks towards the figures. When he has almost reached them, the figures escape and a complicit legion of soldiers captures him and his companions. Before his hands are tied, the twin removes his clothes. With this gesture, he seems to be identifying with the idealized figures. His first and last words, spoken just before being left to be eaten alive by wild dogs, are repeated four times: 'I killed my father, I ate human flesh, and I quiver with joy.' These are the only comprehensible words in the whole of the twin's narrative, spoken in its last moments, pointing to another crucial step in the process of symbol-formation. Approaching the end of the mansion episode, during the business merger celebration, Julian is seen walking outside towards the pigsty. Soon after, a group of servants announces to Mr Herdhitze that Julian is dead; they report that Julian was devoured by the pigs. The film ends with Mr Herdhitze urging the servants: 'Shhh . . . not a word to a soul.'

Bion concludes his article by stating that Klein's belief in the earliness of the Oedipal situation could be confirmed if psychological stages of development are thought to be linked with physiological development: oral sadism with the eruption of teeth, and the Oedipal phase with the development of vision (pp. 21–2). It is interesting to think about this last point if Bion's later developments of the Oedipus myth are taken into account: the development of vision as an addition to the instruments for investigation is consistent with the centrality of the element of curiosity or epistemophilia that Bion assigns to the myth.

Bion's second thoughts on his article, which were written and published 17 years after he read it to the British Psychoanalytical Society, recognize a growth pattern on the emergence of the Oedipal situation that corresponds to a configuration that he was formulating at the time: the catastrophic change, the image of a rigid container struggling to contain the contained, of an explosive contained threatening to destroy the container (1967, p. 135). But, in another passage in his commentary, Bion considers the usefulness of the notes he used to take after the sessions with the analysands in question (a practice he later abandoned) in the following way:

> The value of the notes lay not in their supposed formulation of a record of the past but in their formulation of a sensory image evocative of the future. The notes did not make it possible to remain conscious of the past but to evoke expectations of the future.
>
> (p. 124)

Bion's notion of caesura seems to be germinating here, although the past is as important as the future in the understanding of the concept as it will be formulated. In the notes that described the analysands' past and present – a present in which the turbulent emergence of the Oedipus situation was taking place – Bion finds, years later, images that evoked the future. In the processes of binocular vision made possible by the analysands' imaginary twins, a contact was established between different time and space dimensions.

The temporal and spatial (dis)continuity of *Pigsty* is the binocular vision at work, the contact with different times and spaces; it is an articulation of the caesura. Early in the film, Julian declares: 'The last lurid experiment . . . is done'; but this scene is actually followed by the first of the crucial events that take place in the volcanic scene (the killing of the father). Also, it is only after this statement that he retreats to his bedroom. This evidence of an ambiguity in relation to the time in which events are taking place is further encountered, in both narratives, in the following flash-forward scenes: Julian, back from his retreat, eating avidly, speaks to Ida of the business partnership, but this happens before the conversation between his father and Herdhitze reaches the 'impossible to say', and the 'impossible to hear'; and the twin is seen ascending the mountain towards the village, in shackles, before the moment in which he and his companions are captured.

Robert S. C. Gordon comments on the disruption of temporal continuity that many of Pasolini's films produce, observing that it 'moves the function of narrative itself away from sequential cause and effect towards metaphor and metanarrative' (1996, p. 245). And one of the functions of metaphor in Pasolini's cinema, for Gordon, is that it 'figures the transience and alterity of the subject in crisis' (p. 234). Gordon's observations are pertinent here: the disruptions in *Pigsty* disturb a sense of causality and they convey a sense of Julian's emotional turmoil, a sense of crisis in the ability to know or articulate with clarity what is past, present or future. The volcanic episode could be interpreted as a form of events that have happened in the distant past of Julian's childhood, on which his retreat, and the events that will occur between Julian and his parents after it, already cast their shadow. These scenes are intertwined with Julian's external world in the present, in an alternating, binocular vision.

'Idleness, unemployment, exile': this is how Mr Klotz describes his son's retreat, as he can make no profit from it, and indeed only loss in the end. But the product of Julian's retreat is of another kind; it is the product of the creative pair he forms with his twin. Julian's retreat enables him to gain a binocular vision of his internal and external worlds so that he can then finally attempt to bring them together. The intertwining of both narratives is a process of investigation of the self, and the self's relationship to others, in a moment of transience, of caesura. Pasolini shows that such process of investigation has no value within the values of the capitalist bourgeoisie that he criticizes, as it ends in a tragedy that is silenced; but he also shows the invaluableness of that process each time his film speaks.

Form as attention and inquiry

In my conclusion to this study of *Pigsty* I consider Bion's later developments on the myth of Oedipus, as they are not only interesting in their affinity with the model of binocular vision, but they are also relevant to my interpretation of the film.

I begin by pointing out that my focus on the form of the film as being given by Julian's binocular vision and caesura contrasts with Pasolini's own theories on the meaning of editing. In the introduction to the publication of the script of his film *Oedipus Rex*, Pasolini writes:

> Oedipus is dead. Death has sanctified a perfect and by now unalterable version of what he once was. Death is the necessary condition *to make a story from his life*. As much as to 'compile' a film of his life.
>
> (1971, p. 7)

This idea that the subject has to die for meaning to emerge recurs in other texts by Pasolini, coupled with the idea that films have to be edited for the same reasons. In 'Observations on the Sequence Shot', Pasolini states that 'Editing [. . .] performs on the material of the film [. . .] the operations that death performs on life' (1967, p. 237). These words are among those cited by Vighi (2006, p. 15) in order to posit, in Pasolini's cinema, editing as death-drive. On the particular case of *Pigsty*, he writes that 'what editing ultimately sutures is not just a series of symbolic correspondences, but crucially, the non-symbolisable object of drive' (p. 54).

On the same issue, Gordon relates life to filming, and death to editing: 'Editing, signifying, and thus concrete expression, is a form of dying that gives out a dim echo of being' (p. 218). But Rohdie opens the function or the meaning of editing to other possibilities, affirming a certain joyfulness in the cut:

> The loss that the cut had engendered was not simply to be mourned; it was also to be celebrated, as the cannibal celebrates in *Porcile*: 'I have killed my father. I have tasted human flesh. I tremble with joy.' [. . .] More crucially, it was a way to return to the Mother (historically) and to his mother (personally) by gathering up the crucial instrument of procreation of the father in an act first of delicious castration and then of an even more exquisite cannibalism.
>
> (p. 69)

Rohdie suggests that Pasolini's 'disarticulated' language, his refusal to rearticulate the cuts he makes on the material of film, is a refusal to obey the linguistic and social code; it is an act against the Symbolic and the father.

Bion's conceptualization of Oedipus inspires a different understanding of the editing in *Pigsty*. Bion draws attention to certain elements of the Oedipus myth and gives these elements certain functions. The pronouncement of the oracle is considered to resemble a pre-conception, as it is yet to be 'saturated' with the realization of the story; Tiresias represents the barrier against anticipated anxiety or against the pursuit of truth; the Sphinx is seen to stimulate curiosity, but at the same time to threaten with death if this curiosity is not satisfied, thus it both stimulates and threatens against curiosity; and Oedipus is regarded as the triumph of the thirst for knowledge over intimidation, therefore he represents the investigatory tool (Bion, 1963, pp. 48–9). These components lead Bion to consider the myth in terms of constitutive *functions* of the mind, rather than *content* of the mind. He writes: 'Features that can serve as symbols for the mechanics of thinking contribute to my suspicion that it is inadequate to regard the Oedipus situation as a part of the *content* of the mind' (ibid.). The myth of Oedipus is then recognized as a part of the apparatus of the subject's armoury of learning (p. 66); and the theory of Oedipus is now extended to functions of the mind such as attention and inquiry (Sandler, pp. 536–7).

These developments of the theory of Oedipus are consistent with the model of binocular vision, as they both entail, or admit, a dynamic between K and −K, the expression and suppression of curiosity. But Julian's binocular vision is undoubtedly an expression of curiosity, an expression that his retreat signifies and enables. It is in the space and time of his retreat that Julian is able to let the space and time of his internal world emerge. Within the 'disarticulated' articulation of the caesura, editing in *Pigsty* is an expression of the epistemophilic instinct.

What Bion's theory of Oedipus does to a theory of *Pigsty* is to foreground the function of the form of the film, rather than its content; it foregrounds the form of the film as resolute attention and inquiry; it gives the cuts in the film an investigatory function, as they bring together that which has been pulled apart, not as an attempt to find causal relations, but to make meaning emerge. The content of *Pigsty* – the 'scandalous' love, the killings, the deaths – ultimately remains difficult to pinpoint. And this is precisely what Julian alludes to with his wondering: 'Who knows the truth of dreams, beyond that of making us eager for the truth.'

Notes

1 The DVD edition I will refer to was released in 2003 by Water Bearer Films, and has been supervised by the association 'Fondo Pier Paolo Pasolini'. The English translation of the dialogues is by William Weaver. There are more recent DVD releases by Tartan Video and Eureka Entertainment in which the flash-forward scenes mentioned later in the chapter are edited in linear time.
2 The cycle comprises *Oedipus Rex* (1967), *Theorem* (1968), *Pigsty* and *Medea* (1969).
3 At this point Pasolini's portrayal of the poor is warm and romanticized, set in stark opposition to that of the bourgeoisie. In this regard, also consider the preceding film of the mythical quartet, *Theorem*, in its contrasting treatment of the reactions to the visitor by the members of the family and the servant Emilia.
4 (My translation). Herdhitze (Ugo Tognazzi) is the German industrialist who, using his knowledge of Julian's secret, forces Julian's father into merging their businesses.
5 The translation of the whole excerpt quoted by Brisolin reads:

> but the essential thing is to remain alive and to keep the code vigorous; suicide creates a void which is immediately filled by the worst quality of life; while *excessive transgression against the code finishes by creating a sort of nostalgia for it.* Revivals are always based on a real fact, which is precisely the general nostalgia for a code which has been too poorly and "extremistically" violated.
>
> (Pasolini, 1970, p. 273)

6 Julian's dream has similarities with a dream of the Wolf Man, the dream in which he cuts through one of his little fingers while playing with a knife, and sees that it is only hanging on by skin, feeling great terror but no pain; this dream is interpreted by Freud as being related to the Wolf Man's fear of castration by his father (see Freud, pp. 85–6).
7 Ryan-Scheutz quotes from Pasolini's 1968 poem titled 'The PCI to the Young!!' (see *Heretical Empiricism*, pp. 150–4) in which Pasolini, addressing the Italian students who had demonstrated in Rome against the education system, takes the side of the police because they were children of the poor (Ryan-Scheutz, pp. 121–3).
8 Greene has mistakenly identified this character as being played by Ninetto Davoli (p. 137). This character denounces the cannibals to the village authorities, while the character played by Davoli in the volcanic setting is a mere observer (though an important one) of the events. Davoli is the only actor in the film who appears in both the volcanic and the mansion settings; in the latter he is a servant named Maracchione, who will relate the circumstances of Julian's death in the final scene.
9 This 'almost point-of-view shot' can be related to Pasolini's concept of the 'free indirect point-of-view shot' as defined in 'The "Cinema of Poetry"' (1965).
10 Meltzer's notion of the 'explosiveness of the truth' might be recalled here.

References

Bion, W.R. (1950). The imaginary twin. In: *Second Thoughts: Selected Papers on Psychoanalysis*. London: Karnac, 2007.

Bion, W.R. (1963). *Elements of Psycho-Analysis*. London: Karnac, 1989.

Bion, W.R. (1967). Commentary. In: *Second Thoughts: Selected Papers on Psychoanalysis*. London: Karnac, 2007.

Bion, W.R. (2005). *The Italian Seminars*. Translated by P. Slotkin. London: Karnac.

Brisolin, V. (2010). Martyrdom postponed: The subject between law and transgression and beyond. Reading Pasolini's *Porcile* with Lacan. *Italian Studies*, 65 (1), pp. 107–22.

Duflot, J. (1970). *Entretiens avec Pier Paolo Pasolini*. Paris: Pierre Belfond.

Freud, S. (1918). From the history of an infantile neurosis. *SE* 17: 7–122.

Gordon, R.S.C. (1996). *Pasolini: Forms of Subjectivity*. Oxford: Clarendon Press.

Greene, N. (1990). *Pier Paolo Pasolini: Cinema as Heresy*. New Jersey: Princeton University Press.

Klein, M. (1930). The importance of symbol-formation in the development of the ego. In: Klein, M. (ed.) *Contributions to Psycho-Analysis: 1921–1945*. London: Hogarth Press and the Institute of Psycho-Analysis, 1950.

Meltzer, D. (1978). *The Kleinian Development*. Strath Tay: Clunie Press, 1985.

Pasolini, P.P. (1965). The 'cinema of poetry'. In: *Heretical Empiricism*. Translated by B. Lawton and L.K. Barnett. Bloomington: Indiana University Press, 1988.

Pasolini, P.P. (1967). Observations on the sequence shot. In: *Heretical Empiricism*. Translated by B. Lawton and L.K. Barnett. Bloomington: Indiana University Press, 1988.

Pasolini, P.P. (1970). The unpopular cinema. In: *Heretical Empiricism*. Translated by B. Lawton and L.K. Barnett. Bloomington: Indiana University Press, 1988.

Pasolini, P.P. (1971). Why that of Oedipus is a story. In: *Oedipus Rex: A Film by Pier Paolo Pasolini*. Translated by J. Matthews. London: Lorrimer.

Pasolini, P.P. (1981). *Les dernières paroles d'un impie: Entretiens avec Jean Duflot*. Paris: Pierre Belfond.

Rohdie, S. (1995). *The Passion of Pier Paolo Pasolini*. London: British Film Institute.

Ryan-Scheutz, C. (2007). *Sex, the Self and the Sacred: Women in the Cinema of Pier Paolo Pasolini*. Toronto: University of Toronto Press.

Sandler, P.C. (2005). *The Language of Bion: A Dictionary of Concepts*. London: Karnac.

Viano, M. (1993). *A Certain Realism: Making Use of Pasolini's Film Theory and Practice*. Berkeley: University of California Press.

Vighi, F. (2006). *Traumatic Encounters in Italian Film: Locating the Cinematic Unconscious*. Bristol: Intellect.

Vighi, F. (2007). Liberation hurts: Violence, masochism and anti-capitalism according to Pasolini. *Italian Studies*, 62 (1), pp. 61–77.

Filmography

Hawks and Sparrows (1966). Directed by Pier Paolo Pasolini. [DVD] Italy: Arco Film.

Medea (1969). Directed by Pier Paolo Pasolini. [DVD] Italy/France/Germany: San Marco/Les Films Number One/Janus Film und Fernsehen.

Notes for a Film on India (1968). Directed by Pier Paolo Pasolini. [DVD]

Oedipus Rex (1967). Directed by Pier Paolo Pasolini. [DVD] Italy/Morocco: Arco Film.

Pigsty (1969). Directed by Pier Paolo Pasolini. [DVD] Italy/France: IDI Cinematografica/ Orso Films/INDIEF/CAPAC.

Salò, or the 120 Days of Sodom (1975). Directed by Pier Paolo Pasolini. [DVD] Italy/France: Produzioni Europee Associati/Productions Artistes Associés.

Theorem (1968). Directed by Pier Paolo Pasolini. [DVD] Italy: Aetos Film.

5

THE CAESURA AND THE IMAGES OF THE POINT, THE LINE, AND THE CIRCLE IN *A MAN ASLEEP*

> A sleeping man holds in a circle around him the sequence of the hours, the order of the years and worlds. He consults them instinctively as he wakes and reads in them in a second the point on the earth he occupies, the time that has elapsed up to his waking; but their ranks can be mixed up, broken.[1]
>
> Marcel Proust, *The Way by Swann's*

Introduction

A Man Asleep (1974),[2] the title of the film made by Georges Perec and Bernard Queysanne, which is also the title of Perec's book on which the film is based (1967), is borrowed from the beginning of the above citation.[3] In this citation, Proust traces the images of a circle, of lines and of points, that are references to space and time. In the film, images of the point, the line and the circle recur, perhaps most strikingly visually; but also in the text, spoken entirely in voice-over,[4] and in the sounds, which are often repetitive like a series of points arranged in a linear sequence, sometimes later repeated as if part of a loop or a circular pattern. What the presence of these geometrical figures in the film might mean will be discussed in this chapter, considering Bion's use of the same figures in order to investigate thinking.

Bion observes that the point and the line are visual images that remain invariant under a number of possible situations, but in his own conjectures he often uses or interprets them as marking 'the place where something was' (1965, p. 121). The narrator in Proust's novel is able to think of the position he occupies in space and time with points, lines and a circle, but he adds that the sense of these coordinates can become muddled or broken. In *A Man Asleep*, the protagonist (Jacques Spiesser) retreats when he appears not to know anymore where he is, because something that was there before is no longer. The voice speaks: 'Something has snapped. You no longer feel secure: something that until now fortified you and warmed your heart begins to fail, the sense of your existence, a feeling of belonging to the world, of being immersed in it.'

Chris Andrews, who explores the intertextual dimensions of Perec's novel, makes a distinction between the somnolent state of Proust's narrator and Perec's protagonist:

> Proust is interested in the transition from sleep to waking and the way it allows a space for the operation of involuntary memory, while Perec is concerned with the visions and half-dreams which intervene to frustrate the transition from waking to sleep. His protagonist has cut himself off from the past and hardly has memories at all. As [Claude] Burgelin has written, he is engaged in an attempt to escape from his own history and history in general.[5]
>
> (1996, pp. 783–4)

In the film, Perec's man asleep is undoubtedly an insomniac; but I would argue that only to a certain extent can he be said to have cut himself off from his past, and from the world in which he lives. Bernard Queysanne notes that the time of the film is the time of the protagonist, that is, an absence of time, or the time of a mental experience (2007, p. 48). But this mental experience is a caesura; and from this caesura there are glimpses of other caesuras: 'long pants, first cigarettes, shaving rash, drinking, the key under the doormat on Saturday night, your first woman, your first flight, the baptism of fire'. As I will discuss in more detail later, images and words in the film are put together in such a way that they correspond with each other only in certain moments, and in my view the above passage in the text is read in one of such moments. This sequence begins with a car driving away, followed by the interior of an empty countryside house and the surrounding woods. There is a sense that this is the house of the protagonist's childhood.[6] Significantly, it is an empty house, and the voice will speak of 'inert blurred images, overexposed snapshots, almost white, almost lifeless, almost petrified'; but these fragile traces of memories are still part of a past that is being brought up in the present, and so are some of the important experiences of adolescence and early adulthood.

The past also manifests itself in less explicit ways, perhaps because it is more distant, or preverbal. For example, his room can evoke at times the maternal womb, a space that is protective, but that becomes increasingly claustrophobic: 'nine feet seven inches long, five feet eight inches wide, just over fifty-four square feet'; 'you sit on a couch, too short for you to stretch out to your full length at night, too narrow for you to turn over without being careful'.[7] The changes that occur in the experience of this space, as well as of the other spaces in the film, both interior and exterior, point to the containment and the problems of containment in the relationship between the protagonist and the spaces that surround him. The image of the circle is related to the distinction between inside and outside, a distinction that in certain instances cannot be made (in analysis, but also in the film).

Questioning his position in the world, when the sense of it has broken, entails the questioning of his ambitions and desires, and with this the character is also questioning the world in which he lives. 'To be undesiring' could be seen as a shadow cast by a future that has not yet happened: the traces of the future in his caesura. The questioning of his ambitions is something that is largely carried out on the level of language, which begins amidst the clutter of connotation characteristic of a consumer society, and attempts to arrive at a perception of things in which things appear literally as what they are.[8] In a way, it is as if the character finds himself living in a world of foreign languages, a confusion of tongues; and in his retreat he attempts to understand these languages, to deconstruct them, to find his own language.

The myth of the tower of Babel is one of the models of mental growth cited by Bion, a myth that in my interpretation of the film is implicitly evoked from several perspectives. In one of his considerations of the myth, Bion writes:

> In the Babel myth the use of the tower is to effect an entry into realms regarded by Jahweh as his own – heaven. The outcome is exile, as in the garden of Eden and Oedipus myths, but an important precursor is the destruction of a common language and the spreading of confusion so that co-operation became impossible.
>
> (1963, pp. 64–5)

In the above passage an image of the film can already be recognized: the protagonist is 'exiled' from a world pervaded by demands, by the creation of questionable needs and values, in which participation becomes impossible. Other images of the myth that can be identified in the development of the film will be explored towards the end of the chapter.

In addition to the above mentioned main themes in which the retreat as caesura is articulated in *A Man Asleep*, there is a more general structural line in the form of the film in which the caesura finds expression. It can be discerned in the structure of the film's script, the publication of which accompanies the DVD edition of the film. The titles of the seven sections that comprise the script are, in order: 'Rupture', 'Apprenticeship', 'Happiness', 'Anxiety', 'Monsters', 'Destruction' and 'Return'. 'Rupture' marks the beginning of the retreat, and the beginning of 'Anxiety' signals the eventual necessity of ending the retreat. This structure dictates the structure of this chapter, which will consider the first three sections of the film, then the following three, and conclude with an examination of the last section. But I will precede this analysis with a survey of some material that raises issues that are pertinent to my argument, and which will be explored later through Bion's work.

Species of spaces and things

There are no in-depth, dedicated studies of this film to date. David Bellos's biography of Perec (1993) is perhaps the source that contains most information on the project, providing an account of the circumstances in which it was initiated, developed and received, but also referring to a few important formal aspects of the film.

Bellos (p. 479) cites two films that featured in the authors' preliminary discussions on how to make a film of the book. *Hiroshima mon amour* (1959) by Alain Resnais and *Life Upside Down* (*La Vie à l'envers*) (1964) by Alain Jessua resonated with what Perec and Queysanne planned to do: the first film in its fragmented form, the last in its theme.[9] In *Life Upside Down*, after a series of events, the main character decides to throw most of the furniture out of his room and to shut himself in there, apparently drawing strength from one of Pascal's *Pensées*: 'I have often said that the sole cause of man's unhappiness is that he does not know how to stay quietly in his room' (1670, p. 37). Pascal believed that humans endlessly seek distractions and thus often put themselves in danger (hence the unhappiness) in order to forget their miserable and mortal condition. Essentially this idea is not much different from another thought by the same philosopher, quoted by Bion more than once: 'The eternal silence of these infinite spaces fills me with dread' (p. 66). In *Transformations* Bion refers to it as expressing the fear or intolerance of the unknown, which can translate as fear of the undiscovered unconscious (p. 171). In the subsequent book, *Attention and Interpretation*, he comes back to it, this time to express a psychotic, terrifying realization of space into which the analysand's state of 'non-existence' is evacuated. 'Non-existence' is derived from the annihilation of the place where an emotion was. The evacuated state of 'non-existence' is felt to be a terribly hostile object, envious and destructive towards anything endowed with existence (1970, p. 20). It could be that something close to this extreme state of depersonalization is experienced by Perec's man asleep, but only in the later stages of his retreat. What is interesting to note if the two cogitations by Pascal are brought together is that a circumscribed space becomes associated with the experience of an infinite space, or with the unknown; and such infinite, unknown, frightening space could be the internal world in moments of dramatic change.

According to Bellos (p. 541), at the time of the film's release, Perec and Queysanne consistently told the press that the work had a musical structure. Bellos points out that the visual material in the film is the same in all its sections, yet shot from different angles and ordered in a different manner; and he remarks that image, sound and text are edited in such a way as to shift out of phase with each other and come together again at what seem to be random moments (p. 539). Such method of filmic composition appears indeed to draw from music, minimalist music in particular, which was developing in the United States since the 1960s, and which has audible affinities with the music in *A Man Asleep*, composed by Philippe Drogoz and Eugénie Kuffler (who named their ensemble '010'). Terry Riley and Steve Reich are pioneers of minimalist music who experimented with tape loops, exploring for example the effects of playing two identical loops perfectly synchronized with each other in the beginning, in two tape machines playing at slightly different speeds, so that the loops phase out, but eventually become synchronized again (Potter, 2000, p. 117, p. 166). These repetitive, circular patterns that characterize much of the minimalist music movement find a curious example in one of the versions of Terry Riley's *Keyboard Study no. 2* (1967), which reflects 'its free-wheeling, open-form aspect by transcribing the piece's pitch modules in concentric circles' (Potter, p. 126). The piece's modules are to be performed repeatedly and continuously for long, variable periods of time.

Several authors who write on minimalist music draw parallels with concurrent artistic movements, especially with Op art, suggesting that the experience of its optical illusions is comparable with the psychoacoustic effects of minimalist music (pp. 7–8, 11).[10] In the film there is a sequence that could be described as somewhat hypnotic (Figures 5.1 and 5.2) and which could evoke a painting by Bridget Riley such as *Blaze 1* (1962). The sequence begins with the circle in Figure 5.1 taking up most of the frame, the camera slowly zooming out and revolving around an axis that is gradually displaced, so that the image is replaced by the image in Figure 5.2. Space is spinning, surrounded by darkness, unsupported. The sound of a bell chiming is heard throughout, and is referred to in the text, compared to the water dripping from the tap on the landing. The repetitive sound of water dripping is the first sound in the film, heard once the initial credit sequence is over. This sound produces an image that is in fact never seen but is spoken: 'concentric circles of ever-present sounds stretch out' like ripples on the surface of the water created by a drop. But the image of the tap dripping water is seen several times in the film, and at times this image coincides with the sound of water dripping, and at one point it coincides with the sound and the words that are spoken ('the dripping faucet on the landing'). Sometimes this sound becomes similar to the sound of a clock (for example during the exam), then becomes again distinctly the sound of a drop, and then it is assimilated into the chime of the bell. Images, sounds and words recur, in a circular pattern, phasing in and out with each other. In their script notes (no date, p. 49), Perec and Queysanne refer to the *décalage* between the different filmic components as something that conveys the protagonist's gradual loss of the sense of time passing. The repetitive sounds that are like points arranged in linear or circular sequences can also evoke the sound of a heartbeat, an element that can be connected to the aural landscape of an intra-uterine or a preverbal stage.

A project that Perec carried out alongside the shooting of *A Man Asleep* is a reflection on space, titled *Species of Spaces* (1974). It begins: 'The subject of this book is not the void exactly, but rather what there is round about or inside it' (p. 5).[11] The reader is then directed to look at a figure on the opposite page, which is a blank square, almost as wide as the page itself. The page is the first space to be investigated, and from there, the bed, the bedroom, the apartment, the apartment building, the street, the neighbourhood, the town, the countryside, the country, Europe, the world and lastly, space. But in the last section of this last species of space, what is described is a mental space:

> I would like there to exist places that are stable, unmoving, intangible, untouched and almost untouchable, unchanging, deep-rooted; places that might be points of reference, of departure, of origin [. . .]. Such places don't exist, and it's because they don't exist that space becomes a question, ceases

> to be self-evident, ceases to be incorporated, ceases to be appropriated. Space is a doubt: I have constantly to mark it, to designate it.
>
> (Perec, p. 91)

In an almost circular movement, Perec returns to the space of the page, as the space that can be marked with writing, with a form that can be designated, with a memory that can be retained: 'To write: to try meticulously to retain something, to cause something to survive; to wrest a few precise scraps from the void as it grows, to leave somewhere a furrow, a trace, a mark or a few signs' (p. 92).[12] *Species of Spaces* closes with this statement, on the space of the page.

Species of Spaces is part of a larger project that Perec initiated early in 1973, which proposed an observation and description of what goes generally unobserved: everyday habits, rhythms, spaces and objects (Bellos, pp. 521, 523–4). This was Perec's proposal to look at the 'infra-ordinary', and, although of course in its specific way and with its specific purpose, this interest in the 'infra-ordinary' is also visible in the film *A Man Asleep*. In fact, Bellos (p. 522) writes that this project for a new 'endotics' (as opposed to 'exotics') gives coherence to virtually the whole of Perec's oeuvre, from the earlier novel *Things* (1965) to the works he published subsequently.

Andrew Leak notes that Perec considers the two novels *Things* and *A Man Asleep* to represent the 'light' and 'dark' sides, respectively, of a single reality (2009, p. 124). Leak argues that Roland Barthes's *Mythologies* (1957) – a collection of texts that Perec acknowledges to have used while working on *Things* – can in fact provide a basis for the study of both novels, in relation to the reality they share. In *Things*, Jérôme and Sylvie are caught in a perpetual pursuit of things deemed desirable, or even essential, by the society in which they live, not because of the things' real value or use, but because the two characters are prey to the mythical discourses

FIGURES 5.1 AND 5.2 Stills 5.1 and 5.2 from *A Man Asleep*. During the sequence from which these stills are taken, the voice in the film speaks: 'This is where your kingdom begins and ends, and around it concentric circles of ever-present sounds stretch out, your only link with the world, the drop of water from the faucet of the water outlet on the landing, the noises your neighbour makes, the town's endless hum.'

through which those things are made desirable. On the 'dark' side of this reality, the man asleep attempts to dismantle such discourses:

> Whereas Jérôme and Sylvie are defined by their massive, largely unconscious, investment in rhetoric, the man asleep is characterized by his apparently conscious disinvestment in connotation: he aims, by a long and patient ascesis, to transform his very perception of the world into the physical analogue of a purely denotational language.[13]
>
> (Leak, p. 136)

In the text of the film there can be found a statement that would seem to support Leak's contention: 'Indifference dissolves language and crosses signals.' Perec often uses the term 'indifference' in the characterization of the retreat of the man asleep, but from 'indifference' to 'long and patient ascesis' there seems to be a long way. At least at one level, Leak connects the protagonist's indifference to a desire for a certain neutrality, a desire to not respond to the continuous solicitations of the world, a desire to divest his everyday actions of certain values (p. 138). The film as a whole reflects this, and its voice articulates it explicitly in the following passage:

> Your purpose isn't to rediscover the robust pleasures of illiteracy, but to read without making any distinction in your reading matter. Your purpose isn't to go naked, but to dress without any implication of either fussiness or neglect. Your purpose isn't to let yourself die of starvation, but just to keep yourself nourished. Eating, sleeping, walking, and dressing, such things should only be actions, matters of course, not proofs, not tokens: your clothing, your food, and your reading matter, are no longer meant to speak for you.

In his retreat, he attempts to liberate his everyday actions from the nauseating excess of connotation; in a similar manner he tries to liberate the objects of his perception of the same excess. In one of the street scenes, the protagonist sits on a bench in front of a tree, and gazes intently at it for some time. The camera alternates between shots of the tree and shots of the protagonist that gradually get closer, until only a small circular shape on the bark of the tree and a close-up of his eye are seen. The voice speaks: 'you learn to look at paintings as if they were parts of a wall, and at walls as if they were pictures where you effortlessly decipher thousands of routes, unavoidable labyrinths, languages no one dares read, ruined countenances'. This scene in the film appears to be a reworking of an episode in the book that takes place in the countryside, in which the protagonist's contemplation of a tree reaches the point at which nothing more can be said about the tree other than it is a tree; that no other truth, moral or message can be derived from it (Perec, 1967, p. 153). Leak (p. 142) points out that this is a recognizable reference to the episode of the chestnut tree in Jean-Paul Sartre's *Nausea* (1938).[14] This novel has the form of a diary written by a man named Antoine Roquentin, a man whose perception of things reaches a nauseating realization of their sheer existence, of their beingness. The beingness of things cannot be represented or described through concepts, thus things become denuded of meaning, their absurdity and meaninglessness is revealed:

> The root of the chestnut tree plunged into the ground just underneath my bench. I no longer remembered that it was a root. Words had disappeared, and with them the meaning of things, the methods of using them, the feeble landmarks which men have traced on their surface. I was sitting, slightly bent, my head bowed, alone in front of that black, knotty mass, which was utterly crude and frightened me.[15]
>
> (Sartre, p. 182)

When the man asleep sits in front of the tree, he may be reading 'languages no one dares read', he may be stripping it from the outworn metaphors of 'strength' and 'majesty', but he does not seem to have reached yet the disturbing vision that Roquentin has in his encounter with the chestnut tree. Nevertheless, Roquentin's 'thinking without words, *about* things, *with* things' (Sartre, p. 185) describes a problem in thinking about things through representations, and I believe this problem is eventually experienced by the man asleep. This is a problem Bion addresses in his investigation of the point, the line and the circle, to which I will now turn.

Rupture, Apprenticeship, Happiness

Bion writes that the realm of thought can be conceived of as a space filled with no-things. The place where a no-thing is can be marked by a representation such as a word or a visual image (1965, p. 76, 106). Bion conjectures that in their origin, geometrical constructions sought to represent emotions (p. 105). The point, for example, is an image that appears regularly in clinical material in the form of dots or spots (p. 78), and its presence is sometimes felt to be intolerable (p. 55). Bion proposes to use geometrical concepts to investigate the emotional realizations from which he believes these concepts originate. He notes that the point was an object of disagreement when it came to naming the concept in the field of geometry:

> According to Proclus, objection was raised against the term στιγμη [*stigmi*] by Plato on the grounds that it meant puncture and therefore suggested a background of reality that was not appropriate to geometric discussion. The objection resembles that of a patient to the visual image of the point because of its unwelcome penumbra of associations.
>
> (Ibid.)

It seems that in order to fulfil its role in geometric operations, the point should be divested of inadequate associations. The objections raised suggest that 'the importance of a definition is to mark a constant conjunction without the evocation of feelings' (p. 77); but Bion adds that 'something seems real only when there are feelings about it' (ibid.). Thus, if 'point' or '.' is to be usable in K (knowledge) it has to lose the penumbra of associations surrounding it, that is, it has to be developed into a pre-conception. The pre-conception can then be saturated by a realization that approximates to it, and this will be an emotional experience that can then be represented by 'point' or '.'.

Mathematicians are able to solve problems in the absence of objects. They can dispense with the presence of concrete objects, yet are still able to use them through a system of notation. But sometimes these or similar operations cannot be performed. Bion contends that the term 'point' or the visual image of a point can *represent* the place where the breast was, or they can actually *be* the no-breast (p. 82). The presence of this non-existent breast can be felt to be intolerable, and preclude learning and development. What should be what is usually understood as a thought becomes a thing, an actual breast, an actual no-breast present, an actual penis, which are then used in complex relations with real objects as part of acting-out. Bion remarks that 'such procedures do not produce the results ordinarily achieved by thought, but contribute to states approximating to stupor, fear of stupor, hallucinosis, fear of hallucinosis, megalomania and fear of megalomania' (ibid.).

The problem that Bion formulates is that of a breast that has disappeared and has left a point in the place where it used to be, a point placed in a certain relation to the mind (the circle). Again, in order to solve this problem (in order to be able to think about the breast in its absence), the observed phenomenon (the point) has to be developed into a pre-conception, which means that the possibility of its meaninglessness has to be acknowledged. Donald Meltzer explains:

> [Bion's] experiment in describing psycho-analytical observation, thought and communication in terms of the means by which observation is transformed into thought which can grow in complexity, sophistication and level of abstraction, and in doing so accrete meaning, has been narrowed down to experiences of absent objects and tolerance to the pain of acknowledging their continued existence, this being contingent on the ability to be curious about the meaning of the phenomenon by acknowledging that it might be without meaning.
>
> (1978, III, p. 80)

The possibility of meaninglessness may be too painful to tolerate, because the breast, which is the source of all meaning, is felt to have been destroyed. The analysand fears not only that all meaning has been destroyed, but also that he or she has ceased to exist, since existence is dependent on the breast (Bion, 1965, p. 81).

Bion comments that Aristotle's discussions on the relation between the point and the line attest to the relatedness of both concepts (p. 56). Bion notes that phallic symbols may be represented by a line, and so the line can mark the place where the penis was (p. 76). In other instances, Bion wonders whether the point and the line should be regarded as two separate entities or as different manifestations of the same entity (p. 89). Lines and points can become points and lines respectively if submitted to certain geometrical manipulations. In the film *A Man Asleep*, these manipulations are suggested in a large number of images, of which Figures 5.3–5.6 are examples. Not only lines and points are prominent compositional features within the frame, but they are also described or represented by the protagonist, the camera, and their movements. For example, in an outdoor shot the protagonist is walking in a straight line in the middle of a road, towards the camera, as the camera moves faster in reverse tracking and the protagonist becomes a point that recedes in the distance.

'Your room is the most beautiful of desert islands, and Paris is a desert that no one has ever traversed.' The film could be seen to happen inside a circle: inside a mental experience, as Queysanne states. Nevertheless, there are moments in the film in which the distinction from inside and outside the circle is ambiguous, and this disturbs the sense of what is happening inside or outside the mind. In the first three chapters of the film, with which I am concerned in this section of my argument, there are four scenes in which the camera describes a circle or fragments

FIGURES 5.3 AND 5.4 Stills 5.3 and 5.4 from *A Man Asleep*. Two examples of the recurrent and striking use of lines converging into a point.

FIGURES 5.5 AND 5.6 Stills 5.5 and 5.6 from *A Man Asleep*. Two examples in which lines appear constituted by points or in which points appear in a linear sequence.

of a circle, and there are significant events taking place either inside or outside, or both inside and outside the camera's movement.

In the first of these scenes, the protagonist walks in a straight line inside an arcade, a movement that is underlined with the sound of his footsteps (again, a series of points), while the camera describes a tangential or almost tangential curve to his path. In a subsequent scene, he is standing by the river throwing pieces of matches into the water, while a train passes on a bridge in the background; the line is again outside, but now he is inside the circle, inside the concentric circles he is creating on the surface of the water (which, again, are not seen) and enveloped by the curved movements of the camera around him. In another instance, he is sitting on a bench opposite an older man who is also sitting, while the camera travels around them. Both appear to be inside the circle; however, the voice of the film describes the older man's stillness, wondering whether his attention is focused on following his own shadow as the Sun turns around him. This is a circle from which the man asleep is excluded: 'You want to be like him, nevertheless, no doubt it's one consequence of being such a very young candidate for old age, you lose patience all too quickly.' In the last of these scenes, significantly towards the end of this first part of the film that comprises the first three chapters, the man asleep walks around a monument in the centre of a traffic circle, in the opposite direction to the circular movement of the camera. At one point, after which the camera will continue its trajectory for a few more turns until it leaves the circle, he disappears from behind the monument and is not seen again until the following scene.

What could these relationships between circles, lines and points mean? Bion provides an illustration that helps to understand points that are 'complex conjugate', 'real and coincident', and 'real and distinct', which correspond to three different situations in which a line can be positioned in relation to a circle. He begins by describing a situation in which two breasts have disappeared leaving only two points in their place; the subject in this situation may be able to tolerate these points or, instead, perceive them as hostile no-breasts. Bion continues:

> As he watches they appear to come together until they are coincident with each other and the boundary of his personality. They might just as well have travelled towards each other in a straight line and so coincided without touching him. But suppose they have travelled towards, or been drawn towards, him at the same time: then the line along which they travel to meet each other has been pulled into a curve that touches his personality at the point of coincidence. Then they disappear. Where have they gone? If he had an inside or an outside they might have gone inside him or gone out the other side.
>
> (1965, p. 87)

Earlier in *Transformations* Bion remarks that whereas to some personalities the circle is a visual image that marks a distinction between inside and outside, to the psychotic personality the circle is evidence that there is no such distinction (p. 82). So Bion proceeds with his illustration thus: 'But suppose they are not inside or outside. Worse still, suppose there is no inside or outside, that he himself is only a place-where-he-used-to-be, a place-where-inside-and-outside-used-to-be?' (p. 87). This particular image of the circle comes to mean 'no-inside-or-outside' and to be connected with the concept of depersonalization. The fourth and last scene described above, the scene of the disappearance of the protagonist in the traffic circle, brings into focus, with its circular camera movement, that he is no longer inside nor outside the circle, and that the circle is now only the place where he used to be.

To return to the meaning of the relationships between a line and a circle, Rafael López-Corvo summarizes the three possibilities in the following passage of his dictionary on the work of Bion:

> (i) *Real and distinct* [. . .]: inside the circle, in the internal world; would represent a relationship in which analyst-analysand work harmonically in search of O and its transformation in K. (ii) *Real and coincident* [. . .]: when the line is a tangent equally inside and outside of the circle. It represents a relation dominated by feelings of omnipotence and idealization resistant to change. (iii) *Conjugate complex*: when the line is completely outside the circle. Represents narcissism: a mirror representation in which the external is compensated by the internal.
>
> (2003, pp. 55–6)

These definitions support an interpretation of the earlier three scenes of the film described above as representations that correspond to situations of either omnipotence and idealization, or narcissism. These scenes seem to function as representations of defences against the painful realization of the possibility of meaninglessness, and they signal the onset of anxiety.

'Something has snapped', the voice says in the beginning, and what follows is a search for meaning, for a meaning that is no longer where it used to be. This is the moment of 'Rupture', followed by 'Apprenticeship', which Perec and Queysanne note is the protagonist's systematic, methodical investigation of his everyday life and the city around him (pp. 53–4). Among the inside and outside spaces he explores (both of which relate to the external and internal worlds), the real and distinct points inside the circle – the 'search of O and its transformation in K' – are manifest as he deciphers 'languages no one dares read'. The man asleep is learning to strip his surroundings of connotations, of a penumbra of associations, he is developing them into pre-conceptions. But in order to be able to think about such objects, to give them new meanings, their meaninglessness has to be acknowledged and tolerated as a possibility.

'Apprenticeship' is followed by 'Happiness', which Perec and Queysanne consider to be 'the centre of gravity' of the film (p. 57). They write that at this point the city is rediscovered by a questioning gaze, a gaze that rediscovers its mystery. They note that their purpose was to bring a sense of wonder to images of the everyday, an emotion that is normally precluded by habit or familiarity. At the editing stage, their plan to assemble these images was to organize them in a sequence in which 'their juxtaposition, opposition, articulation, continuity, break with scale or tone, will unmask the everyday incessantly, giving way to delight, fascination, or anxiety' (ibid.).[16]

The emotion in these three initial sections of the film is somewhat toned down – 'You have everything to learn, everything that can't be taught: solitude, indifference, patience, silence' – but there are already signs of anxiety and intolerance of the possibility of meaninglessness. These occurrences, of which I will give more examples in what follows, can be considered to be part of the articulation of the caesura: in the midst of real and distinct points inside the circle, there are already images of a lack of containment, of points and lines tangential to circles or 'missing' the circles, that are beginning to articulate a future crisis. And it could be that this future lack of containment was already projecting its shadow, in some form, in the distant past.

Anxiety, Monsters, Destruction

After some time in his retreat, solitude begins to become unbearable to the man asleep. His increasing anxiety is visible for example in his not being able to leave his room on one occasion. This agoraphobia is conveyed also through images of crowds and surveillance cameras, in high-contrast black and white, and often distorted through a fisheye lens; the sound, like drumming, becomes faster and threatening; the tempo of the editing and the movement within the scenes also accelerates; the voice, in a harder tone, describes the monsters that the city and its people have become. But the room also becomes claustrophobic: he is bored of playing card games, he bites his nails, he is unable to sleep, and so he goes out at night.

As part of the psychoanalytic discussion that I have used so far in this analysis of the film, Bion reflects, even if briefly, on agoraphobia and claustrophobia. He wonders whether these two different terms relate in fact to the same configuration. Bion considers the invariant in these two situations (though it could be applied more widely) to be 'space' or 'place where the thing was' (1965, p. 124). Joan and Neville Symington expand on Bion's observation:

> The space, either inside the object as in claustrophobia or outside the object as in agoraphobia, is intolerable. This space represents emotions indistinguishable from the 'place where something was', that is, in these patients who cannot tolerate the absence of the object there is a present non-existent object which renders the 'space' frightening, whether experienced as inside or outside the object. Panic is being trapped in this space with no means of escape, that is, there can be no thought by which escape could be effected.
>
> (1996, pp. 118–19)

In the text of this second part of the film there can be found the words 'there's no way out, no miracle, nothing was revealed', which could be interpreted here as 'there is no escape from the space where the no-thing was revealed'. The space is rendered frightening with the presence of the non-existent object. Bion writes that 'the rule that a thing cannot both be and not be is inadequate' (1965, p. 102), referring to objects that are perceived to not exist, but which nevertheless exist to the point of being endowed with the characteristic of non-existence; such contradiction can also be felt by a subject who feels non-existent but who nevertheless exists sufficiently to feel that way.

The crescendo of anxiety in the film is brought to an end by an image of the protagonist that gradually becomes smaller and finally dissolves into whiteness. The chapter titled 'Destruction' follows, in which the building where his room existed appears in ruins and the interior of his room appears destroyed. The protagonist encounters these ruins and runs away, runs through the city, and at one point he is seen, repeatedly, walking through the corridor of his childhood house, unlike the earlier scene in which his presence in the house was not visible. The text in the chapter 'Destruction' is both poetic and descriptive, and worth reproducing here in its entirety:

> There are no more places of refuge now. You're afraid, you're waiting for everything to stop, the rain, time, the flow of traffic, life, people, the world, you're waiting for everything to collapse, walls, church towers, floors and ceilings; for men and women, the very old and the very young, dogs, horses and birds to fall to the ground one by one, paralysed, plague-ridden, or epileptic; for marble to crumble, for wood to turn to dust, for buildings to be silently flattened, for floods to wash the paint from every surface, squeeze out the pegs of century-old cabinets, dissolve the ink of newspapers; for a flameless fire to eat away the planks of staircases; for streets to give way at their midpoint and reveal the gaping labyrinth of the sewers; for rust and mist to overrun the city.

There are several ways in which this passage can be related to Bion's formulation of the state of 'non-existence'. This formulation occurs in a discussion that has already been considered in Chapter 1, which is that of a situation in which the analysand experiences pain but does not suffer it. The encounter with the 'no-thing' arouses an emotion that is felt to be indistinguishable from the 'no-thing' itself, so effectively this means that a 'no-emotion' takes the place of emotion – in other words, an emotion (for example indifference) the function of which is to deny another emotion, replaces emotion (Bion, 1970, pp. 19–20). This situation is the result of a progression Bion refers to: 'breast → emotion (or place where breast was) → place where emotion was' (1965, p. 105). The place where the no-thing is, or the no-emotion is, which is also where time was, is then annihilated, and from this the realm of the non-existent is created. The object has disappeared, the emotion has been replaced, and the place where the emotion was is destroyed:

this is how the analysand achieves the state of 'non-existence'. This is followed by the evacuation of 'non-existence', which 'immediately becomes an object that is immensely hostile and filled with murderous envy towards the quality or function of existence wherever it is to be found' (Bion, 1970, p. 20). This destructiveness is poignantly expressed in the protagonist's apocalyptic vision. ' "Space" ', Bion continues, 'either as a representation, or the realization the term derives from or represents, becomes terrifying or terror itself' (ibid.). The space in ruins where the protagonist finds himself is terrifying, it cannot be contained; it is at once an explosive 'contained' (floods, fire, rust, mist) and an exploded container ('marble to crumble', 'streets to give way at their midpoint'). This is the culmination of a problem between container and contained of which the film has given several indications in the course of its development.

Perhaps the earliest visual indication of this problem is a series of travelling shots from medium close-up to medium shot and vice-versa of the protagonist sitting on his bed, facing the camera, with a reproduction of René Magritte's *La Reproduction interdite* (*Not To Be Reproduced*) (1937) on the wall behind him (Figure 5.7). In Magritte's painting, the mirror reflects the objects in the space correctly, apart from the figure of a man who is facing the mirror but can see his back instead. This is an image of an impossible containment. Michel Foucault (1973) comments on a similar painting by Magritte, titled *Les Liaisons dangereuses* (*Dangerous Liaisons*) (1935), in which a naked woman is leaning against a wall, facing the viewer, and holding a mirror in front of her that impossibly reflects her image. In addition, the space between the mirror and the wall is too narrow for her to be able to actually be there; and the shadow on the wall is missing the shadow of her hand holding the mirror. Foucault notes that 'through all these scenes glide similitudes that no reference point can situate: translations with neither point of departure nor support' (p. 52). Places that might be points of reference or departure were being longed for by Perec in *Species of Spaces*; circular spaces without support are revolving, suspended in darkness, in *A Man Asleep* (Figures 5.1 and 5.2).

FIGURES 5.7 AND 5.8 Stills 5.7 and 5.8 from *A Man Asleep*. Examples of 'impossible' or parasitic relationships between contained and container.

FIGURES 5.9 AND 5.10 Stills 5.9 and 5.10 from *A Man Asleep*. The 'exploded' or non-existent contained and container.

Without point of departure or support, and suspended in darkness, is also the image of the man asleep reflected into infinity in mirrors (Figure 5.8), another '*mise en abyme*' framed with a similar gliding movement to the earlier shots with Magritte's painting in the background. Here it is as if the container/contained is leaking, like the dripping tap on the landing and its ever-present sound. Another indication of a broken container/contained is the image of the protagonist reflected in the small broken mirror in his room, the same object that will later reflect the 'exploded' debris.

Thus, as in the isolated examples of the relationship between the circle and the line that have already been discussed, there is evidence in the film of the existence of parasitic relationships between container and contained, which culminate in the destruction or non-existence of both (Figures 5.9 and 5.10). As suggested above, this last situation seems to arise from the encounter with the 'no-thing', in its turn arising from intolerance to the pain associated with the absence of the object. The realization of the absence of the object, or the absence of meaning, is there from the beginning of the retreat, and is being tolerated and thought through: meaning is being searched for. But there are moments in the retreat in which this absence of meaning cannot be contained, until eventually meaninglessness is encountered in an excessive, unbearable way, perhaps not in a dissimilar way to Roquentin's experience in *Nausea*.[17] I will now consider the last chapter in the film, and provide some concluding remarks on these parasitic and symbiotic relationships between container and contained.

Return

Serene music accompanies the final sequence until the end, and the image begins with the man asleep walking on a street. Soon he is out of frame, as the camera begins a long, contemplative look over the urban landscape, around one axis, zooming in and out, but always moving; then, before completing a full circle, it dissolves into another shot that begins where the other ended, and it searches again the same landscape, but in a different light, and with different movements, until it finds the protagonist again, who is walking down another street until he disappears in the distance. Ending with the same panoramic view of the city as the opening credits shot, the final image is nevertheless different in that it reproduces a very slight lulling movement, perhaps indicating that the protagonist's insomnia is finally over. The text of this last chapter is that in which intertextuality is most recognizable. It appears to be made almost exclusively of allusions to various literary works. But overall it functions as a negativistic reflection on the protagonist's retreat, which can be summed up in the following: 'You've learnt nothing, except that solitude teaches nothing, that indifference teaches nothing. [. . .] The world is still there and you haven't changed. Indifference has not made you different.' The text's last two enigmatic sentences give the film an open-ended closure: 'You're afraid, you wait. On that crowded square you wait for the rain to stop falling.'

Interpretations of the ending, and overall meaning, of *A Man Asleep*, differ, and I will have to refer here, as I have done at other points in my argument, to studies of the book rather than the film. Michael Sheringham, who is concerned with the work's investigation of the everyday, views the protagonist's experiment of radical deconditioning as valuable from the perspective of a widening of perception, which brings the everyday into visibility (2006, p. 254). Sheringham also describes how he conceives of indifference in this work: 'The postulate ("propos") of indifference does not rest on hostility or ignorance; the aim is not to regress to some illusory innocence but to refrain from the kinds of choice that indicate taste, distinction, and "personality"' (p. 255). For Sheringham, 'the ending suggests that the protagonist has understood the need to return to the world' (p. 256). Thus, Sheringham conceives of the protagonist's retreat as a gesture sharply opposed to regression or evasion; it is rather an experience that has widened the protagonist's perception of the world and of his place in it, though it eventually becomes necessary that this new perception is used to re-engage with the world.

David Bellos provides his and other views of the ending, noting that its open-endedness calls for a different approach to the earlier work *Things*:

> What does it mean, to wait on Place Clichy for the rain to stop falling? Suicide, obviously, some readers say. Why no, the whole of life! others reply. 'You' have learnt that nothing comes from nothing; 'you' accept that the rain falls on you, too, that you share simple things with others, and that 'you' must live amongst them. Perec's second major work does not lend itself, like the first, to political appropriation, but its resolute inconclusiveness invites (indeed, provokes) psychological projection.
>
> (p. 361)

Bellos's conclusions on *A Man Asleep* would appear to read the protagonist's retreat, at least to some degree, as an omnipotent, narcissistic gesture. Paul Schwartz draws a similar inference, regarding the retreat as an attempt at a self-sufficient mastery of time and space:

> He assumed an attitude of superior indifference in order to master time and space by denying them. [. . .] Neither aloof nor invulnerable nor indifferent, nor even different, he finds himself in the novel's final lines terrifyingly at the mercy of time and space.
>
> (p. 29)

Perec's text does indeed make explicit references to being able or unable to master space and time. But in my view there is an issue here that is symptomatic of the recurrence of a myth in which 'the logical formulation of the problem points to a conflict between omniscience on the one hand and inquiry on the other' (Bion, 1965, p. 58).[18] Through the Proustian allusion it can be understood that the man asleep is in a transitional space and time, in a transitional state, in which the sense of his position in space and time has broken; therefore, during this transitional state, this caesura, his relation to space and time is being changed. The myths of the tower of Babel, the garden of Eden and the Sphinx, Bion notes, sustain the idea 'of a god inimical to the gaining of knowledge by human beings whose search is felt to imperil his supremacy' (1963, pp. 64–5). If the protagonist's attempt at recognizing and understanding his position in time and space is viewed as a hubristic act of defiance, thinking is being understood as the attainment of a sort of mastery over something, rather than as painful submission to the absence of the object. The first becomes parasitic if the pain of the absent object is omnipotently denied. And although the protagonist's retreat seems to be punctuated with moments of omnipotent denial, it is also apparent that its motive and reason for existing are epistemophilic; and, contrary to the statements proffered in the last chapter of the film, the widening of perception to which the retreat leads means that growth can be recognized in it. This idea can be further explored through a closer consideration of the myth of the tower of Babel as a model of mental growth.

Bion remarks that the deity's hostility to human beings' curiosity or search for knowledge is manifested in the attack on speech, 'the infliction of confusion of tongues' (1970, p. 92). Bion devotes particular attention to the presence of this attack within the analytic pair, but this situation is also observable within the group or within the individual; growth takes place if communication and understanding can be established among the parts that make the whole, parts that speak different languages, as it were.

In an interview, Perec states that *A Man Asleep* is not about the impossibility of communicating (Schwartz, p. 19), but his film actually says much about the difficulty in articulating and understanding something that is preverbal. Bion refers to this difficulty in the analytic situation when he writes that the 'ability to use points, lines, and space becomes important for understanding "emotional space", for the continuance of the work and avoidance of a situation in which two inarticulate personalities are unable to release themselves from the bondage of inarticulation' (1970, p. 15). The presence of the point, the line and the circle in the film – a film which is trying to represent the mental experience of its protagonist – seems to be an attempt to articulate something that belongs to a distant past, which is part of an articulation of the protagonist's caesura. This could be said to be a situation in which parts of the protagonist's self are trying to communicate with his whole self.

But the retreat in *A Man Asleep* is not at all only about the individual: it is also about the world in which he lives. It is a sociology book he was reading in his room when 'something snapped', and a sociology exam to which he did not go. It is not about the difficulty of communication with others, but it is about the difficulty in understanding the insidious messages continuously discharged by dubious ideologies, about the difficulty that discerning 'Nature' from 'History' can present, as their languages are 'confused at every turn' (Barthes, p. 11). This confusion of tongues is a situation common to or shared with others, but it is also one in which the individual is likely to feel isolated. It is difficult to imagine that the protagonist's period of turbulence in his relation with the world he inhabits will not have an impact on his future perceptions and decisions, and that these would not in their turn have an impact on others, even if limited; but his future is something that the end of the narrative leaves only to be imagined.

These two images of the myth of the infliction of confusion of tongues – within oneself and in the relation between self and others – suggest that if the protagonist is to build his own tower, and a collective tower, in the world, he needs to learn multiple languages. In my view what he did in his retreat was precisely to learn to articulate and understand a multiplicity of languages, languages from inside and outside, from the past, present and future.

I will conclude with a quotation from one of Bion's papers on the caesura, in which he reflects on the state of being awake and the state of being asleep:

> The change from the state of mind in which we are when asleep (S-state) to that in which we are when awake (W-state) is reminiscent of the change from watery fluid to gaseous fluid, pre-natal to post-natal. We have a prejudice in favour of the W-state: people, without hesitation, talk about having had a dream, often meaning that therefore it did not really happen. But I would say that that is a prejudice of a person who is in favour of the voluntary musculature, who does not attach importance to where he can go unless he can do it by the use of his voluntary muscles. We do not hear much about the places we visit, the sights we see, the stories we hear and the information which is available when we are asleep – unless we translate it into being awake. Who or what decides the priority of the W-state over the S-state?
>
> (1979, p. 327)

This passage could speak, metaphorically, of the retreat of the man asleep. The experience of this man was sufficiently important to the author who decided to write a book about it, and then, with others, to make a film.[19] It was an experience sufficiently important to be considered worthwhile sharing with others, in all its rich detail, first in the language of books, and then in the language of film.

With their film, Perec and Queysanne decided to give priority to the sleep state, translating the places their protagonist visited, the sights he saw and the stories he heard, into languages that want to be understood.

Notes

1 Proust, M. (1913). *In Search of Lost Time: The Way by Swann's.* Translated by Lydia Davis. London: Penguin Books, 2002. p. 9. Translation and editorial matter copyright © Lydia Davis, 2002. General Editor's Preface copyright © Christopher Prendergast, 2002. Reproduced by permission of Penguin Books Ltd.

2 I would like to thank Romain Beck for having introduced me to this film.

3 For references to the allusion see for example Claude Burgelin (1988, p. 67), or Paul Schwartz (1988, p. 24).

4 The geometrical figures can occur in the text as exact terms or terms that evoke their images. 'You follow on the ceiling the winding line of a thin crack' is an example of the first instance, while an example of the second could be 'As always, you make yourself a cup of instant coffee; as always, you add a few drops of condensed milk.' Excerpts from the transcript of the English version of the film (read by Shelley Duvall) will be used throughout the chapter, and are reproduced by permission of Bernard Queysanne.

5 Andrews, C. (1996). Puzzles and lists: Georges Perec's *Un homme qui dort. MLN*, 111 (4), pp. 783–4. © 1996 The Johns Hopkins University Press. Reprinted with permission of Johns Hopkins University Press. For a Deleuzian account of the transitional state of Proust's narrator and its cinematic resonances see Patrick ffrench (2009).

6 This view is corroborated by the original text, in which the character visits his parents' house in the countryside.

7 The maternal analogy has also been drawn by Schwartz, p. 25.

8 This idea is explored by Andrew Leak in an article that I will refer to later in the chapter.

9 Jean-Michel Frodon (2008, p. 68) points out that Perec's development of his work between writing and cinema had only one significant parallel at the time: the work of Marguerite Duras, who wrote Resnais's film. For a list of Perec's projects in film and for television see Bellos, pp. 740–3.

10 See also Wim Mertens (1983, p. 15). Mertens ascribes the analogy to Herman Sabbe.

11 Perec, G. (1974). Species of spaces. In: *Species of Spaces and Other Pieces.* Translated by John Sturrock. London: Penguin Classics, 1997, 1999. Translation and Notes copyright © John Sturrock, 1997, 1999. Espèces d'espaces copyright © Editions Galilée, 1974. This and subsequent excerpts from this work are reproduced by permission of Penguin Books Ltd.

12 For the importance of memory in Perec's work from an autobiographical perspective see Michael Sheringham (1993).

13 Leak, A. (2009). Phago-citations: Barthes, Perec, and the transformation of literature. *Review of Contemporary Fiction*, 29 (1), p. 136. Reproduced by permission of Dalkey Archive Press.

14 The connection to Sartre's book is confirmed in the last chapter of *A Man Asleep*, when Roquentin's name appears alongside other names of male leading characters in literary works (p. 217).

15 Sartre, J-P. (1938). *Nausea.* Translated by R. Baldick. London: Penguin Classics, 2000. p. 182. Copyright © Librairie Gallimard 1938. This translation copyright © Penguin Books Ltd. 1965. This and subsequent quotations from this book are reproduced by permission of Penguin Books Ltd. and New Directions Publishing Corp.

16 (My translation). The original paragraph reads:

> Notre ambition est de faire apparaitre, sous la quotidienneté des images, un étonnement, une émotion, que l'habitude nous empèche de ressentir. Nous pensons y parvenir, à la fois en restant totalement disponibles par rapport aux images que nous

allons filmer, et en les soumettant, au niveau du montage, à une organisation rigoureuse où l'enchainement des images, leur juxtaposition, leur opposition, leur articulation, leur continuité, leur rupture d'échelle ou de ton, démasquera sans cesse le quotidien, laissant place à l'enchantement, à la fascination, ou à l'angoisse.

17 'But that richness became confusion and finally ceased to be anything at all because it was too much.' Sartre, p. 187.

18 I have already quoted this statement in Chapter 1 in my exposition of the conflict between K and −K.

19 The nameless character of *A Man Asleep*, or a close version of him, will resurface in Perec's novel *Life: A User's Manual* (1978) as Grégoire Simpson. See pp. 234–41.

References

Andrews, C. (1996). Puzzles and lists: Georges Perec's *Un homme qui dort*. *MLN*, 111 (4), pp. 775–96.

Barthes, R. (1957). *Mythologies*. Translated by A. Lavers. London: Vintage, 1993.

Bellos, D. (1993). *Georges Perec: A Life in Words*. London: Harvill.

Bion, W.R. (1963). *Elements of Psycho-Analysis*. London: Karnac, 1989.

Bion, W.R. (1965). *Transformations*. London: Karnac, 1984.

Bion, W.R. (1970). *Attention and Interpretation*. London: Karnac, 2007.

Bion, W.R. (1979). Making the best of a bad job. In: *Clinical Seminars and Other Works*. London: Karnac, 1994.

Burgelin, C. (1988). *Georges Perec*. Paris: Seuil.

ffrench, P. (2009). Proust, Deleuze and the spiritual automaton. In: Bryden, M. and Topping, M. (eds.) *Beckett's Proust/Deleuze's Proust*. Basingstoke: Palgrave Macmillan.

Foucault, M. (1973). *This Is Not a Pipe*. Translated by J. Harkness. Berkeley: University of California Press, 1983.

Frodon, J-M. (2008). Oú gît votre sommeil rêvé. *Cahiers du Cinéma*, 631, p. 68.

Leak, A. (2009). Phago-citations: Barthes, Perec, and the transformation of literature. *Review of Contemporary Fiction*, 29 (1), p. 124–47.

López-Corvo, R.E. (2003). *The Dictionary of the Work of W.R. Bion*. London: Karnac.

Magritte, R. (1935). *Les Liaisons dangereuses*. Oil on canvas, 73x54 cm.

Magritte, R. (1937). *La Reproduction interdite*. Oil on canvas, 81x65 cm.

Meltzer, D. (1978). *The Kleinian Development*. Strath Tay: Clunie Press, 1985.

Mertens, W. (1983). *American Minimal Music: La Monte Young, Terry Riley, Steve Reich, Philip Glass*. Translated by J. Hautekiet. London: Kahn & Averill.

Pascal, B. (1670). *Pensées*. Translated by A.J. Krailsheimer. London: Penguin, 1966, 1995.

Perec, G. (1965). Things: A story of the sixties. In: *Things: A Story of the Sixties & A Man Asleep*. Translated by D. Bellos. Boston: Godine, 1990.

Perec, G. (1967). A man asleep. In: *Things: A Story of the Sixties & A Man Asleep*. Translated by A. Leak. Boston: Godine, 1990.

Perec, G. (1974). Species of spaces. In: *Species of Spaces and Other Pieces*. Translated by J. Sturrock. London: Penguin Classics, 1997, 1999.

Perec, G. (1978). *Life: A User's Manual*. Translated by D. Bellos. London: Vintage, 2008.

Perec, G. and Queysanne, B. (no date). *Un homme qui dort*. Fonds Bernard Queysanne. [script notes]

Potter, K. (2000). *Four Musical Minimalists: La Monte Young, Terry Riley, Steve Reich, Philip Glass*. Cambridge: Cambridge University Press.

Proust, M. (1913). *In Search of Lost Time: The Way by Swann's*. Translated by L. Davis. London: Penguin Books, 2002.

Queysanne, B. (2007). Un homme qui dort: Histoire du film. In: *Un homme qui dort: Texte intégral inédit du film.* Paris: La Vie est belle films associés. [accompanying booklet of the DVD edition of the film]

Riley, B. (1962). *Blaze 1.* Emulsion on hardboard, 43x43 in.

Riley, T. (1967). *Keyboard Study no. 2.* For piano. Circular version.

Sartre, J-P. (1938). *Nausea.* Translated by R. Baldick. London: Penguin Classics, 2000.

Schwartz, P. (1988). *Georges Perec: Traces of His Passage.* Birmingham, AL: Summa.

Sheringham, M. (1993). *French Autobiography: Devices and Desires: Rousseau to Perec.* Oxford: Clarendon Press.

Sheringham, M. (2006). *Everyday Life: Theories and Practices from Surrealism to the Present.* Oxford: Oxford University Press.

Symington, J. and Symington, N. (1996). *The Clinical Thinking of Wilfred Bion.* London: Routledge, 2008.

Filmography

Hiroshima mon amour (1959). Directed by Alain Resnais. [DVD] France/Japan: Argos/Como/Daiei/Pathé.

Life Upside Down (1964). Directed by Alain Jessua. [DVD] France: A.J. Films.

A Man Asleep (1974). Directed by Georges Perec and Bernard Queysanne. [DVD] France/Tunisia: Dovidis/Satpec.

6

THE CAESURA AND THE COMPARTMENTS OF THE INTERNAL MOTHER IN *THE CONVENT*

Introduction

'You who enter into this monastery/Neither hear nor see nor speak': these words, neither heard, nor seen, nor spoken by any of the characters in Manoel de Oliveira's film *The Convent* (1995),[1] appear superimposed on the image of its opening scene. Perhaps not as evidently in the English translation, the words in the original are understood as an admonition or warning, similar to a 'do not swim' sign encountered on a beach with a tumultuous sea. But in the convent there are no visible signs of danger. If the visitors to the convent –Professor Michael Padovic (John Malkovich) and his wife Hélène (Catherine Deneuve) – were to encounter such mysterious words upon entering it, they would probably think they referred to a method of religious contemplation. The statue of a blindfolded, hooded monk in one of the convent's courtyards, the image of which punctuates the film at several key moments, would favour this interpretation. Nevertheless, to neither hear, nor see, nor speak, could also be thought to describe the intrauterine state. And, as I shall argue in this chapter, the various spaces inside and surrounding this convent have distinctly maternal qualities, or more specifically, qualities that can be attributed to the inside of the internal mother in the early relationship with her.[2]

Recalling that in his writings on the notion of caesura Bion inquires how much could be left in the adult mind of an 'embriological' intuition, visual or auditory, conjecturing that the foetus may indeed see and hear *something* through differences in pressure in the amniotic fluid,[3] it can also be asked how much of the influence of these primal intuitions may be operating in the characters' experiences in the convent. At times some of the characters seem to be aware of something that is beyond their sensory abilities, or they seem to perceive something that they cannot quite grasp or articulate. 'I can't begin to describe how wonderful it was', says Piedade (Leonor Silveira), the convent's library assistant, attempting to relate what she believes was a dream she had. These divine, and devilish, visitations (or projections) that impregnate this place of retreat seem to be related to the emotional turbulence of the characters, to their transition from one state of mind to another. Michael and Hélène seem to be going through a crisis in their relationship, exacerbated through the force of the encounters with Piedade and Baltar (Luís Miguel Cintra). These encounters have a powerful impact on all the characters involved, stirring desire, jealousy, envy and contempt. And the determination with which Michael pursues his research project, which may have arisen from an attempt to come to terms with his mortality, is persistently ridiculed by Baltar, and sometimes by Hélène. It is in this emotional landscape that the Eden myth, cited by Bion as one of the models of mental growth, finds expression, since to eat the fruit from the Tree of Knowledge of Good and Evil is found to be a punishable act. It appears to be part of the punishment that ignorance must prevail, especially when it comes to trying to distinguish between good and evil. In one of the scenes in the library, Michael responds to Piedade's dutifulness with 'I wish you weren't so pure, it's cruel'. Michael's statement is an example of how the conflict between good and evil in this film is most often played through ambiguity. This conflict has been identified by several authors as a crucial aspect of the film.

But there are other prominent aspects to *The Convent* that invite a psychoanalytic reading. In my interpretation, Michael's and Hélène's caesuras, and a certain form of the Eden myth, are articulated as an emergence of parts of their personalities from the inside to the outside of the internal (maternal) object; the 'views-of-the-world' engendered by these two different positions in relation to the object have been theorized by Donald Meltzer, whose work I will turn to in this last chapter. His investigations on the phenomena of projective identification and claustrophobia will be particularly useful to explore the film's numerous acts of intrusion and the resulting stagnant, claustrophobic atmosphere of some of the film's circumscribed spaces, as well as to illuminate the more positive uses of these spaces, motivated by the characters' epistemophilic instinct and an aesthetic relation to the object that respects the privacy of its interior.

Meltzer, in collaboration with his colleagues, made significant developments in the area of the pathological use of projective identification. This mechanism, which had hitherto been characterized in terms of a quantitative nature such as 'massive', 'excessive' or 'normal', begins to be distinguished in its qualitative forms, which are dependent on its motive or use (Meltzer *et al.*, 1986, p. 69). He proposes the following differentiation:

> It has often been argued that the pathological use of projective identification, that is as a mechanism of defence, would better be called 'intrusive identification' since this term catches the essential motive of invasion of an alien personality and body as originally described by Melanie Klein. In that case the term, projective identification, could be reserved for the more Bionic use, as a primitive and largely unconscious mode of communication central to learning from experience.
>
> (pp. 66–7)

Communicative projective identification thus differs from intrusive identification, which enters the object violently or stealthily. Furthermore, Meltzer brings a new depth to the discovery that this mechanism also operates with internal objects. The internal mother, and particularly the inside of her body, is the 'privileged' locus for the operation of such mechanism, as Meltzer notes that intrusive identification with the father seems to happen only as a means of access to the mother (1992, p. 72). Because the intruding part of the personality enters the object uninvited, it suffers claustrophobic anxiety inside the object. The object then becomes what Meltzer defines as a 'claustrum' (pp. 69–71).

The claustrum is the interior of the object seen by the intruder (or intruding part of the personality) from the inside. This omniscient construction is opposed to an imaginative conception construed from the outside, which respects the privacy of the object. Hence the same object, the same space, can be invested with very different qualities, depending on whether it is seen from the inside by the intruder, or construed from the outside.

Observing that the geography of the internal mother is divided into separate compartments according to the functions she performs, Meltzer formulates – drawing on clinical material but also on poetry and painting – the conceptions of these different compartments seen both from the outside and from the inside. The internal mother is compartmentalized into a top area (inside chest, breast or head), front-bottom (genital), and back-bottom (rectum) (Meltzer *et al.*, 1986, p. 66).

As I will argue, some of the spaces in *The Convent* evoke Meltzer's identification and description of these maternal compartments. The same spaces in the film are susceptible to change, and to acquiring different qualities, depending on the quality of the projective or intrusive mechanism of the characters who dwell on or who intrude into those spaces. Michael's and Hélène's experiences in the spaces of the convent confront them with aspects of themselves that appear to be ensconced in claustra, but that will eventually emerge.

The Convent is loosely based on the ideas for a book written by Oliveira's long-time collaborator Agustina Bessa-Luís, titled *As Terras do Risco* (*The Lands of Risk*) (1994). The two works have different titles because the film should not be considered an adaptation. Eager to begin shooting, Oliveira did not wait for Bessa-Luís to finish writing the novel, and so he wrote the script himself. Yet the works have things in common. For example, as Didier Coureau rightly points out (2006, p. 208), their titles attest to the importance of 'place'. For Jean Gili (1995, p. 25), the set is in fact the main character in Oliveira's film. Terras do Risco is the name of a region in Arrábida, the same wider area on the coast of Portugal that provides all the locations in *The Convent*. In her book, Bessa-Luís refers to the etymology of the word 'Arrábida': it possibly originates in the Arabic *ribat*, a place of retreat built for prayer and the 'Holy war' (p. 19). Several hundreds of years later, the Arrábida convent is still a place separated from the 'outside world', but what brings the professor to this place, writes Bessa-Luís, is his curiosity (p. 10); and here, as in the film, is established an important connection to Goethe's *Faust*, which becomes explicit in various ways. Randal Johnson (2007, p. 89) cautions against a close transposition, as it is Hélène and not Michael who makes a pact with the 'devil'. However, Goethe's version of the Faust legend will be referred to in the course of my argument as it can help to explore possible meanings in the film.

It would be fallacious to regard *The Convent* as an isolated example of the significance of place, and space, in Oliveira's work. Places often have religious, historical, biographical or autobiographical significance. Space is often circumscribed, enclosed, confined or claustrophobic: it is a space that signifies, for example the difficulty that the characters have in expressing their emotions and in acting according to them. Both place and space are created not only with images, but also with words, sounds and music. Oliveira (2005) states that in his films none of these elements is ancillary to the others, they all have equal importance. *The Convent* will be better understood if examined in conjunction with some of his other works; thus I will now consider these with the help of existing scholarship and Oliveira's own comments, while drawing some thematic and psychoanalytic correspondences.

Spaces of retreat in the films of Oliveira

Between 1972 and 1981 Oliveira made four films that are commonly referred to as the tetralogy of frustrated love.[4] João Bénard da Costa, who wrote extensively on Oliveira and acted in several of his films,[5] notes that already in these early works the characters find themselves in closed and restrictive environments – houses, convents, prisons, cabins – and seem incapable of getting out of them (1981, p. 8). Oliveira explains that it is not love which leads some of these characters to their deaths, it is society; society imprisons them, yet he states that society can only imprison their bodies, not their souls: they are in fact free to love and to desire. He adds that ultimately it is the impossible or unattainable that seduces human beings (Oliveira *et al.*, 1981, p. 42).

In a later article, Bénard da Costa mentions the tetralogy of frustrated love as the beginning of the appearance of a theme in Oliveira's work he believes can be found in *The Convent*, and the subsequent film *Party* (1996). This theme is the nostalgia for the lost original unity of man and woman, and the harmonious state of being it implies, in the garden of Eden (da Costa, 2008a, p. 166).[6] Both these later films deal with the disintegration of a couple or couples, with the impossibility of man and woman being one flesh and one soul: men and women are born, and die, parts of a part. In *The Convent*, Piedade reads a passage of *Faust* to Michael, in which Mephistopheles introduces himself in this way:

> If man, that tiny universe of folly, usually considers himself to be whole, I know I am a part of that part which existed at the beginning of everything; a part of that darkness, which gave birth to proud light, which now quarrels with the night that mothered it.

Piedade's reading of this passage bears a connection with what initially was to be the title of *Party*. The initial title was *The Part of the Part that Was Lost in the Garden*

Party (da Costa, 2008b, p. 36). Like good and evil, these parts of the part are not always easily identified.

In my view, there is another connection between these two films, and that is that their spaces can be read as maternal spaces. In *Party*, when Leonor (Leonor Silveira) drives Michel (Michel Piccoli) down to the seaside – where he will fall in love with her – she says to him: 'Look. The pool was dug out of rock, a present from my mother-in-law [to her son]. It symbolizes the womb.' This space of retreat, separated from the garden-party, is where they are transformed as they encounter the unknown in each other, and perhaps in themselves (Leonor's words express her emotion at this encounter: 'I'm afraid'); the space's liberating quality is conveyed through the images and loud sound of the waves crashing against the rocks. When they return to the party and join their partners, Michel reveals he is in love, and then a strong wind begins to blow. Leonor speaks: 'This island has strange powers. Volcanoes sigh like women, as though they had women inside.' Irène (Irene Papas), Michel's lover, responds: 'Island hysteria. This wind! It affects young women.' Indeed it appears to affect Leonor, who is the only protagonist who attempts to get out of the restrictive environments in which she lives: she wants to run away before the guests arrive, she leaves the party to go to the seaside, she stands in the rain outside her house, and she stands outside ready for Michel to take her away with him. But in the end, as Michel departs with Irène, Leonor goes back inside the house with her husband. As in *The Convent*, a space of retreat that can be read as a maternal space is the setting for transformative experiences; those experiences constitute the core of the narrative, a crisis or a pivotal moment in the lives of the characters, a caesura.

Party is followed by *Voyage to the Beginning of the World* (1997), which could also be considered to be about the caesura. Most of this film alternates between dialogue scenes inside a car, in which the characters travel to the 'beginning of the world', and shots of the road left behind as they drive. The latter are similar to images of driving forward, being rewound: they are at once going forward, and going back to the point of departure. For two of the characters (a director and an actor), the 'beginning of the world' is located in various places around northern Portugal; for the director (Marcello Mastroianni) this journey means revisiting places of his childhood and youth (now changed, or derelict), and for the actor (Jean-Yves Gautier) it means discovering the place where his father was from. Randal Johnson writes:

> Oliveira's journey to the beginning of the world involves travel to a time of identity formation, seen in both retrospective and prospective terms. It is a film of return, reminiscence and *le temps perdu* as the director moves inexorably toward the end of his life. At the same time, it is a film of discovery, hope and transformation as one of the actors connects with his roots and begins to understand his own identity in a way that he never had before.
>
> (2005, p. 209)

The characters' age difference places a different emphasis on the orientation of each of their journeys. But to be confronted with the loss of the past is also to be confronted with the question of what will remain in the future; and to discover a past that can become part of the future is also to encounter a part of the past that will remain forever buried. The latter is expressed by the difficulty in communication between the actor and his aunt, and the sense that she can only repeat what he already knows from his father. The journey is a transitional time in the lives of these two characters, in which their emotions – *saudade*, expectation, disappointment, discovery – can sometimes only find expression in their silences.

It is in this film and the following that Fausto Cruchinho (2008, p. 58) identifies two figures who belong to a matriarchal dimension that he believes cannot be found elsewhere in Oliveira's work. Although mother characters are recurrent, in *Voyage to the Beginning of the World* and *Anxiety* (1998) there are two matriarchal figures who seem to live outside time: in the first film this figure is the actor's aunt (Isabel de Castro), in the second it is the Mother of the River (Irene Papas), who performs, inside a cave, an initiation ritual for a young woman who will take her place. Thus *The Convent* can be seen to be the first of four films that follow each other in Oliveira's oeuvre in which appear, implicitly or explicitly, a maternal space associated with the space and time of a transitional stage.

The last of the films that I would mention in this connection was made 3 years after *Anxiety*, and is titled *I'm Going Home* (2001). 'I'm going home' are the words spoken by the main protagonist, an actor by profession (Michel Piccoli), as he abandons the film set on which he is working, because he cannot remember his lines. This is one of the final scenes in *I'm Going Home*, a film about a man who is suffering the tragic loss of most of his family in an accident. In an interview, Oliveira explains what the gesture of 'going home' means for him:

> 'To go home and have a rest' is a commonly used, simple sentence. [. . .] But this association between resting and going home is very important, because . . . home is a place where . . . it's a private place, where one retires to, where one detaches from the world and becomes free with him or herself. And of course that is important to someone who is tired of crowds, of socialising and needs his or her rest. Or else when . . . something tragic happens, as in the case of *I'm Going Home* [. . .]. And in that case the sentence has another meaning. And that meaning is . . . the return to the mother's womb, which is the only place where a human being is conceived in absolute peace.[7]
>
> (Oliveira, 2001)

At first, the retreat seems to be associated with having a rest from others or from society, and with freedom, a certain personal freedom gained from privacy. But then, in other instances, it becomes associated with tragedy, in which case Oliveira construes the retreat as a return to the mother's womb: a place where peace is (or is hoped to be) found. Shortly after, he continues:

> The same way it could happen with a man, it could happen with society [. . .]. A civilization which may fall into chaos, tragedy, and which therefore [. . .] wishes to go back home, that is, back to those heavenly days when it had peace. But it is always difficult or impossible. It is a subterfuge, an interruption, people are merely fooling themselves, almost giving up their own lives. It is a postponement of living life. In other words, if you will, a tragedy. *I'm Going Home* is . . . it is the tragedy of our civilization. The reason why so many people falter, why they don't know what to do any more, why they have nothing to do, and have even a more serious problem: they don't know how to go back home. And that is the greatest despair in society today.
>
> (Ibid.)

Here Oliveira states his belief that when something tragic happens, to try to find peace in the retreat is an illusion. The retreat is seen as an interruption, a postponement of a life that should be continuing instead. Nevertheless, his conclusion seems to be that it is a tragedy that people (have to) retreat, but an even bigger tragedy that they do not know how to. It is unclear from the development of the interview the exact sense of his conclusion. Oliveira could mean that he believes that people today do not feel the necessity to retreat, or perhaps that they do feel it but there is something that prevents them from doing it. Oliveira's views on the tragedies surrounding the retreat or the lack thereof are ambiguous in his comment on *I'm Going Home*, but the theme and the images of retreat undoubtedly recur in his films.

In his study of *The Convent*, Didier Coureau (p. 218) also identifies the image of a return to the mother, while quoting Mircea Eliade on the mythical significance of entering the archetypal spaces of the cavern and the labyrinth.[8] For Coureau, the spaces of the convent, its courtyards, chapels, stairs and terraces, suggest the idea of labyrinth, especially because of the way they are filmed: through the use of a complex and rigorous system of shot/reverse-shot, which establishes numerous points of view. Often the observed is constituted as observer and vice versa: statues seem to be endowed with vision, protagonists seem sometimes petrified (pp. 214–15). The sequence in which Baltazar shows 'the sacred space' to Michael and Hélène, positions some of the points of view inside the monks' cells and chapels. This evokes the imaginary of the gaze of the cave, also present in the second part of Goethe's *Faust*: the gaze of the Phorcyads, one-eyed monsters who observe Helen and Faust as they retreat inside the rock caverns (p. 217).

These mysterious points of view in the film have also been noted by other authors. Laurent Roth (1995, p. 48) writes that the camera seems to reproduce the vision of the dead, of the saints who once inhabited the cells and chapels. Mariolina Diana (2001, pp. 85–6) further notes in these scenes that the camera anticipates the arrival of the protagonists: the eye of the camera seems to coincide with the point of view of a mysterious invisible entity that is already expecting the visitors. Diana also recognizes this transcendent look in the forest, a look that seems to come from the 'abyss of instincts' in which Piedade will be lost. It is indeed

Oliveira's use of these points of view that to my mind endows space with a certain corporeality, a corporeality with eyes and orifices, and which pre-exists the arrival of the characters; these orifices are penetrated by the characters with their look, their voices and their bodies, and this conveys and reinforces the idea of intrusion that is central to my interpretation of the film.

However, as I have already pointed out, there are more positive relationships to the object in *The Convent*, not just intrusive relationships. Patrícia da Silva Cardoso (2010, p. 219) focuses her reading of the film in the opposition between good and evil, which she sees as the film's theme. She begins by citing Oliveira's comment on the meaning of the 'normal life' referred to in the end as the life that Michael and Hélène were supposed to be leading after their stay in the convent: 'a normal life cannot be other than that in which the two opposing forces [of good and evil] are evenly balanced, in a perfect or ideal symbiosis' (ibid.).[9] Cardoso argues that the conflict between these forces is based on the relationship between nature and psyche, taking Bessa-Luís's opening sentence in her novel as a thematic point of contact between the novel and the film. The sentence reads: 'Those who let themselves be moved by a landscape are hiding their innermost desires.' (Bessa-Luís, p. 7).[10] Supporting her thesis with a citation from a dialogue between both authors, Cardoso writes that the conflict between good and evil is articulated in the striving to overcome that which is animalistic in humans, something that cannot be differentiated from nature:

> Evil is what is instinctive or impulsive in human beings, it is what leads them to act with the purpose of satisfying themselves, without thinking about the possible consequences for themselves and others, it is what hides behind those 'innermost desires' of which speaks the narrator in *The Lands of Risk*. Thus, the ecstatic contemplation of an exuberant landscape would be a way to contain the turbulence of the bound instincts, perhaps even the only non-aggressive way to maintain the link between nature and humankind.
>
> (p. 226)

It would appear that it is the containment of instincts that keeps good and evil balanced in a perfect symbiosis, here epitomised in a certain emotional containment in the contemplation of a beautiful landscape. But is this symbiosis, achieved through a containment of instincts, related to the symbiotic relationship between container and contained? In other words, can such relationship of wonder at the beauty of the object be related to a growth relationship between container and contained? I will draw on the work of Donald Meltzer to address these questions, as well as suggest ways in which the distinction between good and evil in the film might be made. Although Cardoso seems to define evil in clear terms in the above quotation, she will towards the end of her article underline the equivocal nature of what goes by the names of 'beauty, intelligence, scientific spirit, dedication to a cause, desire, curiosity' (p. 233). Meltzer's investigations on the aesthetic conflict can contribute to a less ambiguous understanding of these notions as they suggest themselves at different points in the film.

The aesthetic conflict and emergence from the claustrum as caesuras

In *Transformations*, Bion observes that his conviction that mental growth appears to depend on truth as a living organism depends on food may belong to the realm of the Aesthetic as it cannot be supported by scientific evidence (1965, p. 38). In a later passage he reflects on his analysand's thought process in the following way: 'When I thought I grasped his meaning it was often by virtue of an aesthetic rather than a scientific experience' (p. 52). The aesthetic aspect of the mind and of the analytic process will gain increasing significance in the later work of Bion, culminating in *A Memoir of the Future* (1975–81). Meltzer, in collaboration with Martha Harris, Meg Harris Williams and others, develops this dimension of Bion's legacy with the formulation of the concepts of the aesthetic conflict and the claustrum (though the latter concept, despite its link with the first, has been discussed by Meltzer in the context of his investigations of the *geographic* aspect of mental functioning). Meltzer notes that the visual relationship between infant and mother, and the aesthetic impact of the external world on the infant, has been for the most part overlooked in psychoanalytic theories of development (Meltzer *et al.*, 1986, pp. 182–3). The conflicts of separation from and absence of the mother are in fact regarded by Meltzer as possibly secondary to the 'aesthetic conflict' in her presence, a conflict he defines thus:

> The beauty of the world and its epitomisation in the figure of the mother, the breast, the face, envelops the baby but brings in its train the most acute pain of uncertainty in the three-dimensional area. To what degree does the beauty of the exterior of the object correspond to the goodness of its interior, its feelings, intentions, durability? In a word, is it a 'truthful' object?
>
> (p. 182)

The hidden interior of the object is seen to be a powerful stimulus to thought. Meltzer considers the possibility that it may be more powerful than the absence of the object as the latter carries anxiety while the former invites passionate exploration (p. 183). But on the level of the aesthetic conflict there is a distinction to be made, as the pain of uncertainty can be dealt with in different ways; this relationship does not always have a passive, expectant quality, which surrenders to the mystery of the object:

> This view, that differentiates active and passive attention, 'penetration of' from 'envelopment by' the object, also draws a sharp line between intrusive curiosity and thirst for knowledge. [. . .] That intrusive curiosity which seeks the faults and defects of the object, stands in marked contrast to the awe and wonder at the beauty of the world which seeks to know and be known by the object.
>
> (p. 182)

This same differentiation could be made between Bessa-Luís's opening of her novel and Oliveira's opening of his film. Bessa-Luís follows the emotional contemplation of the landscape with words on the languor with which nature envelops the senses, on the understanding of a religious soul, and on the eyes of the animals that let their mysterious innocence be known. Oliveira follows Michael and Hélène entering a chapel of the convent before they meet their hosts, encountering on their way various mutilated statues. These statues have a beauty of their own, but while looking up at the mouldy dome of the chapel, Hélène says, 'You were wrong my dear, this is not it', and Michael replies, 'I know, I know . . . let's go.' The diegetic sound of birds is replaced at this point with a sombre non-diegetic music.[11] This opening sets the general atmosphere of the film, as mostly there is a sense that these characters are intruding in a space to take something from it, often finding faults and defects on their way. The state of dereliction of the buildings and statues, the stolen 'Blonde Virgin' mentioned by Baltazar, and the signs of vandalism such as the missing tiles in one of the chapels, are evocative of Melanie Klein's theories of the phantasized sadistic attacks on the mother's body, and the stealing and spoiling of the riches in her interior (Meltzer, 1992, p. 7). Before Baltazar guides the visitors through these spaces, he announces at the stone gate 'This is where the sacred space begins', and as soon as the characters pass through it, an even more disturbing music is heard, giving a sense of intrusion that is repeated in the aforementioned points of view from inside the chapels. And before the visitors are introduced in this way to the spaces of the convent, Baltar introduces himself to Hélène by entering the car she is in with the upper part of his body to kiss her hand. This intrusive gesture is his first attempt of several throughout the film to come between the couple and to seduce Hélène. One evening, when Michael and Hélène enter or try to enter each other's bedrooms (Michael seems to feel this as an intrusion as it interrupts his work), Baltar is spying on them, and finally tries to enter Hélène's bedroom himself. Piedade's bedroom is intruded into twice while she sleeps, the first time by Baltazar and Berta (Heloísa Miranda) and the second by Michael. These are some of the most striking examples, but there are others that are equally important, and also the exceptions to the rule. Before I examine these, I will provide some introductory remarks on the geographic aspect of the mind as theorized by Meltzer.

Meltzer (p. 117) divides the geography of psychic reality into four areas: outside, inside, the interior of internal objects and the interior of external objects. There is also a fifth area that has no links with the others, the 'nowhere' of the delusional world. In the introduction to *The Claustrum*, which is largely a project for the amendment and amplification of the concept of projective identification, Meltzer points out that the reason for his dissatisfaction with Klein's article 'On Identification' was its tendency 'to continue treating projective identification as a psychotic mechanism and one which operated with external objects, primarily or exclusively' (p. 13). Already in 1966 Meltzer gives evidence that projective identification operates with internal objects, and that this type of mechanism bears a particular connection with anal masturbation and character formation.[12] In retrospect, Meltzer (p. 30) remarks that this early work does not yet recognize the claustrophobic aspects of the material, because the interior spaces described in it are still not viewed as life-spaces. Later, with more clarity and precision, the interior spaces of the internal mother penetrated by omnipotent intrusive phantasies are not only seen to have implications in character pathology, but to generally interfere with the maturational process, forging the structure of the self and of the subject's 'view-of-the-world' (pp. 61–2). From the earliest years of life, the outside world begins to mould the qualities of these phantasized interior worlds, yet parts of the personality can become ensconced in them, casting their influence on how the outside world is perceived. Meltzer writes that 'In the neurotic patient, and perhaps in most people generally, the existence of an infantile part still inhabiting the claustrum casts its shadow on the person's "picture of his world"' (p. 120).

The mother's internal geography is compartmentalized by the child according to the child's experience of bodily orifices in relation to the functions performed by the mother: for example, the child's eyes are drawn to the mother's eyes, ears to her mouth, and mouth to her nipples, thus bringing the child's head together with the maternal head/breast (p. 63). Ambivalent feelings towards the mother and the uncertainty characteristic of the aesthetic conflict contribute to the unintegration of her interior. Thus the three compartments of the internal mother (head/breast, genital, rectum) whether conceived of imaginatively or penetrated intrusively will tend to remain separate from each other.

The first space in *The Convent* that evokes the maternal compartment of head/breast is the library. It is Baltar, already identified with the devil by having stood in front of an inverted pentagram in an earlier scene, who leads Michael to this space. Before reaching it, they pass through a chapel encrusted with skulls, which seem to function as a silent reminder of mortality, after Hélène had derisively explained to Baltar that her husband's aim with his research was to be immortalized. When they arrive at the library they meet Piedade, and Michael looks entranced by her luminous figure, while Baltar remarks cynically that with Piedade's assistance, Michael will discover wisdom comparable to the knowledge of God. 'Knowledge of Good and Evil', Michael replies, and from Piedade's absent-minded smile, the film cuts to an image of the ocean. This image, to which I will come back at a later point, is filled completely by the ocean and the sky, but it is difficult to see where the ocean ends and the sky begins.

Meltzer defines the imaginative conception of the head/breast compartment as follows:

> Construed from outside, the mother head/breast is seen as an object [. . .] whose primary quality is richness. This richness, at first concrete and related to urgent need for nourishment, becomes diversified in its nuances: generosity, receptiveness, aesthetic reciprocity; understanding and all possible knowledge; the locus of symbol formation, and thus of art, poetry, imagination.
>
> (p. 72)

It is in the library that Michael and Piedade research together and help each other, where they discover poetry, read it and offer it as a gift (Piedade offers Michael a copy of the second part of Goethe's *Faust*), and where they once relate their dreams – or what they believe were dreams – and wonder about their meaning. The reciprocity between them is conveyed through long sequences of shots and reverse-shots of their figures sitting at their desks, their faces lit by the brightness coming from the windows.

But what is also pertinent to observe is how the qualities of this space change dramatically as soon as Baltar or Hélène intrude into it. Baltar, entering unnoticed and eavesdropping on Piedade's reading of *Faust*, interrupts to suggest Michael is working too hard and that he should have some rest (again, cynically). Effectively he separates the two, leading Michael to the shore only to upset him with a different passage of *Faust*, thus leading him away from Hélène; Baltar then departs with her on a small boat to a nearby cave. When Hélène enters the library, towards the end of the film, she has already planned with Baltar the disappearance of Piedade. She takes the copy of *Faust*, sits on Piedade's place, leaves the book purposefully open, and exits. In this whole sequence not a single word is exchanged between her and Michael. The library's atmosphere becomes heavy with unspoken motives and suspicion. Meltzer describes how the qualities of the maternal head/breast degenerate when they are seen from the inside by the intruder: 'Generosity becomes quid pro quo, receptiveness becomes inveiglement, reciprocity becomes collusion, understanding becomes penetration of secrets, knowledge becomes information' (pp. 72–3). And while from the outside the maternal head/breast is 'industrious, burdened with responsibilities, prudent from foresight', from the inside it is 'indolent, carefree, living only in the power of its momentary beauty and wealth' (p. 73). Indolence seems to be Baltar's real perception of the situation as he enters the library. And it is with this quality that Meltzer characterizes the scene in the left panel of Hieronymus Bosch's triptych *The Garden of Earthly Delights* (1500–5), a work which for him is a great depiction of the compartmentalization of the internal mother: 'Bosch's triptych [. . .] displays the indolence, the sensuality and the claustrophobia of the three compartments consequent to the "first disobedience", the intrusion upon the parental prerogatives' (p. 67).[13] In the left panel God is introducing Adam and Eve; in the library of the convent it is Baltar, taking the role of the serpent, who introduces Michael and Piedade, tempting them to eat the forbidden fruit. Baltar tempts but he also spoils, like Mephistopheles who interrupts Faust's enjoyment of the longed-for *Augenblick* (Goethe, Arndt and Hamlin, 1976, p. 266, n.7).[14]

Suggestions of the sensuality of the genital compartment in the film can be found mostly in the cave, but there are also traces of it in the 'Witches' Garden' when Baltar and Hélène are present. These two spaces, the forest and the cave, appear in a scene in *Faust* precisely titled 'Forest and Cave', in which Faust's awareness of his nature is expressed in a self-reflective monologue (p. 377). He speaks: 'You lead me to the cavern refuge, show | My own self to me, and of my own breast | The secret deep-laid miracles unfold' (p. 90).[15] In the cave Baltar falls to his knees and confesses his love for Hélène, and in the forest Hélène can no longer hide her jealousy of Piedade.

It is noteworthy that in *The Convent* the camera is always static – which contributes to the stagnant atmosphere – with the exception of only three separate moments that I will indicate in the course of the text. The first of these moments occurs as Baltar and Hélène enter the cave – a low-angle tracking-in shot (moving forward inside) that shows the cave's dark, uneven ceiling. This shot reinforces the sense of intrusion, of entering the claustrum.

As they penetrate into the spaces of the cave and the forest, Baltar's and Hélène's observations suggest their being in intrusive identification with the internal object. Meltzer writes that 'Internal objects impinge on the self, at various levels, because of both their qualities and their functions. Unlike external objects, emotions are not deployed to these objects, they are evoked by them' (1992, p. 59). This evocative power, as well as a certain emotional detachment, can be found in their comments in the cave: 'All this evokes the infernal', 'A huge vulva, that's what it looks like'; and in the forest (referring to the branches of the trees), 'They are huge arms defending darkness from the sun's prehistoric threat from a time when good and evil were indistinguishable'. Baltar and Hélène want to probe each other, knowing that they need something from the other (love, the secret of the forest, the fall of Piedade), but sensing danger; this seems to be the unconscious intrusive phantasy with the internal object being played out with an external object, a phantasy that manifests itself, for example, in the way the space is perceived. The state of the object is altered by the parasitism (p. 70), and this damage can be seen for example in Baltar's belief that the chapel of the cave served to worship the devil. Baltar's mentioning of the orgies that were said to have taken place in the cave can be linked specifically to the genital compartment:

> Seen from the interior through the eyes of the intruder, [the genital compartment] is Mardi Gras, a festival of priapic religion where the beauty of femininity has the irresistible power to produce the erection that is irresistibly fascinating and craved by every sense and orifice. [. . .] For the essence of this interior view is that the entry of the father's phallus is celebrated and enjoyed voluptuously by all the babies, while the mother calmly receives this homage.
>
> (p. 89)

According to Meltzer, the obsession with sex of the dwellers of this compartment is typical of adolescent communities. The preoccupation with decorating and beautifying the body originates in an obsessive belief in the 'irresistible' object. 'The burning desire is to *be* the irresistible phallus or to have absolute power over it' (p. 88). This phantasy of irresistibility is satisfied through multiple and transient encounters, astute selection of targets, and feelings of triumph over casual lovers' partners (p. 90). In the film, this sort of sexual magnetism riddled with issues of power is found in the forest sequence, when Hélène makes the pact with Baltar.

The irresistible attraction to or seduction into this claustrum is also conveyed when Piedade is lost in the forest, oblivious to Baltar's call. This moment is emphasized by a camera movement, the second in the film: in slow, jagged motion, the camera reverse-tracks, while Piedade moves forward.

I have described several examples of modes of intrusion that appear in the film, such as spying, eavesdropping and entering spaces uninvited. Meltzer points out that the meaning of private/secret is precisely that entry into its area must be invited (Meltzer and Harris Williams, 1988, p. 67). But the boundaries of privacy/secrecy are complicated not only by myriad social and cultural conventions, but also by the fact that the private surface of the body is itself variable. Meltzer writes:

> At all ages the orifices of the body are sacrosanct, even for the infant. This is clearly because we attribute to these entries the significance of portals to the internal world. Yet the senses, particularly the special senses, are also invested with this meaning; this raises a dimension of ambiguity that amplifies the privacy/secrecy equivocation.
>
> (p. 68)

Therefore a distinction must be made between a drive towards intimacy (towards wishing to know more of the private other), and a drive towards a violation of the boundary of privacy/secrecy – an idea that Meltzer uses to develop a concept of violence (p. 69). In the cave, when Baltar comes close to Hélène to tell her that he could provide her with pleasures comparable to those sought in the orgies, Hélène reacts dismissively with 'You really are Mephistopheles!', and this is followed by Baltar's violent laughter. The intimacy that Baltar cannot achieve with his words is followed by the violation of privacy with his laughter. The laughter is experienced as violent to such a degree that Hélène covers her ears and begs him to stop. Meltzer writes that every sense and orifice of the body can become a portal for the intruder (1992, p. 71).

From the point of view of intrusion, the relationship between Michael and Piedade is the most benign in the film, for even Michael's intrusion into Piedade's bedroom while she is asleep is surrounded in ambiguity, as the following day he does not seem to remember exactly what happened. There is another ambiguous episode between the two characters, which involves the sense of vision in particular. On their way to the library, Piedade stops to look through a small circular window (at a statue of Mary Magdalene that is inside), which Michael seems to understand as an invitation to look through it as well. When he does this, Piedade has already walked around the building, and positioned herself in front of another opening that is exactly opposite. Both windows are circular or elliptical, ocular shapes that focus the characters' look, and frame their bodies looking back. On seeing her, Michael averts his eyes, which is probably an indication that he feels his look is intrusive. But Meltzer writes that 'the eyes can be entered by exhibition' (ibid.), and so Piedade's positioning herself in front of the window could also be construed as an intrusive gesture. Still, this scene is ambiguous as it is apparent in other moments of the film that Michael desires Piedade, and Piedade in this instance appears to invite Michael's look. It is interesting to note how this fleeting moment of looking and being looked at happens *through* this interior space, with the symbolic presence of the statue of Mary Magdalene positioned inside that space and between them.

The most claustrophobic of all compartments is the maternal rectum, which I believe can be recognized in certain aspects of Baltar's behaviour and speech, and in his room. Meltzer states that in this compartment there reigns an oppressing hierarchy, where survival means conformity or joining a malignant object in leadership (p. 92). He writes:

> We are dealing with the region of psychic reality where the atmosphere of sadism is pervasive and the hierarchic structure of tyranny and submission forebodes violence. For this reason, unlike the other two compartments where comfort and erotic pleasure dominate the value system, in the rectal compartment there is only one value: survival. [. . .] The nameless dread consists in being 'thrown away'. [. . .] It is a region of satanic religion, ruled by the great fecal penis, the world of Orwell's 'Big Brother'.
>
> (p. 91)

The most claustrophobic of the spaces in the convent, Baltar's room is a windowless space filled with red light, decorated with various mysterious objects and detection instruments. A glimpse of his world of tyranny and submission appears in the cave scene, in his violent laughter followed immediately by his kneeling: 'guilt and the yearning for punishment takes the place of regret', writes Meltzer (p. 92). Other qualities of the prisoners of this compartment include cynicism (p. 154) (the hallmark of Baltar's speech) and a frantic ambitiousness (p. 94), which Baltar is constantly projecting onto Michael. The dialogue between Michael and Baltar at the top of a hill, filmed with low- and high-angle shots that surround Michael with the light of the sky and Baltar with the darker colours of the mountain, contains several examples of this projection: 'Just look! The wonder of it! The whole world at your feet. Don't you see, professor, that the glory of your discovery will make you immortal?'; 'Isn't [immortality] what you want? Isn't that what every man worthy of the name aspires to?'; 'Come now professor. Not a genius like you can settle for so little'.

In Goethe's *Faust* there also can be found a satirical view of the aspirations of academic learning. Cyrus Hamlin notes that the confined space of Faust's study represents an existential prison, and the limitations imposed by time and mortality on human beings (Goethe, Arndt and Hamlin, p. 354); and that its dusty books and materials indicate a realm of intellectual sterility removed from the living domain of nature (p. 352). Nevertheless, Faust's striving is, effectively, focused on the achievement of a union with the Feminine, first in his encounter with Gretchen and then in his search for Helen of Troy (p. 454). It is only when he has lost both that his pursuit becomes more identified with a pursuit of power, as he embarks on an urban development project that entails taming the waters of the ocean with the construction of dikes and dams (p. 460). Among the victims of such project are the characters Philemon, Baucis and the Wayfarer. Hamlin comments:

> In the final lines spoken by the Wayfarer [. . .], as he approaches the place where the shore used to be, he indicates that he has gathered in his lifetime of travel a fullness of experience, a sense of 'the boundless ocean', which sustains his 'prayerful devotion' in the face of nature and of life itself. [. . .] But Faust long since abandoned such an affirmative stance and has become obsessed by his land-development project and the illusion of absolute power.
> (p. 470)

In *The Convent*, the sense of 'the boundless ocean' is suggested by the aforementioned image of the sea, in which the sea's limits are out of frame, and the line of the horizon is indistinct. This is the image that immediately follows the first scene in the library, in which Baltar and Michael speak of the knowledge of good and evil that might be found in there, and in which Michael meets Piedade. Similar to the main form that Faust's striving takes in Goethe's drama, in the narrative of *The Convent* Michael's research project is secondary to his involvement with Piedade and his reunion with Hélène. But unlike Faust, Michael does not embark on any sort of violent appropriation of the landscape for the construction of a new city under his rule. In the last moments of the film, when Michael reads from the page on which Hélène left the book open, he is reminded of Helen of Troy's gift of ubiquity and ability to transform herself, and finally understands the connection between Hélène and Piedade.[16] He leaves the library and drives to the shore, and then sees Hélène surfacing from the water. There is a parallel between this scene of Hélène's arrival at the shore and Helen of Troy's journey from the underworld to the stage of the drama, which Hamlin notes corresponds to her journey from the sea to her native land (p. 433).[17] It is Faust who descends into the underworld in search of Helen, in order to bring her from the mythical domain into his own realm. Hamlin writes that '[Faust's] descent to the underworld [. . .] consists primarily in a journey inward, as if to the realm of the unconscious' (p. 428).

The idea that Faust's quest to achieve union with Helen consists, at least from a certain perspective, of a journey inward could be useful to expand possible interpretations of Michael's and Hélène's experiences in the convent. It is not far from Coureau's own reflections on the film, when he considers the disappearance of Baltar and Piedade, and also of Michael and Hélène after they embrace on the shore: he suggests that these characters could be spectres, mental images (p. 223). The psychoanalytic reading of the film that I have carried out here enables a conceptualization of the space and time of retreat as a space and time of the internal world, intimately connected with the thirst for knowledge, and knowledge of the other and the self, at a time of crisis in a relationship. Meltzer's theory of the compartments of the internal mother, specifically, elucidates how the characters' different 'views-of-the-world' invest spaces with different psychic realities; but it can also sustain a reading of the dwellers of the convent as different parts of Michael's and Hélène's personalities, some of them ensconced in claustra, others construing imaginatively the object from the outside, respecting the privacy of its interior. Baltar could be at times that part of Michael's personality which imposes the scrutiny of the motives behind his research, as well as that which personifies his own doubts about those motives. Baltar could also be the part of Michael which once told him that 'thought could not still the oceans'.[18]

The third and last shot in which the camera moves in the film is worth considering here. While the previous two could be seen as intrusion and seduction into the claustrum, the last could be seen as emergence from the claustrum. The camera gently follows Hélène's feet as she walks from the water to the shore, reverse tracking, slightly to the side of the direction of her walk, making way for her to be reunited with Michael, and in a high angle, refraining from exposing her nakedness. And as Michael and Hélène embrace and walk along the shore, leaving their retreat, there is a sense that each is now in the presence of the internal object whose beauty and mystery can be contained; there is a sense that their retreat enabled them to contain the fullness of 'the boundless ocean'. This is clearly not the containment that Faust tried to achieve in his later project, but the containment in Bion's terms, the symbiotic relationship between container and contained; it is also the crossing of a caesura, as they overcome the emotional turbulence of their crisis through experiences that have changed them. These encounters with parts of their personalities formed early in their lives suggest a reorienting influence in their future.

In Meltzer's terms, the symbiotic relationship finds an image in Bessa-Luís's opening of her novel: 'Those who let themselves be moved by a landscape are hiding their innermost desires.' The subject neither wards off the aesthetic impact of the object,[19] nor submits to omnipotent impulses to intrude into it and destroy it, but instead desires to know and understand it, and be known and understood by it; and this entails the regard for the privacy of the object, which is the acceptance of its mystery, or its boundlessness.

The conflict between the epistemophilic and the omnipotent impulse, or between inquiry and omniscience, which Bion identifies in the Eden myth, is developed by Meltzer through distinctions such as those between communication and intrusion, and between intimacy and violence, distinctions that expand the understanding of the geographic and aesthetic dimensions of mental functioning. Both Bion's and Meltzer's developments owe much to Melanie Klein's insights on how the epistemophilic instinct is primordially directed towards the interior of the mother's body. *The Convent* affirms the limitlessness of the object and the limits of human knowledge of good and evil, as to neither hear, nor see, nor speak might be construed as part of a defence against understanding, or as part of the wish to understand without intruding.

Notes

1 The English subtitle version of the films by Oliveira used throughout this chapter, including the interview with the filmmaker, are those available in the Lusomundo Audiovisuais DVD collection of 2008, and are reproduced by permission of NOS Lusomundo Audiovisuais.

2 'Inside of the internal mother' or, in other words, the inside of the mother's body as a psychical construct.
3 See Chapter 3.
4 The tetralogy comprises *Past and Present* (1972), *Benilde or the Virgin Mother* (1975), *Ill-Fated Love* (1979) and *Francisca* (1981).
5 João Bénard da Costa also participated in films by other Portuguese directors, always under the pseudonym Duarte de Almeida. In *The Convent* he plays the role of Baltazar.
6 See also Oliveira's film *The Divine Comedy* (1991), which happens inside the enclosure of a psychiatric institution, and in which there is a sequence that recreates the original sin.
7 This excerpt and the following are faithfully reproduced from the available English subtitle translation.
8 Interesting to note that Luce Irigaray (1985, p. 101) suggests that the word 'labyrinth' shares its etymology with the word 'lips', which derives from *labra*. She writes:

> The labyrinth, whose path was known to Ariadne, for example, would thus be that of the lips. This mystery of the female lips, the way they open to give birth to the universe, and touch together to permit the female individual to have a sense of her identity, would be the forgotten secret of perceiving and generating the world.

9 This and subsequent quotations from Cardoso are my translation.
10 (My translation). Bessa-Luís, A. (1994). *As Terras do Risco*. Lisbon: Guimarães Editores, 1999. Use of translation by permission of Guimarães Editores.
11 Coureau (p. 212) notes that this is an extract of *The Rake's Progress* by Igor Stravinsky, a work inspired by the Faust legend.
12 The article in question is titled 'The Relation of Anal Masturbation to Projective Identification' and is reproduced in Meltzer, 1992, pp. 14–29.
13 In his article on the mirror stage, Jacques Lacan (1949, p. 4) also refers to Hieronymus Bosch's painting, in his consideration of the appearance of the fragmented body in dreams. He writes: '[The fragmented body] appears in the form of disjointed limbs, or of those organs represented in exoscopy, growing wings and taking up arms for intestinal persecutions – the very same that the visionary Hieronymus Bosch has fixed, for all time, in painting'.
14 The note compares the interruption of the consummation of love between Faust and Helen to an earlier episode of intrusion by Mephisto between Faust and Gretchen (p. 89). For a definition of the concept of *Augenblick* see Cyrus Hamlin's interpretive notes on p. 364.
15 von Goethe, J.W., Arndt, W. and Hamlin, C. (1976). *Faust: A Tragedy*. Translated by W. Arndt. Edited by C. Hamlin. 2nd ed. New York: W.W. Norton, 2001. p. 90. Reproduced by permission of W.W. Norton & Company, Inc.
16 Earlier in the film, this connection is apparent in the following instances: Berta tells Baltazar that she believes there is a strange coincidence in Hélène's and Piedade's astral charts; during the night, after Michael has left Piedade's bedroom, both women experience pleasure; Piedade gives Michael Part II of *Faust*, which is mostly devoted to Faust's quest to achieve union with Helen of Troy.
17 The peninsula opposite to the shore at which Hélène arrives is named Tróia.
18 Refer to the dialogue between Baltar and Piedade in the forest.
19 Meltzer relates the developmental failures in autism to 'processes for warding off the impact of the beauty of the world'. See Meltzer *et al.*, 1986, p. 204.

References

Bessa-Luís, A. (1994). *As Terras do Risco*. Lisbon: Guimarães Editores, 1999.
Bion, W.R. (1965). *Transformations*. London: Karnac, 1984.
Bion, W.R. (1975–1981). *A Memoir of the Future*. London: Karnac, 1991.

Bosch, H. (1500–1505). *The Garden of Earthly Delights*. Oil on oak panel. 205.6x386 cm.
Cardoso, P.S. (2010). A estrutura do invisível: Palavra e imagem em Manoel de Oliveira. In: Junqueira, R.S. (ed.) *Manoel de Oliveira: Uma Presença*. São Paulo: Perspectiva.
da Costa, J.B. (1981). O cinema é um vício. In: Cinemateca Portuguesa (ed.) *Manoel de Oliveira*. Lisbon: Cinemateca Portuguesa.
da Costa, J.B. (2008a). Party. In: de Oliveira, M. and da Costa, J.B. (eds.) *Manoel de Oliveira: Cem Anos*. Lisbon: Cinemateca Portuguesa/Museu do Cinema.
da Costa, J.B. (2008b). The touchstone: The so-called eternal feminine in Manoel de Oliveira. In: Overhoff Ferreira, C. (ed. and trans.) *Dekalog 2: On Manoel de Oliveira*. London: Wallflower Press.
Coureau, D. (2006). *Le Couvent* ou l'architecture du mystère. In: Estève, M. and Gili, J.A. (eds.) *Manoel de Oliveira*. Caen: Lettres modernes Minard.
Cruchinho, F. (2008). The woman in the shop window and the man looking at her: The politics of the look in Manoel de Oliveira's oeuvre. In: Overhoff Ferreira, C. (ed. and trans.) *Dekalog 2: On Manoel de Oliveira*. London: Wallflower Press.
Diana, M. (2001). *Manoel de Oliveira*. Milan: Il Castoro.
Gili, J.A. (1995). *Le Couvent*: Entre la méditation et la séduction. *Positif*, 416, pp. 24–5.
von Goethe, J.W., Arndt, W. and Hamlin, C. (1976). *Faust: A Tragedy*. Edited by C. Hamlin. Translated by W. Arndt. 2nd ed. New York: W.W. Norton, 2001.
Irigaray, L. (1985). Gesture in psychoanalysis. In: *Sexes and Genealogies*. Translated by G.C. Gill. New York: Columbia University Press, 1993.
Johnson, R. (2005). *Viagem ao princípio do mundo/Journey to the Beginning of the World*. In: Mira, A. (ed.) *The Cinema of Spain and Portugal*. London: Wallflower Press.
Johnson, R. (2007). *Manoel de Oliveira*. Urbana: University of Illinois Press.
Lacan, J. (1949). The mirror stage as formative of the function of the I as revealed in psychoanalytic experience. In: *Écrits: A Selection*. Translated by A. Sheridan. London: Routledge, 1989.
Meltzer, D. (1992). *The Claustrum: An Investigation of Claustrophobic Phenomena*. London: Karnac, 2008.
Meltzer, D. *et al.* (1986). *Studies in Extended Metapsychology: Clinical Applications of Bion's Ideas*. Perthshire: Clunie Press.
Meltzer, D. and Harris Williams, M. (1988). *The Apprehension of Beauty: The Role of Aesthetic Conflict in Development, Art, and Violence*. London: Karnac, 2008.
de Oliveira, M. *et al.* (1981). Diálogo com Manoel de Oliveira. In: Cinemateca Portuguesa (ed.) *Manoel de Oliveira*. Lisbon: Cinemateca Portuguesa.
Roth, L. (1995). Le Diable amoureux. *Cahiers du cinéma*, 494, pp. 48–9.

Filmography

Anxiety (1998). Directed by Manoel de Oliveira. [DVD] Portugal/France/Spain/Switzerland: Gemini Films/IPACA/Light Night/RTP/Wanda Films.
Benilde or the Virgin Mother (1975). Directed by Manoel de Oliveira. Portugal: CPC/Tobis Portuguesa.
The Convent (1995). Directed by Manoel de Oliveira. [DVD] Portugal/France: Madragoa Filmes/Gemini Films/La Sept Cinéma.
The Divine Comedy (1991). Directed by Manoel de Oliveira. [DVD] Portugal/France/Switzerland: Madragoa Filmes/Gemini Films/2001 Audiovisuel.
Francisca (1981). Directed by Manoel de Oliveira. Portugal: V.O. Filmes.
I'm Going Home (2001). Directed by Manoel de Oliveira. [DVD] France/Portugal: Madragoa Filmes/Gemini Films/France 2 Cinéma.

Ill-Fated Love (1979). Directed by Manoel de Oliveira. Portugal: CPC/IPC/RTP/Cinequipa/Tobis Portuguesa.
Party (1996). Directed by Manoel de Oliveira. [DVD] Portugal/France: Madragoa Filmes/Gemini Films.
Past and Present (1972). Directed by Manoel de Oliveira. Portugal: CPC.
Voyage to the Beginning of the World (1997). Directed by Manoel de Oliveira. [DVD] Portugal/France: Madragoa Filmes/Gemini Films.

Audiovisual Material

Entrevista com Manoel de Oliveira (2001). Interview in the Lusomundo Audiovisuais DVD edition of the film *I'm Going Home* (2001) directed by Manoel de Oliveira. [DVD] France/Portugal: Madragoa Filmes/Gemini Films/France 2 Cinéma.
Manoel de Oliveira 2 (2005). Interview in the Lusomundo Audiovisuais DVD edition of the film *Magic Mirror* (2005) directed by Manoel de Oliveira. [DVD] Portugal: Filbox.

CONCLUSION

In this book I have attempted to delineate some of the possible physical and psychical contours of the retreat in cinema and the retreat in film, while aiming to have expanded some of their possible meanings. It may be useful to extract an overarching conceptualization from the different notions of retreat that have been arrived at during the course of my argument. I will begin by recapitulating those notions, as well as the ones that have been challenged.

The analysis of Baudry's and Metz's theories of the apparatus conducted in Chapter 1 revealed that for these authors the cinema is a retreat from reality, in which the subject is dominated by unconscious mechanisms of wish-fulfilment that keep areas of knowledge or truth distorted or repressed. These mechanisms are seen to be typical of dreams, yet the dream theory relied on narrowly conceives of them as serving only that purpose of wish-fulfilment. The subject is also seen to be under the influence of imaginary pleasures derived from the specular arrangement of the cinema. Such a state of affairs is seen to be perpetuated by widespread, manipulative and pernicious ideologies.

However, an examination of the early stages of thinking that occur in the early relationship with the mother as formulated by Bion, presents a very different model of the mind that can usefully inspire a more positive psychoanalytically driven theory of the cinema, of the retreat, and of the cinema as retreat. According to this model, the operation of the epistemophilic instinct develops in the subject a capacity for tolerating unpleasurable and painful experiences (of which the mother's absence is the prototype) which are seen to be at the basis of thoughts and thinking. The cinema as retreat can then be conceptualized as a space in which emotions can be investigated and assimilated, and which does not shelter the subject from unpleasurable experiences. Mental growth can be recognized in the cinema/retreat, provided pain is *suffered* rather than just felt, to use Bion's terms; but most prominent among the achievements of this introductory chapter is the rethinking of cinema/retreat as a thinking space.

In Chapter 2 the question of mental growth is made more precise in relation to the question of knowledge. Bion's concept of O is used here to further inform a reading of the experience of film in the cinema that was initiated in Chapter 1. In Chapter 2 I argue that the cinema as retreat allows growth in particular, because of its separation from the outside world and its relation to the internal world. This separation from the outside world is not seen in its potential for evasion, but is seen instead in the possibility it offers the subject to encounter the real self, to be or become real (O). This is not only due to the retreat's relation to the internal world, but also because the retreat allows the correlation between the understanding derived from more than one vertex to be made: a binocular vision between the cinema/retreat and the outside world, a means of testing the truth value of an emotional experience from different vertices. Such a binocular vision is not taken into account in Baudry's analogy between the cinema and Plato's cave; and Plato only concedes a binocular vision in his scheme to the prisoner who comes outside through the use of reason and knowledge, disregarding the emotional and experiential capacities that make reason and knowledge possible.

The image of retreat that can be drawn from Bion's theory is one in which knowledge is only possible through the assimilation of emotional experiences, yet knowledge is not sufficient in the process of mental growth, because the subject may know but still resist change: the subject has to be or become real, and this state of atonement with O, or ultimate reality, is only attainable in a state in which there is no memory, desire or understanding. Bion sees memory, desire and understanding as possessions or things that possess, which ultimately hinder the absolute receptiveness to the emotional experience of the present: such is the precondition for potential contact with O, for potentially being or becoming the real self. From Chapter 2 is derived a notion of retreat as a privileged space for growing, for being or becoming the real self, for the recognition and working through of resistances (K→O).

In Part I is also established a connection between the space of retreat and the internal world, a world that, through the lens of object relations, is to a great extent structured by the early relationship with the mother. This connection is evident throughout all the films examined in the chapters of Part II. Specific to this part is a connection between the retreat and the caesura. Bion's concept of caesura is instrumental in challenging common perceptions of the retreat as a regressive movement, because the caesura is seen to make contact with more than one temporal dimension: it makes contact with past, present and future.

In *Through a Glass Darkly*, the religious or messianic question linked to the retreat appears to be inextricable from familial relationships, especially from the maternal relationship. Karin's retreat has been interpreted by Frank Gado as a phantasy of regression to the womb, representing at times a dream of refuge, at others a dangerous delusion. But the world she hallucinates, at times idealized, at others persecuting and vengeful, is one that is undoubtedly connected with *real* situations of her past, present and future. Spaces of retreat assume the function of container and contained: projection/investigation and introjection/assimilation of emotions that probe different times and spaces.

Psychoanalytic approaches to *Pigsty* disregard the presence of the maternal in the volcanic landscape, and consider Julian to be completely overcome by his masochism, ruled by repetition compulsion and the death instinct. But the emergence of his Oedipus situation is effected through a method of investigation – the binocular vision – that is in fact driven by his epistemophilic impulse. Julian's retreat manifests the expression of curiosity, attention and inquiry, elements that are central to Bion's theory of Oedipus. While Julian's father construes his son's retreat as idleness and unemployment, Julian is indeed working with his imaginary twin in understanding his internal and external worlds, at different points in his life, through a binocular vision enabled by his retreat.

In *A Man Asleep*, the protagonist's retreat seems to be initiated by his loss of a meaningful relation to time and space. Some critics read his retreat as a narcissistic attempt at mastering these dimensions. The film gives some signs of the protagonist's omnipotence and narcissism, which appear to be a defence against the painful realization of the possibility of meaninglessness, yet these occur in what is fundamentally a *search for meaning*. Rather than cutting himself off from his past and from history in general as some have argued, the protagonist is trying to piece together his memories, his present situation, his ambitions and desires, and the world around him. His indifference, mentioned in the text of the film, is rather a desire for a certain neutrality, a wish to divest his actions of certain values. He is striving to arrive at a truer perception of things, to learn and understand a multiplicity of languages, from inside and outside, across time. Through its expressive use of the images of the point, the line, and the circle, the film suggests that among these languages there is also something preverbal being articulated.

From a certain perspective, the Faustian aspirations in *The Convent* could be seen to lead to an existential prison, limited by time and mortality, an intellectually sterile retreat removed from the living realm of nature. They could also suggest greed or omniscience, which is a defence against true understanding and epistemophilic pursuit of knowledge. But the spaces of retreat of the convent lead to encounters with unknown others, which carry the possibility of transformation of the self. These others might even be parts of the personality formed early in life that are faced in this turbulent stage and that will have a reorienting influence in the future. Space becomes invested with the qualities of the different maternal compartments in which these parts of the personality live (*claustra* created by omnipotent intrusive phantasies) or which they contemplate from outside (spaces created by imaginative conceptions that respect the privacy of the object). Emergence from the *claustrum* is then motivated by a wish to understand without intruding, associated with wonder at the beauty of the object while accepting the mystery of its interior.

The analysis of the films in Part II achieves a conceptualization of retreat as a space and time of turbulent or dramatic psychical growth. In all the films the retreat was seen to provide the functions of container and contained during a stage of vulnerability and catastrophic change; the retreat provided the space and time to make contact with the internal world, as well as to attain a binocular vision of both internal and external worlds. In all the films the retreat involved painful, conflictual experiences that shifted the characters' views-of-the-world.

Although the different parts of this book placed a different emphasis on a conceptualization of the retreat in film – thinking, becoming, growing – they all bring into view the development of the mind. There is certainly a forward movement implicit in this overarching notion, quite opposed to regression. Still, and concomitant with the psychoanalytic methodology that I have chosen, there was ample evidence of past stages of life in the retreat; but I have shown also that the present and the future are not easily detached, or are indeed impossible to detach, from the retreat. These conclusions offer a way to think about the significance of the notion of 'cinema as retreat' for thinking about the future of cinema.

Perhaps the reason why the notions of retreat that I have challenged throughout this book first came into being and still persist, is that while certain distinctions can be made very clearly with words, they present more difficulties in real situations. A theoretical distinction can be made between omniscience and inquiry, or intrusion and communication; but, as was discussed for example in my analysis of *A Man Asleep*, there were moments of omniscience in the protagonist's search for meaning that could lead to an erroneous interpretation of the retreat as being solely underlain by an omniscient impulse.

Another reason for ambiguity is related to the duration of the retreat. John Steiner, within his conception of 'psychic retreat' as a kind of 'transient shelter', cautions: 'The retreat may become so regular a feature that it is no longer a transient shelter but more a way of life' (1993, p. 88). His statement is worth noting, but it has to be understood in the context of his conception of retreat as an area that provides protection or relief from pain. Steiner explains the danger, and Bion observes, I quote again, that 'mental evolution or growth is catastrophic and timeless' (1970, p. 108), which conveys the difficulty in delimiting the time of a retreat as growth.

This book introduced the important value of the thinking of Bion for film theory and analysis. The work of Bion, and object relations psychoanalysis more widely, are vast and rich territories that are open to further, and in my view necessary, exploration in film studies.

References

Bion, W.R. (1970). *Attention and Interpretation*. London: Karnac, 2007.

Steiner, J. (1993). *Psychic Retreats: Pathological Organizations in Psychotic, Neurotic and Borderline Patients*. London: Routledge.

Filmography

The Convent (1995). Directed by Manoel de Oliveira. [DVD] Portugal/France: Madragoa Filmes/Gemini Films/La Sept Cinéma.

A Man Asleep (1974). Directed by Georges Perec and Bernard Queysanne. [DVD] France/Tunisia: Dovidis/Satpec.

Pigsty (1969). Directed by Pier Paolo Pasolini. [DVD] Italy/France: IDI Cinematografica/ Orso Films/INDIEF/CAPAC.

Through a Glass Darkly (1961). Directed by Ingmar Bergman. [DVD] Sweden: Svensk Filmindustri.

INDEX